A
PEOPLE'S
GUIDE
TO
CAPITALISM

A
PEOPLE'S
GUIDE
TO
CAPITALISM

AN INTRODUCTION
TO MARXIST ECONOMICS

HADAS THIER

Haymarket Books
Chicago, Illinois

Published in 2020 by
Haymarket Books
P.O. Box 180165
Chicago, IL 60618
773-583-7884
www.haymarketbooks.org
info@haymarketbooks.org

ISBN: 978-1-64259-169-9

Distributed to the trade in the US through Consortium Book Sales and Distribution (www.cbsd.com) and internationally through Ingram Publisher Services International (www.ingramcontent.com).

This book was published with the generous support of Lannan Foundation and Wallace Action Fund.

Special discounts are available for bulk purchases by organizations and institutions. Please call 773-583-7884 or email orders@haymarketbooks.org for more information.

Cover artwork, design, and interior illustrations by Tania Guerra.

Library of Congress Cataloging-in-Publication data is available.

10 9 8 7 6 5

Printed in Canada

*To Uri and Tzvia Thier, who instilled in me a knee-jerk reaction to injustice,
and who gave me enough confidence to do something about it.*

*And to Naim, with love, and with the hope that someday you can use
this book to explain to your children what life was like before
we relegated capitalism to the dustbin of history.*

CONTENTS

Introduction 1

CHAPTER ONE
The Birth of Capital 11

CHAPTER TWO
The Labor Theory of Value 27

CHAPTER THREE
Money 49

CHAPTER FOUR
Where Do Profits Come From? 69

CHAPTER FIVE
The Accumulation of Capital 103

CHAPTER SIX
Capitalist Crisis 147

CHAPTER SEVEN
Credit and Financialization 189

CONCLUSION
Capitalism's Gravediggers 233

AFTERWORD
The Coronavirus Crisis 237

Acknowledgments 243

GLOSSARY 245

FURTHER READING 251

NOTES 253

INDEX 287

INTRODUCTION

The world is being ravaged by a coronavirus pandemic as this book goes to print. The virus first reared its head at the end of 2019 and by now, April 2020, the known number of COVID-19 cases worldwide have surpassed a million, leaving over one hundred thousand dead, with estimates that the virus will claim still hundreds of thousands of lives, if not more.

Yet it has become painfully and tragically clear that it is not merely a virus claiming lives. We are also being assailed by a society that has no problem marshaling bombs and fighter jets, but that will not assemble enough ventilators and masks to battle the pandemic. We live in a society in which decades of budget cuts have made a run on overwhelmed hospitals inevitable and which has set countries and states bidding against one another for ventilators on the "free market" rather than devise centralized plans for their production and distribution.

Governments' responses have been uneven across the globe. In countries where authorities responded early on with widespread testing, the transmission of the disease was slowed, as cases were identified, isolated, and quarantined. While the United States, the epicenter of global capitalism, has become also the epicenter of the pandemic. At the first sign of coronavirus-related stock market trouble, the richest country in the world quickly mobilized trillions of dollars to prop up financial capital. But the government did nothing to make testing widely available. We thus faced the obscene reality of hearing about countless celebrities' test results while most health care workers on the frontline battled the pandemic without access to testing.

In Brooklyn, New York, where I live, sixty-eight-year old Theresa Lococo, a pediatric nurse of forty-eight years, contracted COVID-19 on the job and died within days. Her son, Anthony, was asked by the *New York Post* whether widespread testing could have prevented his mom's death. He answered, "I don't even want to hear that—because it would make me feel like someone murdered my mom."[1]

The combination of ineptitude and malice has absolutely had murderous consequences, but the roots of the crisis are deeper still. "The tragedy is immediate, real, epic and unfolding before our eyes," wrote Indian novelist Arundhati Roy. "But it isn't new. It is the wreckage of a train that has been careening down the track for years."[2] The unthinkable scale of the tragedy is the result of a capitalist perfect storm.

First, the increasing number of novel viruses is linked to the rise of factory farming, city encroachment on wildlife, and an industrial model of livestock production.[3] Second, budget cuts and a systematic undermining of health care systems across the world—at varying levels of crisis—have left countries incapable of handling a public health emergency. Finally, as coronavirus rips through our communities, the dark reality of class inequality is laid bare: who will be most vulnerable to infection, who will receive treatment, and who will be left to die? Millions of frontline workers—from nurses to grocery clerks to delivery persons to the homeless largely unprotected and unable to stay home—will bear the brunt of the death toll.

All this is to say nothing of the unprecedented economic crisis that we are plummeting toward. Before the ashes of the health care crisis even clear, we can see beneath them a decimated economy. Again, working people are paying for this. As this book heads to print, a record-breaking 17 million jobs have been lost in a matter of three weeks. During the entirety of the Great Recession, 9 million jobs were lost. The stay-at-home lockdowns rippling through the world have, in the words of Arundhati Roy, brought "the engine of capitalism to a juddering halt."[4] With workers at home, production stands still, and supply chains are broken. Mass layoffs ensue, and millions of unemployed and underemployed workers debilitate demand.

As I frantically set upon rewriting this introduction and adding the afterword to reflect the new reality of a coronavirus-infected world, two things were clear. One, is that an understanding of the way that capitalism works, who it serves and why, is urgently needed. My hope is that this book makes a timely contribution to those discussions. Two, is that at this moment, as the book goes to print, it is impossible to predict how all of this will play out. The biology and evolution of the virus is uncertain, and the scale of the economic crisis is literally unprecedented. In the afterword I attempt to sketch out a few thoughts on the economic ramifications of the pandemic without the pretense of predictions.

The coronavirus pandemic has accelerated economic and social processes that have been unfolding over the decade since the GREAT RECESSION of

2007 to 2009, the longest and deepest crisis in the United States since the Great Depression. That distinction will, of course, be eclipsed by the current crisis. But the devastation wrought by the Great Recession was significant in its own right. And along with the weak and joyless recovery that followed, it fueled new heights of economic polarization.

The Federal Reserve reported that in 2019 the country's top 1 percent controlled a record-high 33 percent of the wealth, while the bottom 90 percent of the adult population shared 30 percent of the wealth. See Figure 1. Even more shocking, the bottom half of the population have had to divvy up 1 percent of the nation's wealth among us.[5] Stepping back to look at the last three decades, the trajectory is even more dramatic. See Figure 2.

FIGURE 1. DISTRIBUTION OF WEALTH 2019

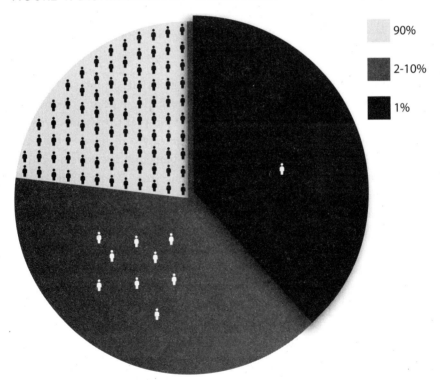

90%

2-10%

1%

Source: Board of Governors of the Federal Reserve System, Distribution of Household Wealth in the US since 1989.

FIGURE 2. DISTRIBUTION OF WEALTH 1989–2019 (IN TRILLIONS)

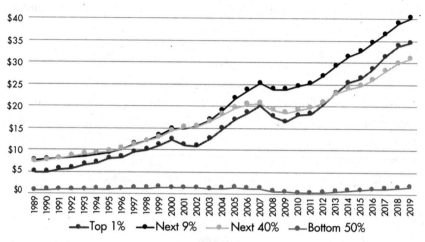

Source: Board of Governors of the Federal Reserve System, Distribution of Household Wealth in the US since 1989.

These conditions have fueled an "age of global mass protests." A 2020 report from the Center for Strategic and International Studies found that mass protests have increased by 11.5 percent per year worldwide, on average, since 2009—from the Arab Spring, to Occupy Wall Street in the United States, to the Indignados' occupations in Spain, to strike waves in China, to pro-democracy protests in Hong Kong and Iran. As the report noted: "Even when accounting for population growth, the relative number of demonstrators over the past three years is likely higher than participation in either the anti-Vietnam War movement or the civil rights movement."[6] The need for isolation and distancing may temporarily put a pause on mass gatherings, but the circumstances that fed them—economic inequalities, planetary crisis, and disgust with political corruption—will only deepen in the years ahead.

Ideological shifts have been as dramatic as the protests on the streets. Even before the pandemic struck, polls consistently showed that the majority of millennials reject capitalism, and in some cases specifically prefer socialism.[7] In the US, where the two-party system has a vice-like grip on the electoral process, Bernie Sanders, a self-proclaimed socialist, won the support of tens of millions of primary voters in 2016, who "felt the Bern" of his anti-corporate political revolution. By the 2020 election, the previously fringe candidate became a front-runner in the national elections and fundamentally shifted the national discussion on every major issue: from health care and climate change to racial justice and class inequality.

Unfortunately, opposition to the rotten status quo has also fed right-wing ideas and movements, from the election of Trump in the US and neofascist Jair Bolsonaro in Brazil, to counterrevolution in Egypt, to the rise of racism and xenophobia in Europe and Latin America, and more. Finally, we have to contend with the precipice of planetary destruction that corporate America has driven us to. We are living through the stormiest of political times in generations, and these times are in equal parts exhilarating and terrifying.

We need a radical theory to address the questions that millions have asked in recent years. Why are resources so easily marshaled for war yet so impossible to rally toward stopping a pandemic from tearing through our communities? Why do profits always trump human lives and ecological sustainability? How can there be a housing glut, when millions are homeless? Why do forty-five thousand people a year die, even pre-coronavirus, in the United States—the richest country in the world—from causes linked to lack of health insurance?[9] How could hunger be the leading cause of death among young children around the world, while current global food production supplies enough to feed more than one and a half times the world's population?[10] Why does money flow to oil, nuclear weapons, and junk food, rather than to fulfill human needs for health care and education? Is this rotten system the best we can do? If these questions are ever raised in mainstream discussion at all, they are presented as unrelated issues.

Contrary to what we are taught, the economic system of capitalism is intimately connected to society's greatest political challenges of war, health and health care, climate change, and oppression. Millennials' turn toward socialism signals an attempt to answer these questions. A new generation is investigating anti-capitalist theories and ideas, which are no longer tainted with the false "socialisms" of the totalitarian states of the past.

Karl Marx, an economist, political theorist, philosopher, and above all revolutionist developed a profoundly radical analysis of capitalism. Having written 150 years ago, he could not be expected to fully predict the ways the system would unfold. Nevertheless, as *Jacobin* editor Bhaskar Sunkara wrote: "The core of the system he described is little changed. Capitalism is crisis-prone, is built on domination and exploitation, and for all its micro-rationality has produced macro-irrationalities in the form of social and environmental destruction."[11]

Marx's economic theory and political method of analysis are critical tools for activists today. Marxism is a means to understand and dismantle the world of the 1 percent, a world that exploits, disenfranchises, oppresses, and dispossesses the many for the sake of the few; a world that may not make it to the next century with our planet and our humanity intact. I wrote this book for those of us who are attempting to make sense of the world in order to change it.

Twenty years ago, when I first picked up a book on economics, I made it about two pages in before I broke down in tears, feeling hopeless that I could ever understand economics. The capitalist system in general, and economics in particular, are purposefully mystified. Analyzing how capitalism works is left to "the experts," and if things look a little askew to you, well, that must be because you don't know any better. This is doubly and triply so for working-class people, women, people of color, and other oppressed constituencies who are daily barraged with the message that we cannot hope to comprehend complex systems and ideas, let alone hope to impact them.

And so, not long after I had my big cry, I decided that I would figure this thing out. Even the study of *Marxist* economics, whose purpose is the *demystification* of the system, is still mostly dominated by men. So I broke open the pages of *Capital*, Marx's seminal work on economics, and discussed it and re-discussed it, and discussed it some more with fellow comrades, until the world started to come into focus. With the benefit of this experience, my hope is that this book will draw Marx's critical ideas into the reach of broader and more diverse audiences and direct readers toward further investigations of Marxist economics. I also hope that it makes the way the system works a bit clearer—and that it only makes you cry tears of joy at better understanding the world.

This book aims to follow the content and arc of Marx's *Capital*. *Capital's* three volumes were written to provide a theoretical arsenal to a workers' movement for the revolutionary overthrow of the system—and to do so on the most scientific foundation possible. As Ernest Mandel wrote in his introduction of it: "Precisely because Marx was convinced that the cause of the proletariat was of decisive importance for the whole future of mankind, he wanted to create for that cause not a flimsy platform of rhetorical invective or wishful thinking, but the rock-like foundation of scientific truth."[11]

In *Capital*, Marx employed a method of scientific inquiry to investigate the inner workings and contradictions of the system. To do so, much as a chemist or a physicist must set up a controlled laboratory, Marx sought to establish a *social* corollary of such a laboratory, but, as Marx wrote: "In the analysis of economic forms neither microscopes nor chemical reagents are of assistance. The power of abstraction must replace both."[13] By distilling, simplifying, and abstracting the key elements of the system, Marx was able to present them in their purest form, isolated from complicating factors. Once he set up the foundations, he built out the layers of complexities so that we are able to apply the deeper concepts to concrete reality. Penetrating beneath the surface appearance of capitalism to its deeper underlying laws and tendencies is central to his method.[14]

At its core, capitalism was defined by Marx as a *social relation* of production. He meant that profits are not the result of good accounting or the inventive ideas of the superrich, but are instead the outcome of an exploitative *relationship* between two classes of people: bosses and workers. In our society, employers and workers meet each other on a very unequal playing field, in which one owns the means to produce value, and the other has no choice but to sell their labor in order to live. No matter how "essential" we discover workers to be, the bosses are the ones that make sometimes life-or-death decisions at workplaces, and, at the end of the day, take home the profits. Capitalism is therefore a system in which production and exchange are determined by these positions of exploitation.

This social order of haves and have-nots is neither natural nor timeless. In fact, the precondition for the early development of capitalism was the violent expropriation of the masses of people from their land in order to create the conditions in which capitalism could develop and flourish. "The expropriation," wrote Marx, "of the agricultural producer, of the peasant, from the soil is the basis of the whole process."[15]

Because class and exploitation are central to understanding capitalism, and because their existence can only be understood within a historical context, I begin *A People's Guide to Capitalism* with the story of the birth of capital. It is perhaps a historical detour to what is otherwise a theoretical exposition of the way that the system works. Here again, I follow Marx, who peppered *Capital* with this same history. My hope is that the first chapter provides a useful context to situate the themes introduced later in the book, and also illuminates the historical, rather than static, reality of these conditions. Looking at the roots of capitalist society also makes it clear from the start that the system is built upon the subjugation of humankind and the planet alike.

In the next two chapters, I come back to the basic, but often abstract concepts where Marx began *Capital*: commodities, value, and money. These are taken up by Marx in the first three chapters of volume 1, and often stump readers who go no further. As Marx warned:

The method of analysis which I have employed, and which had not previously been applied to economic subjects, makes the reading of the first chapters rather arduous. . . . That is a disadvantage I am powerless to overcome, unless it be by forewarning and forearming those readers who zealously seek the truth. There is no royal road to science, and only those who do not dread the fatiguing climb of its steep paths have a chance of gaining its luminous summits.[16]

I do my best to offer enough concrete examples and jargon-free descriptions to clarify the points, which will help you keep climbing with minimal huffing and puffing. The following two chapters get to the juicy questions of where profits come from and capitalism's particular form of exploitation. To do so, it is necessary to unpack vital concepts of capital, labor, and class society. And from there we'll be able to see the system's driving tendencies of competition and accumulation.

The final chapters of the book look at the contradictions embedded within capitalism, which ultimately can lay the basis for a different kind of society. The anarchy of competition, an unceasing impulse to grow, gives way to regular crises and threatens profitability. I end with an analysis of debt and the financial markets, which so thoroughly and grotesquely score our current economic landscape.

The last chapter also includes a substantive analysis of the Great Recession, the world's previous major economic crisis. I write about it in the chapter about finance, not because I think it was primarily a "financial" crisis (as some do argue). In theory, this discussion belongs in the previous chapter on crises, but it is just not possible to explain the ins and outs of the Great Recession without having under our belts the full picture of crisis theory and the role of credit. It is too late in some respects (given printing timelines) and too early in others (being at the very beginning stages of the current crisis) to include a thorough discussion of the coming recession. I therefore sketched some thoughts in the afterword, which I hope will help connect the dots between the capitalist economic system and its literally poisonous effect on people and planet.

The book is peppered with sidebars that offer examples to illustrate points made in the chapters, or which take on related theoretical or historical topics. They sometimes venture beyond introductory material, but will hopefully be of interest to readers. Their content is not required to understand the rest of the chapters' threads. It is up to each reader to decide whether you want to read them in the order that they're placed in the chapters, skip them and come back when you finish the chapter, or pick and choose as you go.

There are also a couple of stylistic issues that I should note. First, I quote Marx's *Capital* a lot, and to a lesser degree some of his other central works. I do this not to overwhelm, but in the hopes that it will make it easier for you to plunge into reading Marx yourself. I use the Penguin version, which I find clearest. But I took the liberty to replace British spellings with American ones (e.g. "labor" instead of "labour," etc.), not as a slight to the British, but because being situated in the US myself, this book's audience is primarily here. (Many of my examples are similarly from the place I live and know best, though capitalism and its impacts are, of course, global.)

I also use "he" or "she" in examples similarly for the sake of simplicity, rather than writing out "he or she or their." By and large I refer to capitalists as "he" and everyone else as "she." This is neither an endorsement of a gender binary, nor a reflection of the way the world is actually organized, but it is a way of denaturalizing men as the de facto subjects of history, while making an exception for capitalists, who are—not in total—in the main, men. Finally, a glossary in the back of the book is a useful reference as you make your way through this book. The terms included in the glossary are also set in small capitals and defined within the body of the chapters.

Lastly, every good book should begin with a disclaimer, so for good measure I'll throw in two. The first is this: This is a book about the way the economy works. The machinations of the economy are inseparable from oppression, imperialism, and the destruction of the environment. Only conventional analysts see economics as numbers. Marxists understand economics as being fundamentally about humans and our lives on this planet. However, each of these matters and their relationship to capitalism need their own book, many books in fact. And sadly, this short introduction cannot do justice to any of them. My hope is to at least paint enough of an outline to make it clear that the one cannot be understood apart from the other.

The second disclaimer is that Marxism is not a simple blueprint, with obvious rights and wrongs. Instead, it is a living, breathing theory, applied to social relations, which themselves are always in motion. There are, in fact, a great number of debates between Marxists about probably every topic covered in this book. I have, of course, represented my own understanding of how to best apply Marx's ideas. In a few instances, I have highlighted where there are particularly contentious debates among Marxists: about the birth of capitalism, about crisis theory, about the role of finance capital today.

Again, they are each topics of many books. My aim is not to adequately represent all perspectives—impossible for a primer on economics—but just to flag that those debates exist. And I encourage you to look more deeply into these questions.

Most of all, enjoy. We live in a world made wretched by capitalism, but which is still beautiful not only for the vast wonders of our planet, but also for the hope that human thought, creativity, and struggle provide. Marx provided a set of ideas that he hoped would not be used to merely interpret the world, but to change it. We have, as he said, a world to win.

CHAPTER ONE

THE BIRTH OF CAPITAL

If money, according to Augier, "comes into the world with a congenital bloodstain on one cheek," capital comes dripping from head to foot, from every pore, with blood and dirt.

—*Capital, Volume 1*[1]

THREE MINUTES OF HUMAN HISTORY

Capitalism, we're told, is a natural—even eternal—expression of the human condition. It seems, the argument goes, that human beings are hardwired to be greedy, hierarchical, and inevitably organized into dog-eat-dog societies. A policy paper from the Cato Institute, for instance, explained: "Property rights are prefigured in nature by the way animals mark out territories for their exclusive use in foraging, hunting, and mating." They concluded, "the human mind is 'built' to trade."[2]

But capitalism is not eternal, and it is not intrinsic to "human nature," if such a thing exists. An exploitative system of commodity production and exchange arose over time, neither inevitably nor smoothly, appearing on the scene only recently in human history. The first traces of modern humans date back to more than two hundred thousand years ago. But it was only in the last five thousand years (i.e. during less than three percent of human history) that the first class societies arose.[3] Modern industrial capitalism surfaced just a few hundred years ago (i.e. in the last 0.25 percent of human history). In other words, if human history took place over the course of a single day, capitalism only unfolded three minutes before midnight.

Throughout most of our history, humankind lived in hunter-gatherer societies, which organized themselves to meet basic needs—food, water, shelter.

Agriculture had not yet been developed, and societies generated little to no excess beyond what was needed for day-to-day subsistence. There was no significant surplus to be hoarded by individuals or communities. Our ancestors tended, in fact, toward common ownership and egalitarianism, and organized themselves by and large into loose-knit collectives with decision-making dispersed among its members.[4]

As anthropologist Eleanor Burke Leacock argued, hunter-gatherer societies required "great individual initiative and decisiveness" among their members. "Decision-making in this context calls for concepts other than ours of leader and led, dominant and deferent, no matter how loosely these are seen to apply."[5] Just as greed and deference to authority are attributes encouraged in our current society, autonomy was a much more useful trait for hunter-gatherers. One example quoted by Leacock was the observation of Jesuit missionary Paul Le Jeune, who came into contact with the Montagnais-Naskapi people in the seventeenth century in Canada. He complained:

> They imagine that they ought by right of birth, to enjoy the liberty of wild ass colts, rendering no homage to anyone whomsoever, except when they like. They have reproached me a hundred times because we fear our Captains, while they laugh at and make sport of theirs. All the authority of their chief is in his tongue's end; for he is powerful insofar as he is eloquent; and, even, if he kills himself talking and haranguing, he will not be obeyed unless he pleases the Savages.[6]

Why and how did it come to pass that hierarchical class societies arose out of communities that had been broadly egalitarian and enjoyed the freedom of "wild ass colts" for many millennia? And out of these hierarchical societies, what were the historical conditions that paved the way for capitalism, in particular, to emerge and to eventually dominate the world we live in? From these broad outlines, we can begin to sketch out a framework that can help us understand the anatomy of capitalism.

FROM SURPLUS TO CLASS

The story begins with the development of agriculture about twelve thousand years ago. The advent of agriculture opened up the possibility of producing a *surplus* of food items, which could be stored for future need. Rather than the precariousness of hand-to-mouth living, the safety of that surplus on hand meant that communities could settle and grow, and some members of the group could specialize in the production of non-food items. Between the third and fourth millennia BCE, towns spread across the globe from Mesopotamia to India to China to Africa.

Throughout several thousand millennia, the need for supervision and control over these surpluses meant that societies became increasingly socially stratified. Initially, this was likely in the interest of the group as a whole, as it provided stability through the ups and downs of weather patterns and access to resources. But ultimately those who maintained and supervised the surplus—and who would eventually appropriate this surplus through violence, taxes, or both—cohered into a social class, distinct from the majority.[7]

It took millennia for conflicting "classes"—groups of people with different relationships to the production, ownership, and distribution of wealth and goods—to form. We'll delve into classes more fully in chapter four. In the meantime, for our purposes here, note that various kinds of societies built upon these divisions—slavery, tributary and feudal modes of production, and later capitalism—developed worldwide. This process was not smooth or automatic, nor one that came about without resistance.[8]

CAPITALISM'S "ROSY DAWN"

Capitalism is one type of class society—the type that dominates the globe today. It first emerged in medieval Europe, where feudal societies had been dominant. Exactly how and why the transition from feudalism to capitalism came about is a highly contested and complex history,[9] and beyond the purview of this book, but it's useful to examine what distinguished capitalism from feudalism in order to look at what makes capitalism unique.

Feudalism essentially divided monarchic lands among local lords. These lords then ruled over the inhabitants of their respective estates. Tied to the lord's estates, serfs (unfree peasants) were put to work. They had to pay their lords with money, or with a portion of their harvest, or by tilling the lord's fields for a certain number of days per week.

In feudal society, peasants generally had access to enough land and tools to sustain themselves and their families. The lord's manor included common lands, where "commoners" had rights to work the land and pasture cattle. As paltry as their subsistence was, it provided some economic independence. Because serfs felt no *economic* compulsion to work (the need for a wage in order to survive), it was ultimately the lord's capacity to mobilize force that prevented peasants from keeping the total fruits of their labor, or from fleeing bondage altogether. Because the enrichment of the lord was dependent on violence, this incentivized each lord to make ever-greater investment in weapons and warfare, rather than develop new, innovative productive techniques (much less tend to the social welfare of his serfs).[10]

When capitalism emerged, it developed a wholly new social order, one that required severing the masses of people from access to land, tools, and resources. Rather than a peasantry violently coerced to turn over goods to their lords, capitalism created a new underclass of wageworkers—a class of people theoretically free to work where and how they pleased, but who would in practice be compelled—by economic necessity—to produce a surplus for someone else nonetheless. Over the course of three centuries (from the fourteenth century until the Industrial Revolution of 1780–1850) the transformation of feudal relationships to capitalist ones created a system of production based on the exploitation of "free" wage labor: a social order of haves and have-nots.

Neither the process, nor the exploitative arrangement that it gave rise to, was "natural" or automatic. As Marx wrote:

> One thing, however, is clear: nature does not produce on the one hand owners of money or commodities, and on the other hand men possessing nothing but their own labor-power. This relation has no basis in natural history, nor does it have a social basis common to all periods of human history. It is clearly the result of a past historical development, the product of many economic revolutions, of the extinction of a whole series of older formations of social production.[11]

What were these "past historical development[s]" that created two types of people—one owning wealth and the means to generate more wealth, and the other owning little more than the skins on their backs? Classical economists like Adam Smith argued that capital came to be through a gradually evolving division of labor, where some people became traders, and some of these traders would eventually—through thriftiness or hard work—save enough wealth to build factories and employ workers. Marx mocked the conventional wisdom of mainstream economists of his time:

> This primitive accumulation plays approximately the same role in political economy as original sin does in theology. Adam bit the apple, and thereupon sin fell on the human race. Its origin is supposed to be explained when it is told as an anecdote about the past. Long, long ago there were two sorts of people; one, the diligent, intelligent and above all frugal elite; the other, lazy rascals, spending their substance, and more, in riotous liv-

ing. . . . Thus it came to pass that the former sort accumulated wealth, and the latter sort finally had nothing to sell except their own skins. And from this original sin dates the poverty of the great majority who, despite all their labor, have up to now nothing to sell but themselves, and the wealth of the few that increases constantly, although they have long ceased to work. Such insipid childishness is every day preached to us in the defense of property.[12]

The division of society into haves and have-nots did not gently come to pass, and certainly not through the frugalness and intelligence of a small elite. It was the outcome of a violent upheaval, which forced large swaths of the population from their lands and traditional means of self-sufficiency. As we'll see, laws and coercive means had to be employed to discipline a new class of laborers. Further, political revolutions discussed below placed a new capitalist elite at the helm of states, which could systematically repress the struggles of the dispossessed, advance markets and plunder abroad, and tend to other needs of the burgeoning elite. The violence, coercion, legislation, and upheavals necessary for the birth of this new system evince just how *un*natural and vicious the road to capitalism was.

WHERE WEALTH ACCUMULATES, AND MEN DECAY

In England, where capitalism gained its first foothold, it did so on the basis of what's referred to as the "Enclosure Movement."[13] Millions of acres of common land were violently confiscated and turned into privately-owned plots during several centuries. Traditional rights to use common land for farming or grazing livestock were revoked, land was fenced in (enclosed) and restricted to private owners—whether through payment, theft, or law. Through this process, land was concentrated into the hands of few landowners, while masses of people were left with no means of self-sustenance, and therefore no means to maintain economic independence.

Forced evictions of peasants left villagers landless and roaming the country seeking livelihood and subsistence. English farmer, journalist, and pamphleteer William Cobbett reported on conditions created by enclosures and disasters that befell everyday people who were left "ragged as colts and pale as ashes."[14] "The day was cold too," he related one day in November, "and frost hardly off the ground; and their blue arms and lips would have made any heart ache but that of a set-seller or a loan-jobber." The next day, he came upon another village, where:

The laborers seem miserably poor. Their dwellings are little better than pig-beds, and their looks indicate that their food is not nearly equal to that of a pig. Their wretched hovels are stuck upon little bits of ground on the roadside. . . . Yesterday morning was a sharp frost; and this had set the poor creatures to digging up their little plats of potatoes. In my whole life, I never saw human wretchedness equal to this.[15]

Landowners benefited greatly from combining many small plots, which previously had been tilled by individual peasants, into large estates that could be more productive. Peasants, meanwhile, were obliged to pay rent and yearly leases, or be forced off the land. Many, unable to pay rent, became agricultural workers on large farms. Yet agricultural work did not keep pace with the growth of the uprooted population. Many more peasants were "set free" to become the "proletarians"—or workers—in burgeoning manufacturing towns.[16]

From the sixteenth to the eighteenth centuries a new system of MANU-FACTURE developed in the towns. Here groups of workers were assembled under one roof with machinery and raw materials, supervised (to avoid the common theft of raw materials at home) and paid a wage to produce commodities. Those that bankrolled the operations—and reaped its rewards—were the nascent capitalists. The BOURGEOISIE—or capitalists—are the class of people who own the means to produce (land, factories, tools, and materials), and employ laborers to do the work of production. The early capitalists were made up of merchants, lords that had become agricultural capitalists, as well as yeoman farmers (richer peasants who owned their land).

In several northern French towns in the eighteenth century, for example, thousands of workers were amassed into factories to make wool fabrics. This process was global, though it happened unevenly across both geography and industry types. Where it took hold, it revolutionized production. According to anthropologist James Blaut, "cities dotted the landscape from northern Europe to southern Africa to eastern Asia." He recounts the emergence of a vast global network of trade and manufacture:

In all three continents we find relatively small rural regions (they were generally hinterlands of major port cities), along with a few highly commercialized agricultural and mining regions, which were clearly being penetrated by capitalism. . . . Among them were Flanders, south eastern England, northern Italy, sugar-planting regions of Morocco, the Nile Valley, the Gold Coast, Kilwa, Sofala (and hypothetically part of Zimbabwe), Malabar, Coromanchel, Bengal, northern Java and south coastal China.[17]

For manufacture to advance, a rising capitalist class needed a counterpart class: laborers who could be employed whenever and wherever industrialists wanted them. These laborers had to be doubly free, in Marx's words: free from serfdom in order to be employed at will, but also free of land and the means to produce their own sustenance. On this basis, they could be disciplined to accept the terms of working for a wage. Marx wrote: "For the transformation of money into capital, the owner of money must find the free worker available on the commodity-market; and this worker must be free in the double sense that as a free individual he can dispose of his labor-power as his own commodity, and that, on the other hand, he has no other commodity for sale, i.e. he is rid of them, he is free of all the objects needed for the realization of his labor-power."[18]

As long as peasants and their families had some economic independence, obligation to serve their feudal lords was quite transparent—landowners and the state had to physically wrest a portion of the peasants' harvest through rent and taxes. Under the guise of freedom and democracy, the new landless wage laborers were "free" to sell their labor-power to whomever they chose . . . or face starvation. Marx described the new setup as wage slavery. "The Roman slave was held by chains; the wage-laborer is bound to his owner by invisible threads."[19] He explained: "The starting point of the development that gave rise both to the wage-laborer and to the capitalist was the enslavement of the worker. The advance made consisted of a change in the *form* of this servitude, in the transformation of feudal exploitation into capitalist exploitation."[20] [emphasis added]

Thus while Adam Smith was writing a capitalist manifesto in *The Wealth of Nations*, and other enlightenment philosophers, economists, and writers were celebrating the rise of capitalist ideals, the ugly underbelly of this new wealth was making itself known. In 1770, just six years before the publication of *The Wealth of Nations*, Irish poet and playwright Oliver Goldsmith wrote "The Deserted Village." His poem condemned enclosures, rural depopulation and the explosive growth of wealth. It read in part:

> No more thy glassy brook reflects the day,
> But choked with sedges, works its weedy way;
> . . . Ill fares the land, to hastening ills a prey,
> Where wealth accumulates, and men decay.
> . . . But times are altered: trade's unfeeling train
> Usurp the land, and dispossess the swain;

Along the lawn, where scattered hamlets rose,
Unwieldy wealth and cumbrous pomp repose.[21]

PRISONERS OF STARVATION: DISCIPLINING THE NEW WORKING CLASS

The expropriated peasants-turned-workers were subjected to a new hell on earth in "dark satanic mills," so-called by poet William Blake. There they were "subjected to inflexible regulations, and driven like gear-wheels by the pitiless movement of a mechanism without a soul. Entering a mill was like entering barracks or a prison."[22] Forcing new laborers into these satanic mills required legislation punishable by beatings, imprisonments, branding, and mutilation.

Freely deployed labor was a necessary component for a rising capitalist system. But creating a new laboring class was a bitter, destructive process. And even the threat of starvation was not enough to prevent "idleness" and "loitering." Towns and countrysides became populated with vagabonds and beggars or day laborers looking for work and at the mercy of wealthy landowners and bosses. In 1739, the Marquis of Argenson, a French nobleman, noted in his memoirs: "For a year now misery has been progressing in the kingdom at an incredible rate; 'men die like flies, poverty stricken and browsing grass.'"[23] Not surprisingly, enclosures were met by riots, the tearing down of fences, the destruction of estates, and full-scale rebellions—such as Kett's Rebellion of 1549, which swelled to sixteen thousand strong and briefly captured the second largest city in England.

The new working class was forged through brutal legislation against vagabondage, joblessness, and begging. "Thus were the agricultural folk first forcibly expropriated from the soil," writes Marx, "driven from their homes, turned into vagabonds, and then whipped, branded, tortured by grotesquely terroristic laws into accepting the discipline necessary for the system of wage-labor."[24]

In England, a law entitled "voluntary criminals" in 1530, for instance, called for:

> whipping and imprisonment for sturdy vagabonds. They are to be tied to cart-tail and whipped until the blood streams from their bodies, then they are to swear an oath to go back to their birthplace or to where they have lived the last three years and to 'put themselves to labor.' . . . For the second arrest for vagabondage, the whipping is to be repeated and half the

ear sliced off; but for the third relapse the offender is to be executed as a hardened criminal and enemy of the common weal."[25]

A statute in 1547 condemned idlers to become enslaved, whipped, chained, and branded with the letter V on their breast.[26]

Marx eloquently summed up how workers were forced to accept their lot as "natural." Over time, the economic relations of capitalism would enforce themselves daily upon the working class as "self-evident natural laws" and, for the most part, without great fanfare:

> The organization of the capitalist process of production, once it is fully developed, breaks down all resistance. . . The silent compulsion of economic relations sets the seal on the domination of the capitalist over the worker. Direct extra-economic force is still of course used, but only in exceptional cases. In the ordinary run of things, the worker can be left to the "natural laws of production," i.e. it is possible to rely on his dependence on capital, which springs from the conditions of production themselves, and is guaranteed in perpetuity by them.[27]

In other words, at capitalism's dawn, the rising bourgeoisie depended heavily on the power of the state to enforce its collective will. Capitalism today still depends on the state and the *threat* of violence, but in its everyday running breaks down resistance through the "silent compulsion" of economic necessity.[28] Lacking our own land, tools, and technology to independently provide for ourselves and our families, we have no choice but to labor for others.

A STATE OF THEIR OWN

Marx wrote that the "economic structure of capitalist society has grown out of the economic structure of feudal society. The dissolution of the latter set free the elements of the former."[29] He meant that the development of capitalist relationships and production grew within feudal society before they broke out into fully capitalist societies. The contradictions between the two forms of societies did not automatically translate into clear conflicts between the old order and the burgeoning new elites. The monarchic states of kings and their lords in fact helped to facilitate the enclosures and laws to discipline the working class, as well as encourage trade and finance factories and new forms of production in the cities.

Yet feudal relationships also fettered the rising capitalist class. The monarchies and the landholding class were more interested in building up riches, weaponry, and their armies, and tended to slow and squander opportunities for economic advances. Society would increasingly divide between forces of economic "progress"[30] and forces that still benefited tremendously from the existing feudal relationships. These contradictions broke out into bourgeois revolutions in Western Europe—the Dutch Revolution of the sixteenth century, the English Revolutions of 1640 and 1688, and the Great French Revolution of 1789. Each in turn provided pivot points, which broke apart feudal tenures and helped to establish the states' intervention on behalf of the capitalist class.[31]

Most critically, the bourgeoisie gained the economic upper hand through the Industrial Revolution in England and through its political counterpart in the French Revolution. *Economic* breakthroughs necessitated new *political* ideology, around which the new bourgeois class, and in some cases lower classes, could be rallied. They propagated worldviews—such as the right to private property, freedom from servitude, and an end to hereditary power. As British Marxist Chris Harman argued: "That class required its own ideas, its own organization and, eventually, its own revolutionary leadership. Where its most determined elements managed to create such things, the new society took root."[32]

The bourgeois revolutions were essential to securing capitalist states. These states defended the new class and its interests, and facilitated the expansion of their economic power domestically and abroad.

A "PRIMITIVE ACCUMULATION" OF WEALTH

Why capitalism first got its footing in Britain and a few other pockets in Western Europe is another source of controversy among Marxists and other radical historians.[33] Whichever the reasons, its eventual domination would not have decisively cohered without the brutal enslavement of as many as twenty million Africans over the four centuries of the Atlantic trade of enslaved people. The monstrous horrors of that trade have been well documented—the buying, breeding, and selling of human beings as though they were cattle; the tearing apart of families;[34] the cruelty of slave drivers in whipping, mutilating, raping, and killing enslaved people; put simply, "the ultimate degradation of man."[35]

American historian Howard Zinn described the capture and journey of Africans to slavery:

> The marches to the coast, sometimes for one thousand miles, with people shackled around the neck, under whip and gun, were death marches, in

which two of every five blacks died. On the coast, they were kept in cages until they were picked and sold . . . Then they were packed aboard the slave ships, in spaces not much bigger than coffins, chained together in the dark, wet slime of the ship's bottom, choking in the stench of their own excrement. . . On one occasion, hearing a great noise from below decks where the blacks were chained together, the sailors opened the hatches and found the slaves in different stages of suffocation, many dead, some having killed others in desperate attempts to breathe. Slaves often jumped overboard to drown rather than continue their suffering. To one observer a slave-deck was "so covered with blood and mucus that it resembled a slaughter house."[36]

These horrors turned into great riches for the wealthy few. In the "new world" of the Americas, slave labor cultivated ever-greater volumes of cotton. Nine thousand bales of cotton in 1791 became half a million in 1822, and five million bales of cotton by 1861.[37] These exponential increases owed themselves to technological innovations in spinning and weaving, and were harnessed by enslaved Africans, who were, in the words of W. E. B. Du Bois, "bent at the bottom of a growing pyramid of commerce and industry." Enslaved people "not only could not be spared, if this new economic organization was to expand," Du Bois continues, "but rather they became the cause of new political demands and alignments, of new dreams of power and visions of empire."[38]

In the "old world," this wealth fueled investments that would spur the Industrial Revolution in Britain. The cash reaped from trading enslaved people, and from the products of their labor on sugar and cotton plantations, was the basis for Britain's banking system, and for investments in many of the labor-saving technologies that propelled British capitalism ahead of the rest. Among others, James Watt's steam engine was financed by the trade of enslaved people. Trinidadian historian Eric Williams's famous account of *Capitalism and Slavery*, described how "the sugar planters were among the first to realize [the steam engine's] importance."[39] The plantations were among the steam engine's most important market.

The trade of enslaved people also encouraged the growth of the iron industry, which supplied chains, padlocks, and fetters for the people's owners, as well as firearms that were traded for enslaved people, and metal used in traders' ship construction. Likewise, the trade of cotton goods stimulated cotton manufacturing by enslaved Africans, and the sugarcane harvested by their counterparts on plantations in turn drove the growth of sugar refinery in English towns. Nearly all of Britain's growing towns and cities flourished as a result of slavery—from seaport towns like Liverpool, centered on trade of enslaved people, to manufacturing towns like Lancashire and Manchester.

Thus it wasn't the case that Europe developed capital and industrial growth, while the rest of the world didn't. But rather, as Walter Rodney put it, Western Europe developed economically by actively *underdeveloping* Africa and other parts of the colonized world.[40] The development of "free labor" in Europe needed the decidedly unfree labor of plantations. As Marx wrote, "While the cotton industry introduced child-slavery into England, in the United States it gave the impulse for the transformation of the earlier, more or less patriarchal slavery into a system of commercial exploitation. In fact, the veiled slavery of the wage-laborers in Europe needed the unqualified slavery of the New World as its pedestal."[41]

Finally, the unfree labor of the enslaved people could only be set to work on land that was stolen. Yet another violent expropriation was required: this time of the indigenous populations in the Americas. The slave plantations and the colonial settlements were built upon over a billion and a half acres of land inhabited by Native American tribes. Their brutal dispossession and ethnic extermination were nothing short of genocidal.[42]

Lest we think the early capitalists piled up their wealth penny by penny, as in Adam Smith's version of the story, the truth has more to do with conquest, robbery, and pillage—from piracy, to colonialism, to the European Crusades, to the enslavement of Africans.[43] You can get a picture of how early capital was accumulated by looking at a seventeenth century map of West Africa. You'll find Ghana, then called the Gold Coast (called such until its independence in 1957). To its west: the Ivory Coast. And to its east: the Slave Coast.

CONCLUSION

In the chapters that follow we will delve into the features that define capitalism—what makes it tick, what slows its ticking. As a starting point, we can see here that capitalism is not an eternal system embedded in our nature. It has a history and an origin, and therefore, it can have an end.

Just as importantly, as we explore themes of value, exploitation, profits, and the accumulation of capital in future chapters, it will be important to understand these concepts within this historical context. So long as families could produce food and clothing for themselves, they did not have to work for a wage. Once the vast majority of people lost access to their lands, the organizing principles of society would change. Private ownership of lands, resources, and tools was firmly established and concentrated into few hands. On this basis arose wage labor and a dependence on the market for goods and sustenance.

We will see that capitalism is not simply an economic or a political structure, but a system of social relationships, whose foundation is the expropriation of masses of people from the land. The power of the few to extract labor and profits from the many is based on a relationship of economic dependence, which is historically conditioned. Turning a profit is only possible on the basis of private ownership of the means of production, a "free" workforce, and a state of the bourgeoisie to enforce and project the power of the new ruling elite.

Lastly, the fact that the opening shots of capitalism are processes that simultaneously destroy humans and land—expropriation, plunder, slavery, and conquest—give us some indication of what's to come in regards to oppression and environmental devastation wrought by the system (see sidebar: "Capitalism and Soil"). Both soil and worker had to come under the domination of capital. As Marx described, the theft of common land and the "transformation into modern private property under circumstances of ruthless terrorism . . . conquered the field for capitalist agriculture, incorporated the soil into capital, and created for the urban industries the necessary supplies of free and rightless proletarians."[44]

With this historical framework in mind, we'll look next at the defining building blocks of capitalism, beginning with the commodity, its "elemental form," according to Marx. We'll see that once wage labor and markets, which had operated only on the fringes of feudal economies, became central to the economic activity of capitalist economies, they set the rules for how every aspect of the system operates.

CAPITALISM AND SOIL

The violent social transformations that gave birth to capitalism destroyed the traditional ties that existed between humankind and the earth. The forcible expropriation of peasants alienated humanity from the natural world, and led to a "metabolic rift," as Marx described it, beginning a process that has driven us today to the brink of planetary destruction.

Labor and the earth constitute society's "original sources of wealth," Marx wrote. That is, everything that we require to live and thrive derives from the land and from our ability to do work to harness nature's great powers. Through the process of labor, a metabolic relationship has bound humans and nature together.

> Labor is, first of all, a process between man and nature, a process by which man, through his own actions, mediates, regulates and controls the metabolism between himself and nature. He confronts the materials of nature as a force of nature. He sets in motion the natural forces which belong to his own body, his arms, legs, head and hands, in order to appropriate the materials of nature in a form adapted to his own needs. Through this movement he acts upon external nature and changes it, and in this way he simultaneously changes his own nature.[45]

The enclosures in England put an end to collective use of land, and instead turned both laborers and the natural world into mere inputs for agricultural and industrial production. Marx explained that "for the first time, nature becomes purely an object for humankind, purely a matter of utility; ceases to be recognized as a power for itself; and the theoretical discovery of its autonomous laws appears merely as a ruse so as to subjugate it under human needs, whether as an object of consumption or as a means of production."[46]

While the masses of people were dispossessed, the land itself was robbed of nutrients as rapidly increasing output of industrial agriculture despoiled the earth. The soil was depleted of nitrogen, phosphorus, and potassium, which reappeared in the cities in the form of urban pollution, simultaneously poisoning the land and the city dwellers. Marx was profoundly disturbed by this development, and considered it a breach in the natural relationship of humans to the earth. In *Capital*, Marx argued:

> All progress in capitalist agriculture is a progress in the art, not only of robbing the worker, but of robbing the soil; all progress in increasing the fertility of the soil for a given time is progress towards ruining the more long-lasting sources of that fertility . . . Capitalist production, therefore, only develops the technique and the degree of combination of the social process of production by simultaneously undermining the original sources of all wealth—the soil and the worker.[47]

Since Marx's and Engels's time, a far deeper crisis has befallen the earth's ecosystem. Among our most timely and life-threatening challenges is that of climate change. Fossil fuels, which first became the dominant form of energy during the Industrial Revolution, now dominate the world economy, and threaten our planet's survival. We'll discuss some of these critical issues in future chapters. But for the time being we see that capitalism could only break through as a world system on the basis of conquering both humankind and the planet and subjugating both to its profit motive.

CHAPTER TWO

THE LABOR THEORY OF VALUE

A commodity appears at first sight an extremely obvious, trivial thing. But its analysis brings out that it is a very strange thing, abounding in metaphysical subtleties and theological niceties. . . It is absolutely clear that, by his activity, man changes the forms of the materials of nature in such a way as to make them useful to him. The form of wood, for instance, is altered if a table is made out of it. Nevertheless the table continues to be wood, an ordinary, sensuous thing. But as soon as it emerges as a commodity [sold on the market], it changes into a thing which transcends sensuousness. It not only stands with its feet on the ground, but, in relation to all other commodities, it stands on its head, and evolves out of its wooden brain grotesque ideas, far more wonderful than if it were to begin dancing of its own free will.

—Capital, Volume 1[1]

THE CELLULAR STRUCTURE OF CAPITALISM

The opening line of Karl Marx's *Capital* is: "The wealth of societies in which the capitalist mode of production prevails appears as an 'immense collection of commodities'; the individual commodity appears as its elementary form."[2] It may sound prescient of late-stage capitalism's hoarding disorders. But even in Marx's day, as capitalism was developing and growing in pockets of Western Europe, the world was already overflowing with "commodities"—goods for sale on the market. Marx began his study of capitalism by examining commodities, which he saw as its building blocks. In this chapter we'll investigate these blocks, and through their examination, work through the Marxist understanding of *value* and the role of labor.

At first glance, a commodity appears to be simple enough. We are surrounded daily by hundreds of thousands of commodities all about us. From the food that we buy at the grocery store, to knickknacks that clutter our apartments, to the apartments themselves, all these commodities, and an infinite number more, are bought and sold on the market. Simply put: a COMMODITY is defined as something that was made through human labor, satisfies a demand, and is produced for the purpose of exchange. If I bake a loaf of bread to eat, then it's just bread. But if I bake it in order to sell it, then the loaf becomes a commodity.

Production has existed throughout history. Human beings have always labored to make things—tools, food, clothing, shelter—in order to survive. Things manufactured, mined, or grown were not commodities, however, as long as they were made for direct use, rather than to be sold on the market. In hunter-gatherer societies, production was organized for use and consumption by the producers themselves. In feudal societies, peasants were the primary producers. They harvested crops for themselves, as well as a surplus product for the lord. In the current system, goods are not made for the personal consumption of the workers or bosses of a particular business. They are made for the purpose of exchange—that is to be bought and sold. Workers at Apple don't come home with fistfuls of iPhones. Nor did Steve Jobs live in a castle of iPads. Apple products are manufactured for sale on the market.

The separation of production from consumption is unique to capitalism and was inconceivable in earlier times because needs were so immediate. A vast distance now exists between the maker and the user of a particular good. Each is anonymous to the other. As Marxist theorist Ernest Mandel wrote: "Someone who essentially produces [in order to] satisfy his own needs or those of his community, lives by the products of his own labor. Production and products, labor and products of labor, are identical for him, in practice as in his mind. In commodity production this unity is broken. The producer of commodities no longer lives directly on the products of his own labor: on the contrary, he can live only if *gets rid* of these products."[3]

By looking at who produces what and how it will be consumed, we begin the process of uncovering the structure of capitalism. It may seem like a tedious place to start, but it's where Marx begins *Capital*. He explains why in the preface:

> The value-form [the value of commodities], whose fully developed shape is the money-form, is very simple and slight in content. Nevertheless, the human mind has sought in vain for more than 2,000 years to get to the bottom of it, while on the other hand, there has been at least an approximation to a successful analysis of forms which are much richer in content and more complex. Why? Because the complete body is easier to study than its cells.
>
> ... But for bourgeois society, the commodity-form of the product of labor—or value-form of the commodity—is the economic cell-form. To the superficial observer, the analysis of these forms seems to turn upon minutiae. It does in fact deal with minutiae, but so similarly does microscopic anatomy.[4]

THE DUAL CHARACTER OF A COMMODITY

If the defining aspect of commodities is that they are produced for exchange, we are immediately faced with a conundrum: How are they exchanged? What determines their values in relation to other commodities?

Marx distinguished between two different kinds of values that we can attribute to goods: use-values and exchange-values. An item's USE-VALUE is how it is *used*. The use-value of bread is that it provides nourishment. The use-value of a chair is that it can be sat upon. And so on. Regardless of whether that item is sold on a market, it still has a use-value if it is useful to someone. All societies have thus produced use-values, regardless of whether those items have been commodities to be exchanged. And, even in our current capitalist system, some use-values, like air, are still not commodities. A few expensive novelty jars of "fresh air" notwithstanding, capitalism has not figured out how to bottle up and sell us the air that we breathe.[5]

Marx placed no judgment on what it means for something to be *useful*. He wrote: "The nature of these needs, whether they arise, for example, from the stomach, or the imagination, makes no difference. Nor does it matter how the thing satisfies man's need, whether directly as a means of subsistence, i.e., an object of consumption, or indirectly as a means of production [producing other commodities]."[6] At the end of the day, something has a use-value if anyone has want or need for it—whether it is something as vital as bread, as destructive as drone bombers, or as trivial as your 1980s Garbage Pail Kids and 1990s Beanie Babies collections.[7]

Some use-values are universal. We all need air. We all need nourishment of some sort, whether it comes from rice, kale, or cookies. But other use-values are geographically, culturally, and historically determined. Whether there is need or want for a product is not a fixed or evenly determined measurement. People living in the suburbs probably need a lawn mower, hedge clippers, and gardening tools, but someone living in an apartment in New York City is unlikely to have want or space for such items.

The changing and often subjective "utility" of commodities is one of the reasons why it cannot be the determinant of how much something is worth on the market (see sidebar: "A Marginally Useless Theory?" for more on mainstream economics' concept of utility). Since a single commodity can often be more or less useful to different people, each person—the logic follows—would be willing to pay different amounts for a particular good. The muffins at your local coffee shop would have to be sold at varying prices based on the hunger level of each customer. Even accounting for average needs, or in cases where the hierarchy of utility is more fixed, it makes no sense as a measure of exchange-value. If it were, bread would be more expensive than cars, and certainly more so than diamonds.

What then determines the relative value of goods? To answer this question, Marx distinguishes between an item's use-value and its EXCHANGE-VALUE, the quantity with which one commodity exchanges for another commodity. Whereas use-values are qualitative in nature—it matters a lot to me whether something is a chair or a loaf of bread before I sit on it—exchange-values are purely quantitative. How many loaves of bread make up a monetary equivalent of a single chair? Russian revolutionary Vladimir Lenin summed up Marx's approach this way:

> A commodity is, in the first place, a thing that satisfies a human want; in the second place, it is a thing that can be exchanged for another thing. The utility of a thing makes it a *use-value*. Exchange-value is first of all the ratio, the proportion, in which a certain number of use-values of one kind can be exchanged for a certain number of use-values of another kind.
>
> Daily experience shows us that millions upon millions of such exchanges are constantly equating with one another in every kind of use-value, even the most diverse and incomparable.[8]

These millions upon millions (now trillions upon trillions!) of exchanges make up the daily life and breath of capitalism. The process of exchange of commodities is itself a historical condition. So long as trade between tribes or individuals was casual or episodic, there was no need to have clear measurements of relative values. But once regular networks of exchange and local markets took root, so too did the need for precise costs. As Marx explained:

> The exchange of commodities begins where communities have their bound-aries, at their points of contact with other communities. . . . However, as soon as products have become commodities in the external relations of a community, they also, by reaction, become so in the internal life of the community. Their quantitative exchange relation is at first determined purely by chance. They become exchangeable through the mutual desire of their own-ers to alienate them. In the meantime, the need for others' objects of utility gradually establishes itself. The constant repetition of exchange makes it a normal social process. In the course of time, therefore, at least some part of the products must be produced *especially for the purpose of exchange*. From that moment the distinction between the usefulness of things for direct consumption and their usefulness in exchange becomes firmly established. Their use-value becomes distinguished from their exchange-value. On the other hand, the quantitative proportion in which the things are exchange-able, becomes dependent on their production itself. Custom fixes their val-ues at definite magnitudes.[9] [emphasis added]

Capitalist society is organized around the quantitative exchange-val-ues of goods, rather than qualitative human need for use-values. While you or I are primarily concerned with the use-value of items, whether we can sit on a chair or on a loaf of bread, a capitalist does not care what an item's use is, so long as it will make him money. Use-values only mat-ter to capitalists insofar as they know they must produce something that can be sold, and useless things can't be sold. But what matters most is ex-change-value—how much money can be made from selling those goods. Put another way: the use-value of grain and whether there are people that need to eat is not the system's main concern, rather its exchange-value is what matters—whether and for how much grain can be exchanged.[10] And so capitalism is responsible for such grotesque events as dumping grain reserves into the ocean rather than selling at a loss in order to feed hungry people. At the same time, boundless quantities of plastics and disposable ev-erything are churned out without any regard for human and environmental consequences. (See sidebar: "The Waste of Society.")

The question of how exchange-value is determined is, therefore, crit-ical to understanding what makes capitalism tick. The commonsense assumption in our society is that exchange-value is somehow an innate characteristic of a product. An average car, for instance, is unquestioningly just "worth" about $30,000. Yet there is no physical manifestation of this value. You can inspect the materiality of a car all you like, but you won't see or feel or weigh the exchange-value. "So far no chemist has ever discovered exchange-value either in a pearl or a diamond."[11]

Measuring physical qualities clearly does us no good in the realm of exchange. How do you compare a block of cheese with a bike? If we were trading hay for hay, that would be simple. We could put them on a scale against each other and determine an equal weight for a fair exchange. Of course, that would be a pointless exchange! It's the *difference* between use-values that makes them exchangeable. . . and yet we obviously can't weigh a bushel of hay against a vat of soup to determine their rate of exchange. How then can two things that possess incommensurate qualities be compared or equated?

The one property that all commodities have in common, and through which their "value" can be determined, is that each is a product of human labor. In Marx's words: "Despite their motley appearance," commodities "have a common denominator."[12] Commodities can exchange according to the relative amount of labor-time that it takes to produce them. This basic idea is the core concept behind what's known as the LABOR THEORY OF VALUE—explained further below.

But before turning our attention there, one final point about the dual nature of commodities: use-values and exchange-values. The difference, contradiction between, and unity of quality (use-value) and quantity (value) is a recurring theme in volume 1 of *Capital*. One type of value does not cause the other (how useful an item is does not determine its value on the market; nor does its value on the market determine how useful an item may be to us). Yet despite this lack of causality, the two values of a commodity impact each other, and are inseparable. As Marxist economist David Harvey put it, "The commodity, a singular concept, has two aspects. But you can't cut the commodity in half and say, that's the exchange-value, and that's the use-value. No, the commodity is a unity. But within that unity, there is a dual aspect."[13]

A thing can be a use-value without having an exchange-value. If you make a pie, it will be of use to you as you eat it, but unless you put it up for sale, it has no exchange-value. At the same time, a thing cannot have an exchange-value if it does not have a use-value. If you make a bunch of foul, inedible pies for sale at the local market, and if no one has use for foul, inedible pies, then these pies will also have no exchange-value—no matter how long it took you to make them! The item doesn't have to be useful to the person or people who produced them. But they have to be useful to *someone* in order to have an exchange-value. And that's the purpose of having a market—to find a buyer who will have use for what you've created.

In fact, it's precisely the fact that an item has no use-value to its producer that allows it to be an exchange-value. If a tailor sews a coat to wear, she can't very well sell it to someone else at the same time. An item that has a use-value to the tailor can't simultaneously have an exchange-value for sale. But if she makes two coats, and can realistically only wear one, the fact that the second coat is redundant and therefore has *no* use-value to the tailor is exactly what gives it the potential to be an exchange-value.

Simply put, you can either live in your house, or you can sell your house. You can't have your cake and eat it too.

A MARGINALLY USELESS THEORY?

The predominant explanation of value in mainstream economics today is the neoclassical theory of "marginalism." It assumes that a commodity's worth is determined by laws of supply and demand, mediated by what they term "marginal utility." This theory argues that value is established on the one hand by individuals maximizing the amount of "utility" (or benefit) that they get from purchasing a good, and on the other hand, a corporation maximizing the amount of profit they can achieve through producing and selling those goods. Where these two values meet determines the cost of a product. To understand the logic of decision-making in the marginalist model, we look at an economy with just two actors: a buyer and a seller.

Roughly speaking, the basic premise of marginal utility is that consumers demand goods in order to gain maximum benefits from their use. A thirsty person wants a bottle of water in order to quench her thirst. The more bottles of water our thirsty friend buys, the more thirst-quenching "utility" she gains. However, at a certain point, as she gets to feeling more hydrated, each additional bottle of water brings in diminishing returns. While she may have been willing to pay $2.50 or $3.00, desperate for that first bottle of water, by the third bottle she's unlikely to pay more than $1.00, and by the sixth bottle, doubtless she would pay anything at all—thus reaching "maximum utility." If we were to chart the amount of money she is willing to spend on bottles of water, we could construct a "demand curve."

One of the early theoreticians of marginal utility, Stanley Jevons, explained: "Repeated reflection and enquiry has led me to the somewhat novel opinion that value depends entirely upon utility."[14] The more a consumer wants something, the more utility it has for her, the more she is willing to pay for it. "Water," he wrote, "may be roughly described as the most useful of all substances. A quart of water per day has the high utility of saving a person from dying in a most distressing manner. Several gallons a day may possess much utility for such purpose as cooking and washing; but after an adequate supply is secured for these uses, any additional quantity is a matter of indifference."[15]

FIGURE 3. SUPPLY AND DEMAND

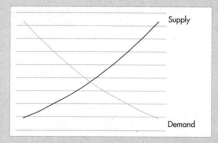

The company producing bottled water, on the other hand, measures its "marginal cost," to see how much it would cost to increase production by each additional bottle of water. The marginal cost then is the cost of producing one more unit of a commodity. It would include any additional costs—more labor-power, more equipment, or factory space—for the next additional unit. Plotting the cost of production for each additional unit allows us to construct a "supply curve." And where the supply curve and the demand curve meet, we find an equilibrium for prices and quantities of goods produced. There are some complicated assumptions involved in going from the two-actor market to the infinite-actor market of the world of "perfect competition," but this simple outline gets to the heart of neoclassical logic.

Unfortunately, this theory raises more questions than it answers. First, the supply curve assumes that the marginal costs of production rise for every output increase. In their model, production costs keep rising and therefore the only factor that can lead a capitalist to increase production levels would be generating higher income from demand. In reality, as we'll discuss in chapter five, this is a faulty claim, as scaling up production usually increases efficiencies and reduces the cost of production per item.

Perhaps more fundamentally troubling to the neoclassical model is that marginalists assume that their model works equally for the commodity of labor-power. But labor-power is a special commodity under capitalism, and workers—the sellers of that commodity—operate with a different set of motivations. Under capitalism, workers are given the "choice" to work or starve. This is a pretty big difference from a company selling water bottles, which can decide to simply walk away from a transaction and not sell if the price drops too low. Depending on the state of the labor market and the level of class struggle, workers' ability to walk away from such a transaction can be very limited. Given the fact that most people living in our society spend our waking lives producing and selling our labor-power as our only commodity, this is a pretty serious flaw in the neoclassical logic.

Above all, the neoclassical theory conveniently assumes that values are not determined by labor-time, but by subjective valuations and desires. Capitalism is reduced, in sum, to individual behaviors and decisions. In this paradigm, explained Marxist blogger Brendan Cooney: "Rather than a theory of classes, we have a theory of pure individuals, all seen as equals in the market."[16] This shift in bourgeois economics was a *deliberate* attempt to undermine the labor theory of value. Classical economics was developed during capitalism's infancy, before class struggles were seen as a threat to the new order; neoclassical economics, on the other hand, afraid of growing working-class power, degenerated into apologetics. As one economist expressed it in 1832: "That labor is the sole source of wealth, seems to be a doctrine as dangerous as it is false, as it unhappily affords a handle to those who would represent all property as belonging to the working classes, and the share which is received by others as a robbery or fraud upon them."[17]

Marx and Engels dismissed marginal utility as just a fancy way of saying that value is determined by supply and demand (prices go up when demand increases and go down when supply increases).[18] "The fashionable theory just now here is that of Stanley Jevons," wrote Engels at the time, "according to which value is determined by utility and on the other hand by the limit of supply (i.e. the cost of production), which is merely a confused and circuitous way of saying that value is determined by supply and demand. Vulgar Economy everywhere!"[19]

NOT BY GOLD OR BY SILVER, BUT BY LABOR

Labor, "the creator of use-values," in Marx's words, has been a permanent feature of the human existence. Some kind of expenditure of physical or mental energy is necessary to create the conditions for our species' survival: shelter, clothes, machines, tools, food, and on. In Marx's words: it is "a condition of human existence which is independent of all forms of society; it is an eternal natural necessity which mediates the metabolism between man and nature, and therefore human life itself."[20]

The wealth of society, argued Marx, comes from human labor *and* from nature. "Labor," he argued at the start of the *Critique of the Gotha Programme*, "is *not the source* of all wealth. *Nature* is just as much the source of use-values (and it is surely of such that material wealth consists!) as labor, which itself is only the manifestation of a force of nature, human labor-power."[21] [emphasis in original] Marx understood "wealth" to mean the things that we need to live, survive, and thrive, as distinct from "value," which is a characteristic we assign to commodities and is socially constructed. As socialist author Paul D'Amato argued, "Value is not really a thing, but a historically evolved relation between human beings that takes the 'fantastic form of a relation between things.'. . . Value is a meaningless category outside of market relations."[22]

We can see that labor is necessary to create the various use-values that make up the wealth of society. But the labor imbued in goods made for sale—commodities—has an added role as a measure of exchange-value. How does it fulfill the latter function?

Some amount of labor is necessary to power the production of every commodity. In that sense, as we've said, it is the common denominator across all goods. The cost to society of making a given commodity—its "value"—can be measured by the amount of labor devoted to its production. And exchange-value is a quantitative representation of that value. Roughly, if it takes ten times as long to make a chair as it does a loaf of bread—that would make a chair about ten times more valuable.

To become an effective means of measurement, the labor imbued in commodities has to become generalized. Specific work like "baking" or "woodworking" has to be replaced with quantities of generic (or abstract, as Marx calls it) labor-time. The real, concrete labor that has gone into producing a commodity is too varied and complex to be used as a measurement for comparison. But all acts of labor can be boiled down, as Marxist economist David McNally put it, to "expenditures of the *general* human capacity to exert muscles, energies and brain cells to create or produce something. Even if all commodities come into being through different acts of concrete labor, they nonetheless all share the property of being products of the generic act of human labor, or what Marx calls abstract labor, i.e., labor as a general power abstracted from all its specific forms."[23] [emphasis added]

Marx used his favorite example of a commodity—linen—to explain the point in *Capital*: "Human labor . . . creates value, but is not itself value. It becomes value in its coagulated state, in objective form. The value of the linen as a congealed mass of human labor can be expressed only as an 'objectivity,' a thing which is materially different from the linen itself and yet common to the linen and all other commodities."[24]

Marx defined this labor-time as HUMAN LABOR IN THE ABSTRACT. Abstract because the exchange-value of a commodity is not determined by *what kind* of specific or concrete labor went into making something, only *how much* of it was required. Whereas use-values are defined by the "how" and the "what'" of labor, exchange values are defined only by the "how much." The market thus reduces specific kinds of labor—for example assembling toaster ovens versus baking bread versus teaching a class—into quantities of generalized abstract labor.

Baking is the type of concrete labor that results in bread. But an hour's worth of "abstract labor" determines that the value of the bread is commensurate with a tenth of the value of a chair. And a toaster oven's price isn't determined by the fact that welding, electronics, mechanics, and assembly went into its production. It is measured only by the number of general or abstract hours of labor this adds up to. Simply put, you don't trade tailoring for mechanics at the store, you trade hour for hour. In Marx's poetic, if not entirely attractive imagery, first labor is abstracted away from its unique, qualitative form, then it "congeals" back into discernable quantities. He wrote:

> The *use-values* coat and linen are combinations of, on the one hand, productive activity with a definite purpose, and, on the other, cloth and yarn. The *values* coat and linen, however, are merely congealed quantities of homogenous labor. In the same way, the labor contained in these values does not count by virtue of its productive relation to cloth and yarn, but only as being an expenditure of human labor-power. Tailoring and weaving are the formative elements in the *use-values* coat and linen, precisely because these two kinds of labor are of different qualities; but only in so far as abstraction is made from their particular qualities, only in so far as both possess the same quality of being human labor, do tailoring and weaving form the substance of the *values* of the two articles mentioned.[25] [emphasis added]

Measurements of abstract labor may be easiest to see in their physical manifestations. The exertion of human energy can clearly transform or combine raw materials into finished products. But the same process is at work if the end result of the efforts is not a physical, but a social, commodity. The product might not be palpably tangible. It might be care performed on a patient. It might be knowledge conveyed to a student. But these outcomes, too, are the product of human labor. And, therefore, the value of those outcomes is determined by the labor-time necessary to generate them, just as it is for physical commodities.

Service labor, just as other forms of labor, also becomes labor in the abstract. An hour's worth of tailoring produces a certain number of coats. Just as an hour's worth of nursing equals some number of patients seen, an hour's worth of a teacher's labor produces a certain number of graded tests, an hour's worth of truck driving to deliver goods covers a certain number of miles, and so on.

Nor is the concept of value as determined by labor-time disproved by the difference between relatively skilled and unskilled jobs. It is true that an hour of labor in a skilled industry does indeed contribute more value to a product than an hour of labor in an unskilled industry. The labor that goes into manufacturing a Boeing 737 jetliner produces more value than the labor that goes into making a hamburger. This is because you are paying for several layers of labor-time. One can quickly master what goes into making a hamburger. But the learning curve that goes into being a machinist is steep.

Therefore the value of a machinist's labor includes the physical hours worked as well as the labor-time that helped produce their skills in the first place: the teachers, textbook makers, trainers, blueprint drafters, etc. who also contributed their labor to the education and preparation of a Boeing worker. (Importantly, this also creates an incentive within capitalism to innovate in order to de-skill labor, thereby making workers more replaceable and lowering the value of the specific labor in that industry.) The point remains that all labor boils down to units of abstract labor, even if they are now multiplied.

Finally, it's important to note that Marx's intent was not to determine specific market prices. Prices form the starting point of bourgeois economics, which incidentally is why mainstream economists confuse more than they explain. We will explore, in future chapters, some of the factors that contribute to the formation of prices. These appear at the surface of the system. But Marx was more interested in uncovering the *underlying* dynamics of capitalism: what drives value, how it is produced, and for whom.

SOCIALLY NECESSARY LABOR-TIME

The labor theory of value—that a commodity's value in relation to other commodities is determined by how much labor has gone into producing it—was not a controversial point during Marx's day. For this reason, he actually spent very little time explaining or defining the concept. The idea that labor is the source of wealth and value in society was considered an obvious point by classical political economists like David Ricardo and Adam Smith.

The first line of Adam Smith's *Wealth of Nations* is: "The annual labor of every nation is the fund which originally supplies it with necessaries and conveniences of life."[26] And if Smith's words could be mistaken to be rhetorical flourish, he flushes the point out more explicitly later in the book:

> The real price of everything, what everything really costs to the man who wants to acquire it, is the toil and trouble of acquiring it. . . What is bought

with money or with goods is purchased by labor as much as what we acquire by the toil of our own body. That money or those goods indeed save us this toil. They contain the value of a certain quantity of labor which we exchange for what is supposed at the time to contain the value of an equal quantity. Labor was the first price, the original purchase-money that was paid for all things. It was not by gold or by silver, but by labor, that all the wealth of the world was originally purchased; and its value, to those who possess it, and who want to exchange it for some new productions, is precisely equal to the quantity of labor which it can enable them to purchase or command.[27]

Ultimately, the classical economists did not delve far enough into this potentially revolutionary concept.[28] Marx spent a lot of time taking apart their theories, showing what was worthwhile, and where they fell short. And modern economists—who today function more as apologists for capitalism than as social scientists—have altogether thrown out the idea, fearing its explosive implications. While Smith, Ricardo, and others developed their ideas in a period before working-class struggle emerged, later economists had seen enough militancy and class struggle to fear the radical implications of working-class power.

That's why mainstream economists today are known as neoclassical, rather than classical, economists. They profess dedication to the likes of Smith and Ricardo but have discarded the troubling labor theory of value. After all, if the producers of wealth are laborers and not the bosses, then the popular slogan of May 1968, "The boss needs you; You don't need the boss," is not abstract hyperbole, but a concrete roadmap for the future.

Marx's understanding of value was clearly more aligned to the classical bourgeois economists, who, writing at the early stages of capitalist development, were still genuinely trying to understand and explain the workings of the system. But where Smith and Ricardo left incomplete theories, Marx continued on, developing a social and economic framework on the basis of the labor theory of value. In order for this theory to be an effective analytical guide to understanding capitalism, Marx added a critical element: that the value of a commodity is determined by the amount of SOCIALLY NECESSARY LABOR-TIME that it takes to produce it.

The socially necessary labor-time is the average amount of time that it takes to produce a commodity "under the conditions of production normal for a given society and with the average degree of skill and intensity of labor prevalent in that society."[29] That is to say: what is the average time, using the common tools and technology within society, that it will take to construct a table? If the average is two hours—then this determines the table's exchange-value.

Without understanding socially necessary labor-time, value would be a completely subjective element. If, for instance, the author of this book, being (hopefully) a better writer than a table maker, decided to go into the table making business, my lack of skill and experience might translate into eight hours of labor to produce a (presumably shoddy) table. But this does not mean that my table would be worth four times as much as a table made by an established firm that produces a quality table in two hours. It would simply mean I've wasted an extra six hours of my life (or all eight, in the likely case that no one wants to buy my shoddy table). Most, if not all, of the time that I took to make the table would be deemed wasted labor by the market.

Socially necessary labor-time, as its name implies, is socially and historically determined. How long it takes to produce something in a given society changes over time. IBM's first personal computer in the 1970s cost thousands of dollars to purchase and could perform relatively few tasks. Today, the technology available to build computers is much more advanced, and therefore necessitates much less labor to create something a lot more complex. Now you can buy a personal computer that is many times more powerful than its 1970s predecessor for less than $300. "Value" under capitalism changes over time, further proof that it is not an inherent quality of the item, but socially determined.

The regulation of value by the socially necessary labor-time required to produce a given commodity takes on a force and momentum akin to the laws of nature. If tables are produced, on average, in two hours, all shoddy and inefficient table makers are forced to step up their techniques or bow out of table making. Marx writes:

> All different kinds of. . . labor are continually being reduced to the quantitative proportions in which society requires them. The reason for this reduction is that in the midst of the accidental and ever-fluctuating exchange relations between the products, the labor-time socially necessary to produce them asserts itself as a regulative law of nature. In the same way, the law of gravity asserts itself when a person's house collapses on top of him.[30]

We'll see how important this force of gravity is as we proceed. But the basic idea here is that if a corporation uses outdated techniques, lackadaisical work routines, or otherwise slow means to produce goods, it will discover bankruptcy as quickly as a house lacking proper construction will discover gravity. As socialist Alex Callinicos put it: "The pressure of competition forces producers to adopt similar methods of production to their rivals, or find themselves undercut."[31] A graphic design company would be historically obsolete if it designed websites from scratch using HTML tables. And a mining company that does not utilize the new and dangerous remote control and automation methods in mining would not be "competitive"—incidentally, a good reason to force safety regulations on industries rather than expecting the "laws of the market" to help companies regulate themselves.

GENERATIONS OF LABOR

The value of a commodity is not solely determined by the labor that directly produced it. The worth of a table, a jetliner, or an iPhone must also include the raw materials, tools, and technology used in the production of these commodities—from wood to turbines to microchips. But these raw materials and machinery are themselves commodities created by labor. As such, they all carry their own labor-determined value into the production of a new commodity. Essentially, their value simply gets passed into the value of the table, jetliner, or iPhone.

To explain the point, it's useful to distinguish between what Marx identified as LIVING LABOR—human labor that goes into the production of a commodity in the present time, and DEAD LABOR—previous generations of labor that carry past value into the process of production.

Let's go back to the table-making example. I said (arbitrarily, but for the sake of simplicity) that it would take, on average, two hours of labor—including design and manufacture—to make a table. But in order to produce a table, a furniture company will also have to buy materials: wood planks, glue, screws; and equipment: power saws, clamps, sanders, factory belts, and computer programs that generate cutting specifications.

Let's say that forty-five minutes of labor produced the amount of wood used and another fifteen minutes of labor generated the glue, screws, etc. used for making one table. That's another hour's worth of labor that is hidden in the production process. The raw materials simply pass on their value into a new product—the table.

Similarly, the value of the equipment used adds a fraction of its value to every round of production. Why a fraction? Take, for example, the value of a factory standard wide-belt sander. It costs about $12,000. Assume (again arbitrarily) that an average sander lasts for about four years before it becomes too worn out to be effectively used. That means that each year, the machine transfers about a quarter of its value to the tables that it sands. During its lifespan it will (the capitalists hope) pass its full value into the goods it's used to produce.

By the time we add in the labor passed on from all the other machinery and rent paid for the factory in which it's manufactured, its value will be greater still. The point of this very hypothetical example is of course not to determine exact prices, but to show how every component and input into production is measured by socially necessary labor-time.

Understanding that previous generations of labor embodied in the equipment and materials are "dead labor" but labor nonetheless, highlights the point that workers create value, not—as mainstream economics asserts—a combination of capitalist ingenuity, technology, and (perhaps) a nod to the workers manning that technology. And insofar as they are dead labor, they pass on only the value that was already imbued in them in the past. They cannot, like labor, create new wealth. As Marx explained:

> A machine which is not active in the labor process is useless. In addition, it falls prey to the destructive power of natural processes. Iron rusts; wood rots. Yarn with which we neither weave nor knit is cotton wasted. Living labor must seize upon these things, awaken them from the dead, change them from merely possible into real and effective use-values. Bathed in the fire of labor, appropriated as part of its organism, and infused with vital energy for the performance of the functions appropriate to their concept and to their vocation in the process, they are indeed consumed, but to some purpose, as elements in the formation of new use-values, new products, which are capable of entering into individual consumption as means of subsistence or into a new labor process as means of production.[32]

MONEY AND FETISHISM

If we start from this understanding of value, rather than with a surface appearance of prices, the real character of money loses its mystique. Value—which is just a crystallization of abstract labor—is represented by money. We'll see in the next chapter that money is itself a commodity, which by custom and circumstance, has become a universal measure against which all other items on the market are exchanged. Instead of saying that it takes an equal amount of time to produce a ballpoint pen as a Life Savers candy, we can simply say that they both have a value of ten cents. Thus by being a portable and universal embodiment of value, money simplifies and mediates the process of trading goods.

In Marx's words, "Money necessarily crystalizes out of the process of exchange."[33] As markets developed, money became a convenient and necessary substitute for simple barters of commodities based on socially agreed upon labor-times. With money, a producer of bread doesn't have to go to the marketplace with ten loaves of bread in order to buy a chair. At the same time, a chair maker doesn't need to exchange her chair for ten loaves of bread if she only wants one today and another loaf later in the week. Money conveniently stores value over time, which its owner can dispense of as he or she sees fit.

Money also conceals the true nature of value, so that when you go to the supermarket, you don't think you're trading an equivalent amount of your "congealed mass of labor" with someone else's. As David Harvey explained:

> You go into a supermarket and you want to buy a head of lettuce. In or-der to buy the lettuce, you have to put down a certain sum of money. The material relation between the money and the lettuce express a social re-lation because the price—the "how much"—is socially determined, and the price is a monetary representation of value. Hidden within this market exchange of things is a relation between you, the consumer, and the direct producers—those who labored to produce the lettuce. . . . The end result is that our social relation to the laboring activities of others is disguised in the relationships between things. You cannot, for example, figure out in the supermarket whether the lettuce has been produced by happy laborers, miserable laborers, slave laborers, wage laborers, or some self-employed peasant. The lettuces are mute, as it were, as to how they were produced and who produced them.[34]

The real social relations of production and exchange are therefore hid-den behind a veil of what appears to be a relationship between money and commodities. Instead of human relationships, we have economic relation-ships between goods. Or as Marx put it: "It is nothing but the definite so-cial relation between men themselves which assumes here, for them, the fantastic form of a relation between things."[35] The hidden relations of pro-duction—wage labor and, as we'll see, exploitation—behind this "fantastic form" are specific and peculiar characteristics of capitalism. They did not exist in pre-capitalist class societies, which, despite their brutality, lacked the cloak of "fairness" that capitalism purports.[36] The process of producing commodities, Marx wrote, "has mastery over man, instead of the opposite."[37]

This is the essence of what Marx dubbed COMMODITY FETISHISM. What other way can you describe the modern worship of every new generation of Apple products than fetishism? We idolize these things that we consider to be outside and external to us, but in fact are our own creations. By using the term "fetishism," Marx was also taking a jab at the philosophers of the Enlightenment, who saw superstition as primitive, and hailed the rationality of capitalism. The thinkers of the Enlightenment promoted science and logic, yet had no problem with a warped reality in which *things* are powerful and valuable, while *human beings* relate to each other through the exchange of those things.

CONCLUSION

We've traced here the basic contours of Marx's theory of value. We can see now that capitalism is a system where social relations are determined by, and subordinated to, the exchange of commodities. Each of these commodities has a use-value, whether good (e.g. fruit), bad (e.g. nuclear arsenal), or indifferent (e.g. Garbage Pail Kids). But it is exchange-value that concerns capitalists, and becomes the criteria through which society determines what is or isn't produced, what is or isn't worth investment.

Yet despite the fact that our lives seem to be at the mercy of inanimate exchange-values, the role of labor in determining these values has powerful and revolutionary implications. We'll explore the role of labor more fully in future chapters. But first, in order to further demystify the machinations of the system, we'll follow the scent of money, and see exactly how it is that the "coagulated state" of value congeals into bills of paper that can be stacked in your wallet or electronically digitized in the bank.

THE WASTE OF SOCIETY

Production has expanded exponentially since Marx's time; our society bursts at the seams with commodities. The drive to make commodities in order to *sell* them—rather than to directly *consume* them—gives us a clue as to why the production of commodities expands over the long term. We'll discuss this further in chapter five. But the essence is that while there may be a limit to how much one feudal lord and his family can consume, production for the market knows no such natural bounds.

Capitalism has left no stone unturned in its quest to commodify all living and nonliving matter on the planet—from those as plentiful and mundane as water, to those as absurd and abstract as Wall Street's financial cocktails.[38] If there is a dollar to be made, capitalism will find a way to package it up and sell it.

One way to measure the phenomenal growth of commodities produced under capitalism is to measure the size of our landfills, which now number about two thousand across the country, logging in 265 million metric tons of waste. Of course, official landfills don't capture the total amount of commodity production and waste, since much of our waste doesn't end up in landfills. One extreme example is known as the Great Pacific Garbage Patch, a floating island of debris in the Pacific Ocean so large it is visible from space. This drifting stew of junk stretches across an area larger than the state of Texas.[39]

Along with the wealth of society comes the waste of society. Every year, the amount of paper and plastic cups, forks, and spoons used in the United States alone could circle the equator three hundred times. There is also a yearly average of about 380 billion plastic bags and wraps (which themselves require twelve million barrels of oil to create).[40] According to Heather Rogers: "Every American discards more than 1,600 pounds of rubbish a year, more than 4.5 pounds per person per day."[41] Starting in 1960, the US government's Environmental Protection Agency (EPA) has measured the country's total Municipal Solid Waste (MSW), essentially the everyday items that make up our garbage (food and yard waste, packaging, office paper, clothing, etc.). In 2017, we produced 268 million tons of waste—up from just eighty-eight million tons six decades ago.[42]

Of course, *municipal* garbage is itself a tiny fraction of the overall waste produced, most of which is generated by industry. But unlike municipal waste, industrial waste is largely untracked. An oft-quoted but vastly out-of-date EPA study in the 1980s found that about 7.6 billion tons of manufacturing waste is created annually.[43] This conservative estimate is the equivalent weight of over twenty thousand Empire State Buildings, but a lot more toxic.

This dramatic increase in annual waste mirrors an overall trend of the system to produce ever-growing amounts of commodities, for sale in ever-expanding markets. Take the automobile industry. According to the Bureau of Transportation Statistics, there were 74 million automobiles registered in the United States in 1960. By 2017 that number nearly quadrupled to 272 million.[44] More than 96 million automobiles were produced worldwide in 2017 alone.[45] Similarly in plastics, 381 million tons of plastic were produced annually around the world in 2015, a two-hundred-fold increase since 1950. To put it in context, wrote researchers Hannah Ritchi and Max Roser, "this is roughly equivalent to the mass of two-thirds of the world population."[46] A 2014 study found that there were more than five trillion pieces of plastic floating in our oceans. That number is surely larger today.[47]

The explosion of goods in modern society is not only the result of a growing number of commodities in any given market but is also a consequence of the number of things which are now considered *marketable*. The *types* of things that are now for sale continue to increase as capitalism commodifies a greater and greater share of our lives. This has happened through the privatization of things like health care and education, which used to be outside the laws of the capitalist market. It has also happened by attaching a price tag to things that previously had none. Rather than finding collective solutions to social problems, all issues are subjugated to the machinations of the market. Corporations can now buy credits to pollute past regulatory standards through the emissions trading market. Thus November 2012 was the unsettling occasion of the country's first ever auction of greenhouse gas pollution credits in California.

The market expands further as it insinuates commercial value to women's bodies and sex on advertisements. And it reaches into every realm of society, taking previously counterculture activities like skateboarding and hawking thousands of magazines, video games, sneakers, and paraphernalia. Kids in the 1980s who made their own ramps to do tricks at home and punks who skated in the 1990s can now buy skateboarding-themed ceramic travel mugs online for $24.95.

Along with this expansion comes the ideology of the market as the know-all and cure-all for society's needs. As David Harvey explains:

> To presume that markets and market signals can best determine all allocative decisions is to presume that everything can in principle be treated as a commodity. Commodification presumes the existence of property rights over processes, things, and social relations that a price can be put on them, and that they can be traded subject to legal contract. The market is presumed to work as an appropriate guide—an ethic—for all human action.[48]

CHAPTER THREE

MONEY

We see then that commodities are in love with money, but
that "the course of true love never did run smooth."
—*Capital, Volume 1*[1]

THE MAN BEHIND THE CURTAIN

"Pay no attention to that man behind the curtain!" said a frazzled old man
standing by a console of levers. Behind the smoke and flames of the tower-
ing, disembodied head of the famed Wizard of Oz stood an ordinary, un-
remarkable old man. Such too is the story of money. Its mysterious power
determines the laws by which we live. Yet behind its frightening mystique is a
simple man-made solution to the demands of a market-based system of trade.

Pieces of paper (or computerized electronic bits in our bank accounts)
representing currency seem to have limitless control over our lives. Whether
you have it, and how much of it you have, determines whether you eat or go
hungry; whether you're entitled to the finest health care money can buy, or
are left bleeding to death at the hospital's door; whether your children will
be treated to an elite educational facility, or patted down routinely by the
cops for living in a "high-crime neighborhood"; whether you are politically
connected and taken care of in the halls of Washington, or whether you have
to fight to even have your vote be counted.

Money is so woven into the fabric of our daily lives that we rarely stop
to wonder how it got to be that these pieces of paper have come to dominate
our lives. Every day it slips in and out of our hands—every time we get on the
train to work or fill up our car with gas, stop for a sandwich, pay the electric
bill to keep the lights on and the internet running, get an item of clothing or

a piece of furniture—each of these things is procured by money. It seems as natural as the air we breathe.

Marx took great pains to break down the processes and logic underlying the physical appearance of money. Money, or the "money-form," as Marx explained, is simply a particular physical format representing the development of "value" in market-based societies. It is a universal measure against which all commodities reflect their value. As we said at the end of the last chapter, we can count the worth of a pen and a Life Savers as ten cents, instead of saying that they both embody an equal amount of labor-time.

Having a universal measure of value is critical to any society that depends on trade and exchange—even relatively simple barter economies. Imagine a marketplace in which the bearers of each commodity—a furniture maker, a baker, and many other producers, have to determine the value of their commodity relative to every other commodity in the market. This would lead to a dizzying number of equations.

Enter money: rather than saying that your chair is worth ten times as much as a loaf of bread, and a hundred times as much as a ballpoint pen, and a quarter of an iPhone case, ad infinitum, it is much easier to say that it is worth ten dollars. If all other commodities are measured this way, the ratio with which they exchange with each other will be easily determined. And if those ten dollars can easily fit into your bag, and be spent whenever you see fit, this eases the entire process.

Mainstream economics assume that money determines the values of commodities, and that somehow through its own power, money creates circulation and exchange. But as Marx argued, the relationship is in reverse. The existence of money is determined by the value (congealed units of socially necessary labor-time) of commodities. Because all commodities have values embodied within them, they can be measured against each other and given a price tag with money.

It is not that money

renders . . . commodities commensurable . . . quite the contrary. Because all commodities, as values, are objectified human labor, and therefore in themselves commensurable, their values can be communicably measured in one and the same specific commodity, and this commodity can be converted into the common measure of their values, that is into money. Money as a measure of value is the necessary form of appearance of the measure of value which is immanent in commodities, namely labor-time.[2]

In fact, money plays several simultaneous roles: Within the circulation process, as we've discussed, it measures and reflects the values of commodities by providing a price tag. It then eases the process of circulation of those commodities by functioning as a convenient and easily portable medium of exchange. Finally, money can also be removed from the circulation process to serve as a store of value over time.

How did money come to play these roles? This is a problem of both history and logic. To understand the *logic* of money—to unveil the man behind the curtain—it's useful to follow Marx in a brief, albeit somewhat abstract, detour through the pages of *Capital*. Following this theoretical illustration, we will then outline a brief history of how money concretely developed over time along with capitalism. Finally, once these foundations are in place, we'll return to the question of the relationship between value, money, and price.

A UNIVERSAL EQUIVALENT

In volume 1 of *Capital*, Marx introduced the equation: "20 yards of linen = 1 coat." This equation was not meant to describe a concrete or historical reality, though it's possible that at some point in some place, one could trade twenty yards of linen for a coat. Instead, "20 yards of linen = 1 coat" served as a launching point for Marx to take us from point A to point B to point C on a theoretical exposition, which ended with an understanding of the role of money.

At face value, the meaning of this equation is self-evident. The amount of socially necessary labor-time that it takes to produce twenty yards of linen is equal to the amount of socially necessary labor-time that it takes to produce one coat. But Marx picked apart this seemingly simple equation by distinguishing between the two poles of this equation. The twenty yards of linen, he explained, is the RELATIVE VALUE, and the coat is its EQUIVALENT VALUE.

By "relative value," Marx meant that the linen's value is the one being determined; it is the active part of the equation. The relative value asks the question: "How valuable (relatively speaking) is twenty yards of linen?" The "equivalent value," on the other hand, is simply an item of equivalent value to the linen; it plays a passive part of the equation—a marker of how much value is embodied in twenty yards of linen. The coat does not have an independent role, it only reflects the value that is embodied in the linen. The equivalent value answers the question, "How valuable is twenty yards of linen?" with the answer: "It holds one coats' worth of value!"

As Marx explained, the relative and equivalent forms are "two insepara-ble moments, which belong to and mutually condition each other."[3] It does us no good to say that twenty yards of linen equals twenty yards of linen. The (relative) value of linen can only be expressed in another commodity's (equivalent) value.

Now if the maker of linen wants to trade her linen for tea, she'll need to measure the relative value of her linen by the measurement of tea. She may find that her twenty yards of linen is also equivalent to 10 lbs. of tea. So, in this case, the tea becomes the equivalent, or the measure of the linen's value. If the linen maker wanted to trade her linen for sandals, she may find that twenty yards finds its equivalent in two pairs of shoes.

"The linen," explained Marx,

> by virtue of the form of value, no longer stands in a social relation with merely one other kind of commodity, but with the whole world of com-modities as well. As a commodity it is a citizen of that world. At the same time, the endless series of expressions of its value implies that, from the point of view of the value of the commodity, the particular form of use-val-ue in which it appears [its equivalent value] is a matter of indifference.[4]

What Marx is saying is that the specifics of whether linen's value is be-ing measured against tea or sandals or coats doesn't matter. What matters is the amount of abstract human labor objectified in each. These items lose their subjectivity as they become simple units of measurements of the value of linen. They can become equivalents only because they, like linen, embody human labor in the form of value. "Despite [the coat's] buttoned-up appear-ance, the linen recognizes in it a splendid kindred soul, the soul of value."[5]

As markets develop, the limitations of these equations become self-evident. Whereas societies that only bartered specific products could do so in accordance with ritual or traditional procedures, generalized exchange and commerce require a great number of such equivalent relationships. As Ernest Mandel explained:

> The relations of equivalence concern no longer just two products, or two categories of product, but an infinite variety of different goods. It is no lon-ger the labor-time of the potter that is compared with that of the agricul-turist; ten, twenty, thirty different crafts have to compare their respective productive efforts from time to time. In order that these exchanges may go on without interruption, the owners of the commodities must be able to get rid of their goods before they have had the luck to encounter purchas-ers who possess the products they themselves want to obtain in exchange for these goods.[6]

Imagine going to the mall to procure a cookbook. You have 40 lbs. of tea with you, and you go up to the owner of the bookstore and pull out a sheet of endless equations, "Well, I see here that my 40 lbs. of tea are equal to eighty yards of linen or four coats or eight pairs of shoes or . . . " and scroll down till you find, "Ah, it's equal to two books!" And then the bookseller has to confirm with her sheet of endless equations, "well, I see my book is equal to such and such and such and such. . . oh and 20 lbs. of tea!"

The problem, Marx argued, is 1) that the equation is "incomplete, because the series of its representations never comes to an end" 2) that it is a "motley mosaic of disparate and unconnected expressions of value": and 3) that each commodity will have its own "endless series of expressions of value which are all different from the relative form of value of every other commodity."

So, the solution to this inefficient and incomplete set of equations is to flip the equation around. So now it would read: one coat or 10 lbs. of tea or two shoes and so on *are all equal* to twenty yards of linen. Now linen becomes not only the equivalent part of the equation, but it becomes a UNIVERSAL EQUIVALENT against which *all* commodities are measured. So, no matter which store I go to, every store owner sells their commodities on the basis of how many yards of linen they're worth.

This equation "imposes the character of universal equivalent on the linen, which is the commodity excluded, as equivalent, from the whole world of commodities."[7] The linen becomes the bearer of abstract, undifferentiated human labor. Again, Marx wasn't making a historical point here about linen's role in the market. He was demonstrating how any single commodity (whether it be linen, cigarettes, cattle, or silver) could be assigned such a role. If we now replace linen with gold and eventually gold with paper bills. . . the absurdity and mystique of money is uncovered. Marx wrote:

> If I state that coats or boots stand in a relation to linen because the latter is the universal incarnation of abstract human labor, the absurdity of the statement is self-evident. Nevertheless, when the producers of coats and boots bring these commodities into a relation with linen, or with gold or silver (and this makes no difference here), as the universal equivalent, the relations between their own private labor and the collective labor of society appears to them in exactly this absurd form.[8]

The role of universal equivalent has, in fact, been filled by different commodities over time. At the dawn of petty commodity production, the first universal equivalents were often those goods that were most commonly exchanged, and were either of fundamental importance to the economies (e.g. food or tools) or were ornaments frequently used.[9] Eventually, as we'll see below, the role came to be played most significantly by gold. As economics professor Doug Orr explained in an article for *Dollars and Sense* magazine:

> The "things" that get used as money have changed over time, and "modern" people often chuckle when they hear about some of them. The Romans used salt (from which we get the world "salary"), South Sea Islanders used shark's teeth, and several societies actually used cows. The "Three Wise Men" brought gold, frankincense, and myrrh, each of which was money in different regions at the time.
>
> If money does not exist, or is in short supply, it will be created. In POW camps, where guards specifically outlaw its existence, prisoners use cigarettes instead. In the American colonies, the British attempted to limit the supply of British pounds, because they knew that by limiting the supply of money, they could hamper the development of independent markets in the colonies. . . To overcome this problem, the colonists began to use tobacco leaves as money.[10]

SWEATING MONEY

The capacity for value to be objectified within a physical entity of money allows for the process of circulation to take place with ease. Yet, certain physical characteristics make some forms of money more or less suitable to grease the wheels of exchange. The more that commerce developed in scale, eventually extending into a world market, the greater became the need for a stable and transferable currency. Metal coins came to supplant other forms, like cattle, because they were more practical to carry around, they didn't age and die, and they could be made relatively uniformly. They could also easily be split into discrete quantities. Exchanging half or a quarter of a cow is considerably more difficult than dividing up ten gold coins into two groups of five.

Precious metals thus established themselves over time as universal equivalents for exactly those reasons. Certain qualities were found to be more suitable for the job by merchants and administrators. As Mandel outlined: "Their high specific weight enables them to concentrate in a modest volume a quantity of metal representing a fairly large exchange value," thus deeming them *transportable*. They are also *durable*, "owing to their resistance to wear and tear, rust, etc." Metals are *divisible*, and "fragments can be easily melted down into larger units."[11] Lastly, they need to be *recognizable*, easy to replicate into known qualities, but simultaneously guarding against counterfeiting through detection of differing weights.[12] These physical attributes make some metals more practical than others. Gold, for instance, doesn't oxidize under normal pressures and temperatures—which means it will not deteriorate in the way that silver or copper or other metals do. The malleability of gold also makes it easy to turn coins into bars or jewelry, thus physically adding or subtracting from the money supply.

By easing circulation, money is thus able to appear, disappear, and reappear again in every exchange. Direct exchange of goods—chair for bread—means that one item is replaced by another. In order to get bread, I have to get rid of my chair. And then both items are used, or "consumed" by their buyers. Yet "money does not vanish" through circulation. Instead it continually passes from hand to hand. "It always leaves behind a precipitate at a point in the arena of circulation vacated by the commodities. . . . When one commodity replaces another, the money commodity always sticks to the hands of some third person. Circulation sweats money from every pore."[13]

From its throne as universal equivalent, money displaces personal or social relations. Cash is inherently impersonal. It sits in a cash register. Where did it come from? What did it buy? You don't need to know the person, source, or where it will go. You can buy a ping-pong table, some diapers and baby formula, or this book from a guy named Jeff Bezos, whom you have never met, but he happens to own Amazon.com and conducts business deals with you on the regular. Behind Jeff are over two million suppliers of goods, and behind them millions of low-paid factory, warehouse, and transportation workers, as well as salespeople, whose names you will never know.[14] Items for sale also lose *their* subjectivity as they are reduced to a single number, their price.

"The circulation of commodities differs from the direct exchange of products," argued Marx, "not only in *form*, but in its *essence*. We have only to consider the course of events." Describing the anonymity and boundlessness of this circulation, he wrote:

> The weaver has undoubtedly exchanged his linen for a Bible, his own commodity for someone else's. But this phenomenon is only true for him. The Bible-pusher, who prefers a warming drink to cold sheets, had no intention of exchanging linen for his Bible; the weaver did not know that wheat had been exchanged for his line. B's commodity replaces that of A, but A and B do not mutually exchange their commodities. It may in fact happen that A and B buy from each other, but a particular relationship of this kind is by no means the necessary result of the general conditions of the circulation of commodities. We see here, on the one hand, how the exchange of commodities breaks through all the individual and local limitations of the

direct exchange of products, and develops the metabolic process of human labor. On the other hand, there develops a whole network of social connections of natural origin, entirely beyond the control of the human agents.[15]

A STORE OF VALUE

Lastly, as Marx's above example may also imply, money can store value over time. Were the Bible-pusher to sell his Bible on Monday, but want to wait till Friday to purchase brandy, the intermediary of cash could be used to hold his earnings until he's ready to spend them. This solves the problem of a "coincidence of wants" of a barter economy, as classical economists dubbed it. I may have a chair to sell today, but can I find a person who wants a chair and at the same time has exactly the equivalent amount of bread to exchange it with? Even worse, my chair may be worth ten loaves of bread, but I only need two and on different days of the week.

Instead of each producer and buyer on the market bringing out all their goods and finding a simultaneous and comparable exchange to meet their needs, trading goods for money allows the seller to use that money when and how they please. So I can sell my chair (or, more likely today, my labor-power) on Friday for $30. I may then get a pint to celebrate the end of the week for $7 at the end of the day. The following Monday and Wednesday, I'll spend $6 for two loaves of bread, and put the rest away to pay my rent at the end of the month.

This simplistic example is meant to highlight a broader point: an artisanal feudal market could perhaps operate several times a year for people to gather and swap their goods. But a market economy, made up of an infinite amount of mass-produced goods, must function with a speed and fluidity that can only be facilitated by money.

The convenience of cash clearly suits the modern capitalists as well. A coffee shop may sell enough drinks to generate a few thousand dollars a day. This capital can be put away and used in part for payroll on Friday, while the rest is saved for a mass expenditure at the end of the year for the newest line of cappuccino maker. Conversely, an agricultural company that sells wheat harvests their crops at the beginning of the summer but will have expenses all year round. Meanwhile hotels make their biggest returns during tourist seasons, and so need to hold on to their revenue in order to pay their bills during off-seasons.

Money can also be a means to preserve wealth during recessions. This is a more complicated question, which we'll take up later on. But in a nutshell, you can see how capitalists would want to hold onto their wealth rather than invest it in new production if they see no potential for profitable investments.[16] In a sense, this is the same idea, but on a larger scale, of a hotel holding on to its savings through an off-season. But rather than ensure that the system continues to function, uninterrupted by on- and off-seasons, withholding investment during a recession achieves the opposite effect: a further breakdown of the economy.

A GLITTERING INCARNATION

The role that gold played as the dominant currency, or universal equivalent, for much of capitalist economic history is implied by mainstream economists to be its natural function. The precious metal's worth is assumed to be as intrinsic to its physicality as the color of its shine. The French postmodernist Michel Foucault philosophized:

> The signs of exchange, because they satisfy desire, are sustained by the dark, dangerous, and accursed glitter of metal. An equivocal glitter, for it reproduces in the depths of the earth that other glitter that sings at the far end of the night: it resides there like an inverted promise of happiness, and, because metal resembles the stars, the knowledge of all these perilous treasures is at the same time knowledge of the world.[17]

A contemporary (albeit less poetic) internet explanation from onlygold.com is a typical illustration of the same principle: "Humans almost intuitively place a high value on gold, equating it with power, beauty, and the cultural elite. And since gold is widely distributed all over the globe, we find this same thinking about gold throughout ancient and modern civilizations everywhere."[18] It seems as though humans all over the world, easily impressed by shining metal, spontaneously attached great value to gold. If this were indeed the case, we are hard pressed to explain why humans seem to be as easily impressed by decidedly unshiny green bills of paper currency.

In reality, while gold is itself a commodity and has always carried its own value—equal to the socially necessary labor-time required to find, mine, and smelt it—its Wizard of Oz-like power grew out of its role as the accepted universal equivalent. As discussed above, there is a long history of other commodities serving that same role. Thus for thousands of years, gold was used alongside many other commodities and types of metallic coins—from

Ancient Egypt to the Greek and Roman Empire, up until the development of modern capitalism in Western Europe in the sixteenth century. Yet by the end of the nineteenth century, gold had become the preeminent universal equivalent.

Countries around the world had developed their own systems and currencies, but the need for a universal equivalent that could be used across countries grew as capitalism became a worldwide system. A global system under a gold standard, whereby local economic units, such as the British pound, could be fixed and convertible to weights of gold, took centuries to unfold.[19] Ultimately its predominance followed the hegemony of Britain as a world power—financially and militarily. As historian Pierre Vilar explained: "If late 17th century England laid the basis for what was to become the world monetary system (the gold standard and banknotes), this can only be understood in terms of the establishment of England's power, especially her international and maritime power, which was then taking place."[20]

British power grew in strength from the sixteenth to the eighteenth centuries, based on its advancing industrial development and a massive upheaval of agrarian relations—the enclosure movements discussed in chapter one.[21] Among the most powerful arms that the state used to establish monetary order was the Bank of England, founded in 1694. The Bank of England issued bank notes as receipts for gold deposits, just as gold merchants had issued "running cash notes" for a similar purpose. But the bank's notes became authoritative and eventually accepted and encouraged by merchants as payments to circulate in the economy. By 1773 the consolidation of the Bank of England's authority was evidenced by the introduction of the death penalty for anyone caught forging its bank notes![22]

In the early nineteenth century, this system of pegging currency to the central bank's gold reserves became an official GOLD STANDARD. Each coin or bank-issued bill was worth a certain amount of gold, which could be redeemed by its carrier from the Bank of England at any point. The value of gold, in turn, reflected the labor-time necessary to produce it as a commodity, fluctuations of supply (where and in what quantity it could be found) and demand (determined by the economy's needs of production and circulation of goods). By the late nineteenth century, most countries tied their currencies to gold. For the decades that it operated, it provided a relatively stable price system, in which currencies were all fixed against the same measurements, and all accounts, across any border, could be settled in gold.

The gold standard eventually crumbled under the pressure of the Great Depression and transformed itself for the needs of a new world order. After World War II, it was resuscitated in a different form. Allied nations met through the United Nations Monetary and Financial Conference and agreed to a system that became known as the Bretton Woods Agreement. Bretton Woods set up the International Monetary Fund (IMF) and required all currencies to be tied to the US dollar at fixed rates of exchange. The dollar, in turn, was pegged to gold.

The postwar system now affirmed and strengthened the actuality of the United States' preeminent economic and political position in the world. The IMF, for decades since, has served as an instrument to serve the needs of the US ruling class.[23] Meanwhile the monetary system solidified the US dollar as the world's premier currency, used for conduct of all international trade. The dollar-centered system still relied on gold as the underlying value behind it, since the US was obligated to redeem any foreign reserves of dollars for gold.

Thus Marx's description of contemporary capitalism remained apt for over a century in one form or another. "Modern society," he wrote, "which has already in its infancy pulled Pluto by the hair of his head from the bowels of the earth, greets gold as its Holy Grail, as the glittering incarnation of its innermost principle of life."[24]

FROM GLITTERING GOLD TO IMAGINED ELECTRONIC BITS

Gold, as we've discussed, was a convenient currency for the purposes of measuring value, easing circulation, and storing wealth. It could easily be melted, formed, measured, and carried. But it reached two limits. First, though its supply could be relatively guaranteed in the long run, in the short-term, gold's supply—and therefore its price—was susceptible to wild swings brought on by gold rushes (such as the discovery of gold in California and Australia in the mid-19th century) or dried reserves (such as the decrease in mining of Brazilian gold due to struggles for independence in the region). Second, at points of economic crisis or war, the need for greater money supplies and credit required surpassing the bounds of gold in supply.

In practice, governments abandoned the gold standard whenever they deemed it necessary. The US did so at the onset of the Civil War, again during World War I when governments around the world inflated their economies to finance the war, and again in response to the Great Depression. In each of these cases, states' abilities to fund wars, stimulate investment, and generally regulate the needs of the economy trumped any formal adherence to pegging currency to gold.

The gold standard was finally discarded in 1971, based on the changing needs of the US ruling class. The weakening of the United States' economic position relative to the other world economies at the time meant that America's trade partners were purchasing less American goods, and accumulating dollars that they did not need. Foreign financial institutions were cashing their dollars for gold. And so, facing a swelling outflow of gold, which the US treasury could neither stem nor satisfy, then-President Richard Nixon announced the breaking of dollar to gold convertibility.

Paper money and global currencies thus became delinked from the traditional commodity money form, which had dominated the capitalist economy until that point. Paper bills had functioned as certificates that represented ownership of gold held by banks or the Federal Reserve, and that gold was itself a commodity, which held value. Since the end of the gold standard, money became more complex and intangible, representing "value" in its own right, though it is made up of no particular substance, with no intrinsic worth. Its effectiveness as a means of payment is dependent on state-enforced standards.

Gold's value as a commodity reflected the socially necessary labor-time required for extracting and processing the metal. Previous commodity forms of money, whether they were linen, oxen, or silver, could similarly measure their value through the labor-time required to produce them. Today's paper money, in contrast, is not a commodity. If its value was measured by necessary labor-time, money would indeed be very cheap, as it is rather effortless to produce. And a one-dollar bill would be worth the same as a one-hundred-dollar bill.

Paper currencies' values are in fact abstracted, based on an agreed-upon faith we hold in their role as representatives of value. This is even more the case today, as physical cash makes up a very small percentage of circulating money in our society. Money is another step removed from physical currency, residing as electronic data in banks' computers. As one radical economics textbook points out: "With modern electronic banking, deposits can quietly change hands, without ever touching hands."[25] Cash and electronic bits are certainly less tangible than gold, nevertheless their origin and the role of money as a universal equivalent to measure, circulate, and store value remains the same. (How easily, and to what extent, society can attach value to any currency system has recently been tested by the rise—and fall, and rise, etc.—of Bitcoins. See sidebar: "What's in a Bitcoin?")

WHAT'S IN A BITCOIN?

Bitcoin, the largest and best-known digital currency, was designed and created by an anonymous programmer (or possibly group of programmers) "Satoshi Nakamoto," and released in 2009. Its aim was to mediate online transactions without financial intermediaries (such as banks) and without direction from any single state. Bitcoin is known as a "crypto-currency" because it uses a "blockchain" technology, which is essentially a virtual ledger of all transactions. The technology behind Bitcoin is beyond the scope of this discussion (and this author), but its outcome is that it can provide reliable, secure transactions without a central authority. The *Economist* described the process:

> Every ten minutes each machine or group of machines [involved in documenting and producing Bitcoins] takes a block of pending transactions, and uses it as the input for a mathematical puzzle. The first to find a solution announces it to the rest, which check that it is right, and that the transactions are valid. If a majority approve, the block is cryptographically attached to the ledger and the computers move on to a new set of transactions.[26]

Solving these mathematical problems also rewards the user with new Bitcoins (this is what's meant by Bitcoin "mining"). But what may have begun as a libertarian's utopia and computer nerd's wet dream, in which individuals are able to "home brew" their own money, has become a highly specialized and environmentally degrading industry. The numbers-crunching power of computers mining Bitcoins requires an enormous amount of electricity—more electricity per year than the whole of Ireland.[27] The *Economist* continued:

> Startups from all over the world began building specialised hardware powered by custom-built chips, known as application-specific integrated circuits (ASICs). Leaving the

amateurs behind, these firms soon became locked in a digital arms race. Microprocessors usually double their power every 18 months, a rhythm called Moore's law. In the case of mining ASICs, this doubling has occurred every six months . . . As a result, new mining computers, which each cost several thousand dollars, have been becoming obsolete in a matter of months.[28]

The colossal infrastructure investments that have gone into "mining" and verifying Bitcoin make it unlikely that this cryptocurrency will suddenly disappear anytime soon, as does the promise of potentially huge payouts. But it seems equally unlikely that Bitcoin will take off to become a currency that millions of people actually use. Ten years since its release, it is still accepted by a very small number of vendors, and most of its recorded transactions are speculative trades of the coins themselves, rather than purchases of merchandise. Analysts at Morgan Stanley recently wrote: "bitcoin acceptance is virtually zero and shrinking."[29] Out of a group of five hundred top online merchants, only three of those merchants accepted Bitcoin as of July 2017. In this sense it plays a role more as an investment vehicle (something we'll discuss further in chapter seven) than a currency.

There are a few reasons why. First, for a currency to be of use to buyers or sellers, it needs to be stable enough to provide a reflection of value and price. (This is also why currencies that go into an inflationary free fall, like the Argentinian peso in the 1980s or the dollar in Zimbabwe in the 2000s, for instance, become useless.) But in a span of two and a half months, between November 2017 and mid-January of the following year, Bitcoin's value went from $5,500 to nearly $20,000 back down to $10,500. By the time this book goes to print, it will have doubtless experienced even greater highs and lows.

Let's say you own a car dealership and are willing to accept Bitcoin for your cars. You accept a single Bitcoin for a car, when it is worth $20,000, but the next week, that Bitcoin is worth $10,000. In a sense, you have sold your car for half its intended cost. Of course you could hold on to the

Bitcoin you've earned, assuming or hoping that its value will rise again. But this is a risky venture, and again, resembles speculative gambling more than the functions of day-to-day high-volume market exchanges.

A currency must also be relatively stable as a store of value. Recall our chair maker, who for the money she received for her chair wanted to buy bread on two different days, and save the rest to pay her rent. But if she saves her income in Bitcoins, who knows whether they'll cover rent at the end of the month. On the one hand, if it seems like the currency's value is dropping fast, she might be inclined to just get rid of the Bitcoins as quickly as possible. On the other hand, if it seems like its price will continue to rise in the long run, she'll be more interested in holding on to them than spending, hoping for higher returns down the line.

Lastly, both vendors and customers have to tolerate slow and costly transaction procedures in order to use Bitcoins. Currently Bitcoin protocols can process a handful of transactions per second globally. Compare this to conventional systems, such as Visa, which can handle ten thousand per second.[30] Currently, a low demand for Bitcoin by consumers means that there is not enough incentive for merchants to invest in Bitcoin infrastructure.

Could this change in the future? It's possible, though in my opinion unlikely. For their part, mainstream economics "experts" understand about as much about Bitcoin's "value" as they do about other speculative bubbles. A senior reporter with the techie news source, *Ars Technica*, for instance, had this analysis to share in December 2017: "I think it's going to continue to be volatile. I think it will probably go up more, but I don't know how much more. And then I think it will probably crash. But I don't know how much—you know, how far down it will decline."[31]

What is clear is that whatever Bitcoin's libertarian roots, its outcome is an absurd spectacle only possible under capitalism. In 2015 the *Economist* reported:

A huge aircraft hangar in Boden, in northern Sweden, big enough to hold a dozen helicopters, is now packed with computers—45,000 of them, each with a whirring fan to stop it overheating. The machines work ceaselessly, trying to solve fiendishly difficult mathematical puzzles. The solutions are, in themselves, unimportant. Yet by solving the puzzles, the computers earn their owners a reward in bitcoin, a digital "crypto-currency."[32]

Thus a hangar which used to hold actual physical goods is now warehousing thousands of computers solving meaningless riddles, at great environmental cost, for the purpose of producing nothing but fodder for risky gambles. The magic of capitalism is at it again.

PRICE AND CURRENCY

Price, Marx argued, is not the same thing as value. While value is determined by socially necessary labor-time, prices tend to fluctuate above and below this value, and sometimes wildly so. In volume 1 of *Capital*, Marx presented a theoretical assumption in which prices and values coincide. He did so for the sake of unearthing the elemental dynamics of value. But this assumption has to do with his method of scientific inquiry, and not his belief that price and value are the same. Confusion about Marx's method has been used to deny the validity of the labor theory of value; critics point out the various examples in the concrete world in which prices clearly don't line up with the amount of labor-time that has gone into producing a particular commodity.

In fact, Marx argued that value merely finds expression through prices, but it does not do so in an immovable way. At its base, PRICE is the ratio between a given quantity of a commodity and its equivalent in money. It would be futile to attempt to find the exact price equivalent of an hour's worth of labor-time embodied in a commodity. Several processes take place between the time that labor imbued it with value and the time that a price tag is slapped on it.

What are the factors that would change the price of a commodity? The most fundamental cause would be a change in the actual base value of a product—that is if it took a greater or lesser amount of time to produce that commodity. For instance, recent developments in chilling and condensing natural gas have made it possible to easily ship gas across oceans. Thus the time associated with, and therefore the cost of, transporting natural gas has dropped, and along with it the price of natural gas itself. But there are other things that could cause a change in the price of a commodity, even if its base *value* remained the same.

Firstly, the impact of supply and demand creates fluctuations in price. If there is a *glut* of oil or gas in the energy market, companies will race to get rid of their products before they are left holding unsellable goods. To do so they may drive down prices below their value to ensure that *their* goods, and not their competitors', are bought first. On the other hand, if oil fields dry up or political fallout against drilling shale reserves causes a *scarcity* of energy products, they can feel secure in being able to jack up the price above its real value.

Price fluctuations react to short-term changes in supply and demand for oil—or gas, or cars, or newspapers, or anything else. But as prices undulate up and down, they average out to a base value and make it clearer where the range of equilibrium lies—its "natural price," as mainstream economists call it. As David Harvey explains: "On a given day. . . price fluctuations will tell you the state of demand and supply for shoes on that day and why it has gone up or down from yesterday. . . The fact that we put money-names on commodities and convert the measure of value into. . . price-form, allows price fluctuations to equilibrate the market, and this brings us closer to identifying a proper representation of value as equilibrium of natural price."[33]

The rise and fall of prices allow for flexibility and fluidity in the determination of value, and in this way allows society to reallocate resources in response to market changes. The process also forces more complex, longer-term adjustments on prices, which we will explore in future chapters. In short, capital flows to more-profitable industries from less-profitable ones. This process tends to increase supplies of commodities in profitable industries—thereby lowering prices, and decreasing supplies in the less-profitable ones—thereby raising prices. The end result is an overall equalization in profits in a way that distorts the base value of goods.[34]

Finally, the price of a commodity is also determined by the value of money itself. Marx explained in *Value, Price, and Profit* that "The *values* of necessaries. . . might remain the same, but a change might occur in their *money prices*, consequent upon a previous change in the *value of money*. Nothing would have changed except the money *names* of those values."[35] [emphasis in original] That is to say, a change in the exchange-value of a particular currency does not change the *value* imbued in a commodity, but it will change the *price*.

Let's return to gold as an example. Its value, we've said, is determined by how much labor has gone into its discovery and production. If the amount of labor-time that goes into producing gold drops in half, its value drops in half. So now a chair, instead of being worth one gold coin, would be worth two gold coins, because each coin is worth half as much as it was before. But that doesn't mean that the value of the chair changed. It just means that the same value is now represented by two gold coins versus one. The price may have doubled, but so, too, have the prices of every other commodity. So its value relative to other commodities is still the same.

It's easy to see how a gold coin can change in value, since it has a base value to begin with. Yet the same principles apply to the more abstract currencies of today. As David Harvey explains:

> Gold, recall, is simply depicted by Marx as a representation of value, of socially necessary labor-time. All that has happened since 1973 is that the manner of representation has changed. But Marx himself also notes multiple shifts in representational forms with coins, paper money, credit and the like, so in a way there is nothing in the current situation that defies his mode of analysis. What has happened, in effect, is that the value of a particular currency vis-à-vis all other currencies is (or should be) determined in terms of the value of the total bundle of commodities produced within a national economy.[36]

Money—whether it be counted in gold, dollars, or yuans—is a *universal equivalent*: one coin may have equaled one chair, ten loaves of bread, one coat, and twenty yards of linen. Now it only equals half a chair, but this change in the coin's value means that it also equals five loaves of bread, ten yards of linen, and so on. Sixteenth century Italian economist Bernardo Davanzati explained this same principle through the words of a peasant who sold eggs: "as money was brought down from twelve to one, so the prices of things were raised from one to twelve."[37]

In short, we would have INFLATION: each monetary unit can buy less goods than it used to. In theory, inflation would also drive up the price of labor-power, so while the cost of goods have gone up, so have the wages to buy them. Values, relative to each other, would then remain the same. In practice, however, wages have *not* kept up with inflation in the United States for the last few decades—just another way that bosses can effectively reduce our wages without it seeming like we are taking a pay cut in dollars per hour.

Changes in the value of currencies also occur unevenly around the world, which means that if, for instance, the value of the dollar drops but the value of the Japanese yen does not, then imports of many commonly used goods will be more expensive for working-class people. And of course, if you're lucky enough to have any savings, the dollars that you have in the bank will now be worth half as much as they were before their value dropped.

To sum up, there are several complex processes that stand between value and price. But as Marx explained, they work together in a way that supports, rather than detracts, from our understanding of the labor theory of value:

> The possibility, therefore, of a quantitative incongruity between and magnitude of value, i.e. the possibility that the price may diverge from the magnitude of value, is inherent in the price-form itself. This is not a defect, but, on the contrary, it makes this form the adequate one for a mode of production whose laws can only assert themselves as blindly operating averages between constant irregularities.[38]

CONCLUSION

There is a lot more to say about currencies and economic policy, but the important point to stress here is that while it is tempting to get hung up on fluctuations in currencies and their impact on prices (indeed, this is the focus of much of mainstream economics), the deeper question lies in the determination of the *values* of commodities—a value which money merely reflects. Ultimately, the only way to change the value of the chair is through reducing or increasing the amount of labor-time that goes into making it.

The relationship *between* values—from chairs to cars to wages—determines the economic conditions of our everyday lives (e.g. the relationship between our wages and the necessities we need to buy). Money expresses these value relationships within the economy, and creates a hierarchy of Dom Pérignon champagnes to simple proseccos, and KitchenAid mixers to wire whisks. Yet the unquestioned authority that society bestows onto money masks the social relationships that determine these underlying values. With this understanding of value and money in mind, we'll next look at the special properties money has for the capitalists, and how money becomes *more money* in their hands.

CHAPTER FOUR

WHERE DO PROFITS COME FROM?

The product [of labor] is the property of the capitalist and not that of the worker, its immediate producer. Suppose that a capitalist pays for a day's worth of labor-power; then the right to use that power for a day belongs to him, just as much as the right to use any other commodity, such as a horse that he has hired for the day. . . The product of this process belongs to him just as much as the wine which is the product of the process of fermentation going on in his cellar.

—*Capital, Volume 1*[1]

REAL WORLD EXCHANGE

Up to now we've discussed commodities and values in a simplified world where furniture makers meet bread makers in a market. Happily, the furniture maker takes her chair to the market and exchanges it for money, which she uses to buy bread or other necessities.

Of course, this is not how things work in our society. Today, the people who produce commodities, by and large, do not own what they've made and therefore they have no power to sell or directly exchange these commodities for other essentials. In fact, most furniture makers are not really "furniture makers," in the sense that they don't make a chair from start to finish, but are lumber handlers, machine operators, assemblers, and finishers who work collectively at a factory. And at the end of the day, they don't take home the chairs they've made; they return home with a paycheck.

The finished products are not owned by these various laborers, but by the furniture company, which put them to work manufacturing chairs. This company then exchanges the chairs on the market for money, which—as we noted —acts as an intermediary representative of value. And while there may still be some local marketplaces, or online venues facilitated by companies like Etsy in which small numbers of artisans craft their own chairs to sell, you'd be hard-pressed to find an individual constructing phones, refrigerators, cars, or the myriad of things that we depend on and which fill our everyday lives.

How did this come about? Answering this question leads us to the crux of the system: exploitation, and the special role played by labor under capitalism. In this chapter, we'll unpack what Marx meant by capital, labor, and class society, and out of these concepts we will build a framework for understanding the particular form that exploitation takes in a capitalist society.

To start, let's look at what makes capitalist exchange unique. In a sense, the "simple commodity exchange" we described above never existed in quite so simple a form. But in pre-capitalist formations, exchanges between communities or individuals were "simple" in the sense that the point of these exchanges was to trade commensurate items. Communities could trade any surpluses they had accumulated in order to obtain different goods of equal value. A tribe could, for instance, trade their surplus of kola nuts for another tribe's iron rods for tool making.[2] This type of direct barter could take place among individuals as well.

Commodity for commodity, or "C–C," represents this basic bartered exchange—say, exchanging a chair for an equivalent value of bread. The more likely scenario would involve money as an intermediary, but the process remains the same. A commodity of one value is traded in for cash, which can then be exchanged for a commodity of a similar value. We can represent these exchanges with the formula: c-m-c: Commodity, C, is exchanged for Money, M, which in turn buys a different Commodity, C.

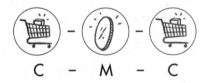

$$C \quad - \quad M \quad - \quad C$$

Marx uses this formula to express simple commodity exchange, which implies that goods exchange for their equivalents. If a chair maker sells her chair for $30, she should be able to get an amount of meat for her $30 that is roughly equivalent in value (or the labor-time that went into producing it). In this setup, no one is extracting more value than what they put in—it is only the *form* of the value that is changing: from commodity, to money, to another commodity. Everything equals out. Therefore "chair = \$30 = 7 lbs. of beef" is the same as saying "\$30 = \$30 = \$30" or "x hours of labor = x hours of labor = x hours of labor."

This is a theoretical example that simplifies the process of exchange in order to better elucidate the processes of capital.[3] The point to note is that the goal of such an exchange is qualitative (gaining new use-values) rather than quantitative (making money). The purpose is to procure a different item, which you did not possess before.

The development of professional traders transformed the goal of exchange from the procurement of like items for use to the accumulation of money. The equation thus changed from C-M-C to M-C-M; or more accurately M-C-M'. The doohickey above the M ("M prime," technically speaking) represents *more* money, or an increase of value above and beyond the money initially invested. In pre-capitalist societies, the basis for this added wealth was, more often than not, pilfering loot. Merchants from more economically developed centers were able to take advantage of societies that did not rely on large-scale internal trade. They could thus purchase goods on the cheap, and then sell them at a higher price in places where these goods were scarce and their values unknown.

M   –   C   –   M'

Not surprisingly, while the merchant class grew and developed, stories from around the world during this time emphasize the thievery, dishonesty, and piracy found at the source of the wealthy man's riches. Yet for all this piracy, the circulation of money, wrote Mandel, "is *sterile* from a global point of view; it does not increase the total wealth of human society. It consists in fact of a *transfer* of wealth, pure and simple; what one gains the other loses, in absolute value. Social value remains unchanged."[4]

THE HIDDEN ABODE OF PRODUCTION

Modern capitalism, on the other hand, is characterized by an immense *expansion* of wealth. Its entire history is marked by growth. The US economy, when healthy, grows by about 4 percent per year. The Chinese economy, until recently, was growing by as much as 10 percent per year. And the world economy as a whole has expanded by roughly 3 percent annually since 1980, according to data from the World Bank. In fact, if any country's output stops expanding, it goes into recession.

How do capitalists generate this ever-expanding surplus? Like the merchant class that preceded them, capitalists produce and exchange goods through an M-C-M' circuit. They start with money (M), invest in the production of commodities (C), and then sell those commodities on the market to get back more money than they started with, (M'). Marx referred to this as "the general formula of capital." Rather than money serving an *intermediary* role, it is the *driver* of the process.

$$M \quad - \quad C \quad - \quad M'$$

Capitalists don't exchange goods for the sake of qualitative enrichment. Steve Jobs didn't decide he had more iPhones and MacBooks than he reasonably needed and therefore might as well trade them for something he didn't have. (What didn't Steve Jobs have?) A capitalist invests for the sole purpose of accruing further wealth. To exchange like-for-like items and wind up with the same amount of money that they started with would be, to use Marx's words, "absurd and empty." The purpose of exchange is the accumulation of *extra* value, or SURPLUS VALUE, which forms the basis of capitalist profit. As Marx argued:

> The simple circulation of commodities—selling in order to buy—is a means to a final goal which lies outside circulation, namely the appropriation of use-values, the satisfaction of needs. As against this, the circulation of money as capital is an end in itself, for the valorization of value takes place only within this constantly renewed movement. The movement of capital is therefore limitless.[5]

The satisfaction of even the most extravagant of needs can only go so far. But the boundless goal of acquiring money through its circulation is an inexhaustible endeavor.

But unlike mercantilism, modern capitalism doesn't depend on a process of "buying cheap and selling dear." Surplus value is produced when capitalists are buying goods for their *true value* and selling them for their *true value.* Capitalists may certainly defraud other players along the way—pay less for inputs or charge more for the final product. But surplus is produced without that duplicity occurring, even when the system is at its most "honest" and "lawful."

Rather than being cunning in the market, the key to surplus value is a production process that creates more wealth than it begins with. Contrary to mainstream explanations (see sidebar: "How Capitalism Explains Capital"), capitalist surplus is not generated within the realm of exchange at all. It is created, argued Marx, within "the hidden abode of production on whose threshold there hangs the notice 'No admittance except on business.' Here we shall see, not only how capital produces, but how capital is itself produced. The secret of profit-making must at last be laid bare."[6]

Wherein lies the secret? Let's look more closely at the circuit of capital. The merchant bought commodities that had already been produced and then sold them for a higher price. However, the capitalist invests not in *finished* products, but rather purchases two different types of commodities: 1) means of production (MP), and 2) labor-power (L). As we discussed in chapter one, the MEANS OF PRODUCTION are the tools and materials that are necessary to make goods (e.g. factories, office buildings, land, machinery, software, IT infrastructure, etc.). The capitalist employs both "inputs" in a production process (P) that creates a new set of commodities, worth more than the combined value of the original inputs. The circuit of capital can thus be expanded to a more precise formula: M-C (MP+L) ... P ... C'-M'.[7]

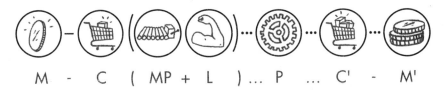

$$M - C \ (\ MP + L \ ) \ldots P \ldots C' - M'$$

The "secret" hidden within the production process lies in a special commodity of LABOR-POWER—the ability to work. Marx explained that the ability to work has become a commodity under capitalism, which the capitalist buys in exchange for a wage (its exchange-value). At first look, this seems self-evident. We wake up, go to work, come home with a wage (or at least the promise of one to be paid at the end of the pay period). We are selling our ability to work—our labor-power. And since selling our old Beanie Baby collection will only get us so far, by and large, for most of us, if we are "lucky" enough to be considered employable, our labor-power is the only commodity we really have to sell.

But what makes this commodity special, and to whom? Marx wrote:

> In order to extract value out of the consumption of a commodity, our friend the money-owner must be lucky enough to find within the sphere of circulation, on the market, a commodity whose use-value possesses the peculiar property of being a *source of value*, whose actual consumption, therefore is itself an objectification of labor, hence a creation of value. The possessor of money does find such a special commodity on the market: the capacity for labor, in other words labor-power.[8] [emphasis added]

The exchange-value of labor-power is paid out in a wage. But the use-value of labor-power is *labor itself*—the source of value, as we discussed in chapter two. What's more, the exchange-value of labor-power, and the value that labor then produces for the bosses, are two very different things. The worker is paid one thing, but then will normally create much more value during her shift than she is paid:

> The value of labor-power, and the value which that labor-power valorizes in the labor-process, are two entirely different magnitudes; and this difference was what the capitalist had in mind when he was purchasing the labor-power. . . . What was really decisive for him was the specific use-value which this commodity possesses of being *a source not only of value, but of more value than it has itself.* This is the specific service that the capitalist expects from labor-power, and in this transaction he acts in accordance with the eternal laws of commodity-exchange.[9]

The key to this golden egg arrangement for the boss is an agreement in which your labor is put under his control for a set amount of time, and you are paid for this time, not for the fruits of your labor. Just as a baker parts with the use-value of bread once she sells it, so too does the worker part with the use-value of her labor-power once she has sold it. As soon as she punches the clock, the conditions of her labor and the products of her labor are no longer hers, but the boss's. Marx thus continued:

> In fact, the seller of labor-power, like the seller of any other commodity, realizes its exchange-value, and alienates its use-value. He cannot take the one without giving the other. The use-value of labor-power, in other words labor, belongs just as little to its seller, as the use-value of oil after it has been sold belongs to the dealer who has sold it. The owner of the money has paid the value of a day's labor-power; he therefore has the use of it for a day, a day's labor belongs to him. On the one hand the daily sustenance of labor-power costs *only half a day's labor*, while on the other hand the very

same labor-power can remain effective, can work, during a whole day, and consequently the value which its use during one day creates is double what he pays for that use; this circumstance is a piece of good luck for the buyer, but by no means an injustice towards the seller.[10] [emphasis added]

In other words, the boss can get away with paying you for just half (or some other fraction) of the day for the "daily sustenance of labor-power" while reaping the full day of your labor. On top of it, he can proclaim it a fair day's wage. The secret to this claim is in the determination of exchange-value of labor-power. Marx explained: "The value of labor-power is determined by the value of the means of subsistence habitually required by the average worker."[11] That is to say, its value, like that of any other commodity, is based on the amount of labor that has gone into producing it. In the case of labor-power, this amounts to the labor-time required to keep the worker alive, to daily reproduce her capacity and readiness to go to work every day, and to keep her children alive, so that they may one day replace her in the workforce. The value of food, rent, clothing, training, and education, along with other necessities deemed essential by society therefore make up the value of labor-power. If, for example, social norms attach an average of $120 to the cost of minimal daily needs, that would loosely translate into the value of labor-power.[12]

The bosses also get a big discount when they purchase labor-power. A good deal of *unpaid* work also contributes heavily toward its reproduction: for instance, childbirth, childcare, food preparation, laundry, and household cleaning, to name a few. As Marxist feminist Tithi Bhattacharya explained, "The working class doesn't only work in its workplace. A woman worker also sleeps in her home, her children play in the public park and go to the local school, and sometimes she asks her retired mother to help out with the cooking. In other words, the major functions of reproducing the working class take place outside the workplace."[13] The free labor, performed largely by women within the home, is not accounted for within labor-power's exchange-value. The realm of SOCIAL REPRODUCTION, as discussed in the sidebar "Outside the Abode of Production," reproduces and regenerates workers at very little cost to the system.

Yet even if we limit ourselves more narrowly to the *paid* labor that goes into producing your subsistence, if all things were fair and just, you would give over to your boss only the amount of time that it takes to reproduce the value of your labor-power. Say it takes four hours to produce $120 worth of goods, the equivalent of your daily wage, you could go home after four hours. But if your boss allowed that, his inputs and outputs would be equal. It truly would just be M-C-M. What would be the point? Why not just keep the money he started with? But all things are *not* fair and just. The capitalist pays you for the cost of your labor-power, not for the value of the goods you produce. Thus your paycheck is worth the *exchange-value* of your labor-power. But the *use-value* of your labor-power is the *production of greater value*.

Let's say you work for Starbucks and they pay you $120 for an 8-hour shift. But you can probably make $120 worth of fancy coffee in an hour, or probably in a half hour at a busy store. Even once you subtract the cost of materials and use of the equipment, Starbucks doesn't pay you anywhere near the value you've created (hundreds of dollars a day). They buy your *labor-power* from you, not the actual *fruits of your labor*. And you make that value back for them in an hour. The rest of your shift, you're basically working for free!

This extra labor they extract from us is called SURPLUS LABOR. While NECESSARY LABOR is that part of the day required to reproduce the cost of labor-power, the surplus labor is the free labor that the capitalist benefits from during the rest of your workday. Thus, if after you finish making $120 worth of coffee, instead of throwing down your apron and going home, you finish out your eight-hour shift, one hour will be necessary labor, and seven hours are surplus labor! (This seven to one ratio is overly simplified because it doesn't yet factor in the machinery and equipment we mentioned above. But we will get to those next!) Marx wrote:

> I call the portion of the working day during which this reproduction takes place necessary labor-time, and the labor expended during that time necessary labor; necessary for the worker, because independent of the particular social form of his labor; necessary for capital and the capitalist world, because the continued existence of the worker is the basis of that world.
>
> During the second period of the labor process, that in which his labor is no longer necessary labor, the worker does indeed expend labor-power, he does work, but his labor is no longer necessary labor, and he creates no value for himself. He creates surplus value which, for the capitalist, has all the charms of something created out of nothing.[14]

In this way, through the "charm of something created out of nothing," capitalism disguises a process of exploitation, of appropriating surplus labor from the working class, as a "fair day's wage for a fair day's work." As we discussed in chapter one, appropriating surpluses was a visible and obvious norm of previous class societies. But in examining capitalist society, we have to go beneath the surface appearance of a "fair day's work," to find the inner essence of exploitation.[15]

HOW CAPITALISM EXPLAINS CAPITAL

Mainstream economists have a number of ways that they explain how capitalists turn a profit.

As we discussed in chapter two, the predominant mainstream explanation is based on the neoclassical theory of marginalism. In this view, profits are generated in the market, not in production. When capital has a "high marginal product," if the demand for goods generates a higher income per unit than the cost of producing those goods, then profits are high. When labor has a "high marginal product," wages rise and profits are low. This clearly pits bosses versus workers, but unlike the labor theory of value, this view sees workers as parasitic—a necessary evil and a drain on profits when they become too expensive. In this model, their labor plays no role in the success or failure of a business. And profits are determined by what's happening in the market.

Another version of this argument is that the final goods don't have any additional or surplus value whatsoever compared to the value of their inputs. Instead, the fact that items can be sold for a greater amount of money than it took to produce them is the result of shrewd buying and selling. The profit created is the result of keen investing—by a capitalist that can pay workers minimally and buy raw materials on the cheap, and then find a way to mark up the price on the final product.

This is a convenient explanation for capitalists because it means that profits are the result of the genius of bosses, a good justification for paying themselves ungodly sums of money. But where this argument fails is that it implies that every sale must have winners and losers. A car manufacturer would benefit by buying materials and parts from suppliers at cut-rate prices. But the suppliers must then lose out, having sold materials for below their worth.

Say, for example, that steel plates are worth $750 a ton. This is the average price paid throughout the market for steel plates by all steel producers and all buyers of steel plates. But our savvy automaker investor is able to cut a deal with their supplier to pay just $650 a ton. That steel is used in the production process and becomes part of the car. Additionally, our automaker, when figuring out the price of the car, prorates the cost of steel in each car at a price of $800 a ton.

But by doing this, our investor hasn't created $150 of new value. All that has happened is that he has stolen $100 from the steel manufacturer and $50 from the car buyer. He has been able to buy something worth $750 for $650. And he's been able to sell something worth $750 for $800. In the process, he is $150 richer, but it has come by taking advantage of other parties.

Plenty of good, old-fashioned fleecing such as this happens in the market economy.[16] And historically it was the basis for mercantilism, an early predecessor of modern capitalism. But at the end of the day, this model would not add money or value. It has simply been redistributed, with the automaker benefiting at the expense of the steel manufacturer and the consumer. One section of society has defrauded another.

If this defined how capitalism worked, our less savvy suppliers would have no profits and be forced out of business, unless somewhere in their production process they, too, were buying their inputs cheaply and marking up the price of their outputs. (But that would merely mean some other company involved in the production of steel was in the position of having no profits and would be forced to shut down.)

So the idea of profits being generated by "buying as cheaply possible and selling as dear as possible," fails to explain how the *system itself* can expand. It denies the reality of capitalism, which is constantly growing in wealth and outputs. If it were just about keen buying and selling, there would be a constant process of roughly half of businesses succeeding while the other half were failing, and no new value being generated.

This explanation also oddly precludes a scenario where the majority of capitalists are turning a profit. In reality, when the auto industry is humming, all of the companies that are involved in the production of cars and in parts supply profit simultaneously. In times of economic boom, investment, employment, and profits all ride high, bosses grow elated, "miracle economies" are declared, and economists proclaim that the days of economic busts are over.

Yet another argument is that profits are a reward to investors for putting their capital "at risk." The logic here is that capitalists are putting up the capital and tying it up into a production process for which they will not be paid back quickly (or perhaps at all). Profit therefore provides incentive to the capitalist for taking this risk rather than sitting on their money, thus the rate of return should be higher than if the capitalist safely tucked their capital away in a low-interest savings account. This explanation essentially equates capitalism with gambling. If a gambler wins at a hand of cards, is this too a profit that is the reward for his risk? Or is it merely the result of someone else losing money? Similarly, if profits are the reward for taking risk, doesn't it imply that there is—somewhere—a loser in the transaction?

The Marxist understanding of capitalism reveals, however, that surplus value is produced when capitalists are buying goods for their true value and selling them for their true value. It illustrates that surplus value, and therefore profits, are rooted in the production process—in the difference between paid and unpaid labor—not in the cunning of market-based exchanges.

DEFINING CAPITAL

Marx called the capital invested in labor-power VARIABLE CAPITAL because it "both reproduces the equivalent of its own value, and also produces an excess, a surplus value, which may itself vary, may be more or less according to circumstances."[17] Labor's use-value is *"a source not only of value, but of more value than it has itself."* That is, its value expands through its use. But *how much* extra value is produced can vary, as we'll discuss below.

Money advanced to purchase equipment and materials, however, passes its value on to the newly created goods without any quantitative change in its worth. Marx called this part of the capitalist's investment CONSTANT CAPITAL. Its value "merely reappears" in the commodities produced.[18] As we discussed in chapter two, the inputs of machinery, resources, and tools embody generations of DEAD LABOR manufactured by previous groups of workers. This value is transmitted as is through the production process. Raw materials transfer their total value when they are consumed by production (Marx called this "productive consumption" of the means of production). Machinery and equipment, on the other hand, pass on fractions of their value during every use. Let's say a piece of machinery was expected to last for a year before breaking down, and it cost the capitalist $365 when he purchased it. Every day, the machine would pass on a dollar's worth of value. In this way, argued Marx, it enters "piecemeal in proportion to its average daily depreciation."[19]

A machine can deteriorate physically, through wear and tear as it's used. Or it can eventually be consumed by the elements while it sits on a shelf unused. "But in addition to the material wear and tear," Marx pointed out, "a machine also undergoes what we might call a *moral depreciation*. It loses exchange-value, either because machines of the same sort are being produced more cheaply than it was, or because better machines are entering into competition with it. In both cases, however young and full of life the machine may be, its value is no longer determined by the necessary labor-time actually objectified in it, but the labor-time necessary to reproduce either it or the better machine. It has therefore been devalued to a greater or lesser extent."[20] [emphasis added] For example, a tractor may lose its value over time through rust and wear of its body in a physical depreciation. Or it can lose value in a "moral depreciation" once newer lines of tractors equipped with wireless maps and monitors of machine data can do more work for the same price. An agricultural company that uses outdated machinery will incur losses because it will require greater time (and therefore higher costs) to do the same amount of work as its competitor.

If we return to Starbucks, perhaps the executives there invest $360 a day in *constant capital*: a store's espresso machines, coffee grinders, refrigerators, dishwashers, cash registers, coffee beans, milk, cream, sugar, etc. The coffee beans and other raw materials pass on the whole of their value as they are consumed. The machinery passes on fractions of its value during every use (which will eventually add up to the full value of the machine getting passed on during its lifetime). They invest another $120 worth of *variable capital* in employing the store's barista. This barista, for her meager paycheck, sets to work on the coffee grinders and espresso machines, producing the first $120 of lattes, cappuccinos, and caramel macchiatos in the first hour, enough to cover her paycheck. She produces another $840 of drinks in the next seven hours, for a total of $960 worth of drinks. After paying out wages and expenses, an extra $480 is left.

By investing in constant (c) and variable (v) capital, the capitalists set in motion a productive process. At the end of the process these values will have replicated themselves, along with an additional surplus value (s). Marx expressed this with the formula: c + v -> c + v + s. In the case of our made-up Starbucks example, this would be $360 (c) + $120 (v) turns into $360 (c) + $120 (v) + $480 (s).

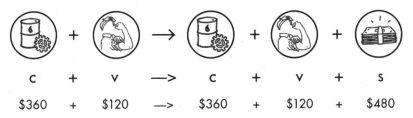

c	+	v	—>	c	+	v	+	s
$360	+	$120	—>	$360	+	$120	+	$480

The RATE OF SURPLUS VALUE measures the rate at which we are exploited (synonymous with RATE OF EXPLOITATION). It is the ratio between that part of the day that creates the value of your wages (v), and that part of the day in which your labor is unpaid (s): in this case $480 (s)/ $120 (v) is 400 percent.[21]

If a 400 percent rate of exploitation seems far fetched to you, consider this real-life example quoted in a 2018 Oxfam report. Oxfam interviewed Lan, a Vietnamese garment worker who explained:

> When I got pregnant, they let me work in the warehouse. There were many boxes full of shoes, and my job was to put the stamp on. Those shoes would fit my son perfectly, they are very nice. I'd like my son to have shoes like these, but he can't. I think he'd want them, and I feel sorry for him. The shoes are very pretty. You know that one pair of shoes that we make is valued more than our whole month's salary.[22]

Finally, while the rate of surplus value importantly tells us the rate at which we are being exploited, what the capitalist ultimately cares about is his rate of profit. The RATE OF PROFIT is defined as the ratio of surplus value to variable *and* constant capital: that is the total amount of capital that was invested. It tells him how much profit he is generating relative to the capital he advanced. In our example $480 (s)/ $ 480 (c+v) is 100%.[23] We'll return to this important concept in later chapters.

For the time being, we can see that CAPITAL is money that is invested in labor-power (variable capital) and materials and equipment (constant capital) in order to produce a commodity whose sale generates a greater quantity of money. It is a self-expansion of value. Marx distinguished again between the *appearance* of capital, which alternates, through the course of its life between capital as money and capital as commodities, and the *essence* of capital, which undergoes a process of self-expansion. He wrote:

> If we pin down the specific forms of appearance assumed in turn by self-valorizing value in the course of its life, we reach the following elucidation: capital is money, capital is commodities. In truth, however, value is here the subject of a *process* in which, while constantly assuming the form in turn of money and commodities, it changes its own magnitude, throws off surplus value from itself . . . and thus valorizes itself independently. For the movement in the course of which it adds surplus value is its *own* movement, its valorization is therefore *self*-valorization. By virtue of being value, it has acquired the occult ability to add value to itself. It brings forth living offspring, or at least lays golden eggs.[24] [emphasis added]

But these golden eggs can only be laid because of capitalism's particular social relation of production, forged through the historical processes we discussed in chapter one. Workers' lack of control over the means of production makes us dependent on capital. We are coerced by the threat of poverty to sell the only commodity we have: our labor-power. Within the "hidden abode of production" our labor then produces more value than our labor-power costs in wages, adding extra value to the final product that the capitalist does not pay for in his initial investment.

Capital therefore reflects a relationship rather than a mathematical formula. Most economists think of capital as things: money, machinery, and labor. But these "things" do not become capital except through a social process in which they are activated to create more value. "Capital is not a thing, but a social relation between persons which is mediated through things."[25] Marx summarized the point in Volume 3 of *Capital*:

> [The capitalist] can convert the value he advances into a higher value only by exchanging it with living labor, by exploiting living labor. But he can exploit labor only in so far as he advances at the same time the conditions for the realization of this labor, i.e. means and object of labor, machinery and raw materials, that is by transforming a certain sum of value that he has in his possession into the form of the conditions of production. Similarly, he is only a capitalist at all, and can only undertake the process of exploiting labor because he confronts, as proprietor of the conditions of labor, the worker as the mere owner of labor-power. We have already shown in Volume 1 [of *Capital*] how it is precisely the possession of the means of production by the non-workers that turns the workers into wage-laborers and the non-workers into capitalists.[26]

OUTSIDE THE ABODE OF PRODUCTION

Capitalism doesn't just control the places where production of surplus value takes place. As is made all too clear by the conditions of our schools, homes, and communities, and the reach that police brutality and a decrepit health care system have into our lives, the system penetrates every layer of day-to-day existence. This is because sustaining the needs of capital accumulation also necessitates the creation, maintenance, and discipline of the working class as a whole.

As a basic starting point, in order for capital relations to produce and reproduce themselves, the owner of labor-power (i.e. the worker) must daily, in the words of Marx, "be able to repeat the same process in the same conditions as regards health and strength. His means of subsistence must therefore be sufficient to maintain him in his normal state as a working individual."[27] The "means of subsistence" is historically and socially conditioned, and determines the value of labor-power. It must also include the maintenance of the workers' children as well, as they will be the next generation of laborers.

But what about the labor necessary to prepare the food, wash the clothing, provide the childcare? This, essentially, is extra labor that is mostly produced *outside* of the sites of capitalist production.[28] While Marx and Engels rightly located the reproduction of labor-power for the system within the nuclear family, they did not delve deeply into this topic. The concept of social reproduction has been theorized largely due to the important work of second-wave feminism (the women's rights movement that, beginning in the 1960s, fought for equality beyond suffrage and legal rights) and Marxist feminists (who incorporated and elaborated on Marx's ideas to explain the roots of women's oppression). In fact, as most women know all too well, the bulk of day-to-day responsibilities for the reproduction of labor at home fall on wives, daughters, mothers, and sisters.

This unpaid labor does not directly create surplus value, yet it is critical to workers' abilities to produce surplus, and therefore necessary to maintaining the profitability of the system. And so it is no coincidence that sexist ideologies that relegate women to second-class citizens emphasize women's nurturing capacity, which make us "naturally suited" to prioritizing husbands and children over our own lives.

One of the leading theoreticians of social reproduction theory, Lise Vogel, situated the theory within Marx's concept of "consumption"—within which he distinguished between a laborer's *productive consumption* and *individual consumption.* "Productive consumption" Marx defined as the process by which workers "consume" the means of production while on the job, not by eating the machinery of course, but by activating it. "Individual consumption" compromises the daily functions—eating, having clean clothes to wear, and so on—of reproducing our ability to live and go back to work the following day. Marx argued:

> The worker's productive consumption and his individual consumption are therefore totally distinct. In the former, he acts as the motive power of capital, and belongs to the capitalist. In the latter, he belongs to himself, and performs his necessary vital functions outside the production process. The result of the first kind of consumption is that the capitalist continues to live, of the second, that the worker himself continues to live.[29]

Vogel added the element of domestic labor to understanding individual consumption. Marx wrote that with individual consumption, "the worker uses the money paid to him for his labor-power to buy the means of subsistence."[30] But, Vogel argued, "he said little about the actual work involved in individual consumption. Here was a realm of economic activity essential to capitalist production yet missing from Marx's exposition."[31] In fact, without this labor, individual consumption could not take place.

As capitalism has increasingly come to rely on women's ability to work outside the home, and to make up a low-wage sector of the workforce, the necessities provided by domestic labor have become strained. All the more so since those elements of social reproduction that *do* take place outside the home—public education, pensions and retirement for the elderly, public transportation—have come under systematic attack over the last several decades. In part this tension has been mitigated by the increasing use of things like laundromats, microwaves, and frozen foods, which reduce the amount of time necessary for domestic labor. But in the main, the contradictory needs of capital to depend on women's labor both inside and outside the home has been "solved" through the ruthless intensification of the double-burden faced by women. More paid and unpaid labor is expected of women, outside and inside the home. So the same woman who is being forced to spend extra hours at work as a teacher also faces increasing pressures as a mom when childcare costs rise out of reach.

DIVERGING RATES OF EXPLOITATION

We simplified the cost of labor-power above to an arbitrary $120 per day in order to distill the basic mechanism of this special commodity. In reality, the cost of the subsistence and reproduction of workers is both socially and historically determined. It reflects the changing cost of producing food or acquiring skills; as well as differences—based, for instance, on the balance of class forces—in what is deemed a socially acceptable requirement for subsistence. For both of these reasons, the cost of labor differs, too, between countries or regions with disparate levels of productivity and histories of class struggle. This is why US-based companies chase cheaper wages to other countries like China or Mexico, or to the closer distance of the "right-to-work" states within the US.[32]

The cost of labor also reflects the injustice of oppression. As of 2019, women in the United States were still paid 79 cents to a man's dollar.[33] (Or in the case of the country's most talented and famous soccer team, the United States women's national soccer team earns 38 cents to their male counterparts, despite generating greater revenue.[34]) Black men are paid 70 cents and Black women 61 cents in comparison to their white counterparts.[35] Latina women earn 53 cents to a white man's dollar.[36] Increased education does little to change this ratio for women or people of color.[37] Blacks, Latinxs, and women at all education levels earn less than white men. Women of color occupy the bottom of the totem pole. American capitalism relies upon women and people of color to populate permanent, low-wage sectors of the labor force.[38]

The disparities in racial and gender wage gaps point to the fact that "socially determined" is not only dependent on public perception of what is acceptable, but is also based on historic and systemic institutions of oppression. People of color, for example, have less inherited familial wealth on average to draw from, and therefore disproportionately suffer from the accumulation of considerable amounts of debt in order to go to college or earn an advanced degree. Combined with the reality of severely underfunded, under-resourced, segregated public schools, this ensures that they never enter a level playing field. Then come long-documented discriminatory practices, which ensure that they are the last to get hired and the first to be fired, contributing to higher rates of unemployment and a more desperate workforce, forced to accept lower wages for equal work.

Capitalism also depends on the superexploitation of immigrants—and particularly those who are not protected by legal documentation. Disenfranchised and disempowered by the threat of deportation, undocumented workers are subject to draconian conditions and wages, and fired if they protest or attempt to unionize. As author Justin Akers Chacón has written, the criminalization of immigration has been "used widely by employers to structure lower-wage tiers within and across whole industries, setting the low-wage standard of 'immigrant labor' by the early 1990s. The declining wage benchmarks for undocumented labor had the further effect of holding all wages down within those same industries."[39]

Inequality has long been built into the core fabric of the American business model. Pitting Black workers against white workers against immigrant workers has been a particularly potent, tried-and-true tactic of employers to drive down all wages. But the cursory sketch laid out here does not even begin to discuss the very many oppressions—of people with disabilities, of gay people, of transgender people, of Native peoples, of elders, and more—that play an integral role in upholding the profitability of US capitalism. In fact, any place where bosses can hold down the wages of one section of the workforce not only ensures a cheaper labor pool among the oppressed demographic, but also, in the words of abolitionist Frederick Douglass, divides both in order to conquer each, so that everyone's wages are pushed down.

Lastly, the value of labor will also vary among industries and skills. One reason is the cost of education and training required for different jobs, and another is the expectation of how stable of a workforce bosses are looking to buy. Fast food workers, home health aides, farm workers, and other low-wage workers are consistently paid wages far short of the cost of living (and therefore their true value). The capitalists bank on getting away with it because they expect, in fact depend on, a high turnover rate and unemployment rate, which will ensure that those positions will fill easily. Bosses see low-wage workers as quickly replaceable commodities, bought and employed as easily as one would buy other cheap "inputs."

Meanwhile, higher paid workers don't suffer the crushing weight of poverty, but this does not mean that they are not exploited. In fact, they often face even greater rates of exploitation if the value of the goods that they produce are significantly higher. A Boeing engineer may earn over a hundred thousand dollars a year, but she contributes to products that sell for millions or billions of dollars.[40] More importantly, varying rates of exploitation make up an integrated web of labor. The extraction of value does not happen on a case-by-case basis, but is a collective process. Google's high-paid programmers work in buildings cleaned by low-paid janitors. The one's work is, in fact, dependent on the other's, and therefore so is the extraction of its value.

THE WORKING-CLASS MAJORITY

Across these experiences, workers collectively make up a class of people exploited to create surplus value for the bosses.[41] A very basic definition of classes as they exist in capitalist society begins with this premise. Workers have to sell our ability to work, and capitalists buy and command our labor-power. You can't understand either the worker's or the boss's class position without understanding that the whole of the system is one in which labor is set to work on means of production, in order to produce a profit for someone else. Class, in other words, is a relationship of exploitation.

This understanding of class as a social relationship is completely absent in mainstream analysis. If class is discussed at all in the mainstream, it is considered in terms of wealth and social stratification. Income levels, education, lifestyles, and patterns of consumption are used to divide people into a society that is mostly middle class, with some rich and poor people around the fringes. Indeed, in most accounts, the majority of us are middle class, and there is no working class at all. We are reminded of this fact at least every two to four years in election seasons, when politicians appeal to the "struggling middle class," a category that apparently includes all "good Americans," or as former president Bill Clinton said, people who "work hard and play by the rules."[42] Bernie

Sanders's presidential campaigns have been so notable precisely because he uttered the words "working class."

An explanation of classes based on levels of wealth also has a more progressive version, as popularized by the Occupy Wall Street movement in 2011. The slogan "we are the 99%" caught on like wildfire as activists identified the top 1 percent of the country's economic elite, which owns about 40 percent of the nation's wealth, as culpable for creating the financial meltdown of 2008 and the Great Recession that followed. While this analysis is a substantial leap forward from that which assumes that we are nearly all middle class, it still assumes that the *quantity* of wealth is the determinant of class positions.

Class and wealth surely have everything to do with each other, but they are not the same thing. A stable, well-paid job (to the extent that these still exist) such as a train conductor in New York City may pay upward of $70,000 a year, and a small bodega owner in the Bronx may earn much less. But the former is a worker—who does not control her own hours and conditions of work, and the latter is a small business owner, charged with his own exploitation, as well as that of others (even if few in number). The numbers on someone's paycheck can't tell you everything. It can't tell you, for instance, that a manager at Starbucks, who makes less than a subway conductor, has the power to fire every worker in the store. We can see then that wealth is just one part of the picture, and one that is more symptomatic of class inequality than explanatory of its origin. In fact, power, control over working conditions, and financial decision-making are the bedrocks of exploitation.

Economics Professor Michael Zweig explained it this way: "By looking only at income or lifestyle, we see the *results* of class, but not the *origins* of class. We see how we are different in our possessions, but not how we are related and connected, and made different, in the process of making what we possess."[43] [emphasis added] The Marxist explanation instead emphasizes that one's position in society is not measured quantitatively, but is determined by a person's relationship to labor, the fruits of labor, and the means of production. Anyone who controls the means of production, has political power, dictates the terms of other's working conditions, or owns capital that can be invested in production, is part of the CAPITALIST CLASS. And anyone who must sell their labor-power for a wage and has no access to the means of production themselves is part of the WORKING CLASS.

This does not just extend to workers engaged in the production of *physical* goods. Teachers and nurses must sell their labor in order to provide services, and thus are part of the working class.[44] As Marx argued: "If we may take an example from outside the sphere of material production, a school-master is a productive worker when, in addition to belaboring the heads of his pupils, he works himself into the ground to enrich the owner of the school. That the latter has laid out his capital in a teaching factory, instead of a sausage factory, makes no difference to the relation."[45]

It is in this sense that Marx and Engels wrote that the "proletarian is without property." PROLETARIANS is another word for workers. And private property does not mean personal belongings, like your TV or laptop, but the means of production—the buildings, machinery, software, equipment, tools, and other materials owned by capitalists. Marx wasn't saying that workers literally have nothing, although that is often and increasingly true. He meant that we are without any means to produce and reproduce our livelihoods, and therefore we are at the mercy of capitalist exploitation. A construction company has mechanical shovels, drills, and dozers, which allow them to exploit laborers and turn a profit. I have a shovel, which I can use to grow flowers or tomatoes.

Historian Geoffrey de Ste. Croix put it this way:

> [Class] is the collective social expression of the fact of exploitation, the way in which exploitation is embodied in a social structure... Class is essentially a *relationship*—just as *capital*, another of Marx's basic concepts, is specifically described by him... as "a relation," "a social relation of production," and so forth. And *a* class (a *particular* class) is a group of persons in a community identified by their position in the whole system of social production, defined above all according to their relationship (primarily in terms of the degree of *control*) to the conditions of production (that is to say, to the means and labor of production) and to other classes.[46]

Using this definition, we see that wealth and poverty do not *determine* class, rather they are manifestations of it. The bosses are thus not defined by the degree of their extravagance. At the same time, society's poor do not represent an "underclass" who, due to lack of employment or wealth, stand *outside* of society. Poverty is an *integral* part of the experience of the working class, and unemployment is just a stone's throw away for most workers. Almost half the US population would not be able to pay their bills if they missed one paycheck, and one in four people report foregoing health care treatment because they could not afford it.[47] A quarter of the population have jobs that are defined as low-wage.[48] Add to this bleak picture the mountains of student debt carried by tens of millions of people and a rising cost of living, and it becomes very clear just how intrinsic poverty is to the fabric of American society.

Capitalism *requires* that there be some level of unemployment at all times, or as Marx termed it, a RESERVE ARMY OF LABORERS. The bosses depend on this reserve army of laborers to ensure that there is always someone else willing to take your job, and can thus discipline the paid workforce into acquiescing to the terms set by employers. High levels of unemployment are certainly a cruel feature of every downturn in the economy, but even when "times are good," unemployment is still a painful reality for millions. What mainstream economists consider "full employment" is in fact about 5 percent unemployment. The introduction of new machinery, a growing labor force due to demographic or migration changes, regular changes in the structure of the economy (what is and isn't produced, and where), can all contribute to unemployment during the "best" of times.

This understanding of society yields a much different picture than the popularized version of the United States as a "middle class country." To be sure, there is a middle class. They do not just live in a glossy alternate universe on television screens. The MIDDLE CLASS is a layer of society that stands between the working class and the ruling class. It includes small business owners, as well as middle managers, supervisors, and professional occupations that have a fair amount of autonomy within the system (such as doctors and lawyers). They are often the daily face of exploitation. You see your manager every day at work. He may reward your work with a raise, or reprimand you for being late, but you will rarely encounter the CEO who profits from this arrangement.

Still, this middle class is much smaller than usually assumed, and many of those traditionally deemed "professionals" are being shoved into the working class (or "proletarianizing") as computer programmers become routine code writers punching timecards, social workers with enormous caseloads spend their days filling out forms, and academic professorial jobs increasingly give way to adjunct positions.[49] Within many middle-class job classifications as well, the differences between the kind of conditions faced by professors at elite colleges versus those at public universities, or doctors with private practices contrasted to those working in emergency rooms, lead to very different levels of control at the workplace. "The bourgeoisie has stripped of its halo every occupation hitherto honored and looked up to with reverent awe," wrote Marx and Engels. "It has converted the physician, the lawyer, the priest, the poet, the man of science, into its paid wage laborers."[50]

Michael Zweig and labor journalist Kim Moody have both estimated that the working class makes up about 63 percent of the US labor force. The corporate elite makes up 2 percent, and in between, the middle class makes up

35 percent.[51] Further, if you include broader society beyond the accounted-for labor force (family members not working, elderly people, people permanently unemployed because of disabilities, etc.), the numbers reflecting the working class would be even higher. As Moody argued: "If working-class people in employment make up just under two-thirds of the workforce, those in the *class* amount to at least three-quarters of the population—the overwhelming majority. As teachers, nurses, and other professionals are pushed down into the working class, the majority grows even larger."[52] This highlights a broader point: classes are fluid and plenty of gray area exists between them. These numbers only offer a general guide to emphasize the broader trend toward increasing polarization. As Marx and Engels wrote in the *Communist Manifesto* over 150 years ago (at a time, incidentally, when the working class was a clear *minority* of the world's population): "Society as a whole is more and more splitting up into two great hostile camps, into two great classes directly facing each other: bourgeoisie and proletariat."[53]

Lastly, one belongs to a class regardless of whether one believes in the notion or identifies with the interests of that class. Whether Democrats tell you that you are part of the middle class they are trying to save or Donald Trump promises tax breaks to the "forgotten middle class," and whether you believe any of them, have little to do with whether you still have to wake up to go to work tomorrow morning, follow someone else's instructions for what to do, and return home with little more than a meager paycheck and a backache.

Class position is therefore determined by material reality rather than ideology. At the same time, the structure of the working class does then lend itself to the development of class-consciousness. In that sense, we can identify a secondary definition of the working class on the basis of its consciousness and activity. Along these lines, Marx distinguished between the working class as a "class *in* itself": defined by a common relationship to the means of production; and a "class *for* itself": organized in active pursuit of its own interests. As Ste. Croix explained:

> The individuals constituting a given class may or may not be wholly or partly conscious of their own identity and common interests as a class, and they may or may not feel antagonism towards members of other classes as such. Class *conflict* (class struggle, *Klassenkampf*) is essentially the fundamental relationship between classes, involving *exploitation* and resistance to it, but not *necessarily* either class consciousness or collective activity in common, political or otherwise, although these features are likely to supervene when a class has reached a certain stage of development and become what Marx once (using a Hegelian idiom) called "a class *for itself*."[54]

THE WORKING DAY

The opposing class positions—and therefore interests—of workers and bosses pits these classes against each other. Bosses try to squeeze more profits out of workers; the working class is always trying in some way to relieve the intensity of exploitation and oppression. As Marx argued, the history of capitalism is, at its heart, the history of class struggle: "carried on an uninterrupted, now hidden, now open fight." It isn't always a clear conflict, like a strike or a protest, and it is never an evenly two-sided fight, but it is an ongoing struggle nonetheless.

The battle between capitalist and worker over the terms of exploitation has historically been centered on the terms of the working day, to determine how much surplus value bosses are able to extract from their employees. If we start with a baseline scenario in which a worker delivers four hours of necessary labor (to replace her own wages) and four hours of surplus labor (to go to the capitalist's profits), the rate of exploitation is 100 percent. Capitalists will attempt to impose faster, more intensive working conditions or lower the value of labor-power in order to extract more surplus labor and a greater profit.

This is not driven by an individual capitalist's cruelty, or a Mr. Burns-like maniacal cackle.[55] To survive and thrive in a competitive market, business owners can get an edge over the competition by raising the rate of exploitation and lowering the cost per unit of their goods. And so the structure of capitalism typically rewards the Mr. Burnses of the world, and puts out of business any bosses who attempt fairness, equity, and job safety.[56]

There are two main roads to increase the rate of exploitation. One is raising the ABSOLUTE SURPLUS VALUE: how much *total* surplus value is created during the day. The other is increasing RELATIVE SURPLUS VALUE: altering the *ratio* of value produced during the course of the day so that less of it goes toward the reproduction of labor-power (paid out in wages) and more of it goes over to the capitalist in the form of surplus value.

To increase absolute surplus value, capitalists lengthen the working day without paying any additional wages. By doing this—forcing workers to toil for two, three, or four additional hours—the capitalist will accumulate additional surplus labor. If the working day is lengthened from eight hours to twelve hours with no additional pay, the rate of exploitation will change from 4 hours / 4 hours = 100 percent, to 8 hours / 4 hours = 200 percent.[57]

In Marx's day, the battle over whether workers would be forced to work twelve-hour days or ten-hour days raged on over decades. Today, working ten or twelve hours is still very much a reality for many working-class people— from restaurant workers, to unregulated sweatshops in the garment industry, to Apple's infamous Foxconn factories. Salaried "middle class" jobs in IT and other office workers regularly work ten- and twelve-hour days without extra compensation.

Even seemingly "secure" jobs with union protections are vulnerable to unpaid increases in the working day. Lengthening the school day without compensating teachers is a common example. Of course it's also completely "normal" for teachers to spend countless hours of unpaid work as it is, grading homework and preparing lesson plans. Just as it is for homecare nurses to spend many unpaid hours filling out reports. On the whole, US workers labor for a month longer per year than our European counterparts. This has been one of the prevailing strategies of American capitalism to increase profitability since the 1970s.

FIGURE 4. ABSOLUTE SURPLUS VALUE

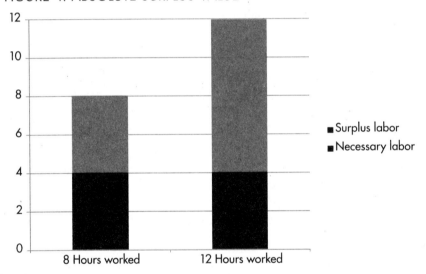

Of course there are human limits to the level to which people can be driven to work. There are, unfortunately for the bosses, a finite number of hours in a day. And the human body can cope with only so much work before it collapses. Indeed, many of the nineteenth-century regulations on the length of the working day stemmed from the fact that the damage done to the working class was so severe as to undermine a sufficient labor pool from which businesses could hire. Marx noted that the British ruling class set limits on the working day and took measures to strengthen the working-class families in order to prevent future generations of laborers from literally being worked to death before they came of age. Bosses gave male workers a "family wage" just high enough to provide for their families.

Most importantly, labor, unlike machinery and other production inputs, is made up of thinking, toiling humans who can organize to fight back against their own ruination. Workers' resistance, as Marx put it, is "that obstinate yet elastic natural barrier" to capital.[58] Thus bosses must rely on a second strategy of increasing *relative* surplus value: that is to change the ratio of who gets what from the fruits of the working day. In this case, the length of the working day doesn't change, but how much surplus value is produced does.

"The prolongation of the working day beyond the point at which the worker would have produced an exact equivalent of that surplus labor by capital—this is the process which constitutes the production of the absolute surplus-value," wrote Marx. "For the production of relative surplus-value," he continued, "the necessary labor is shortened by methods of producing the equivalent of the wage of labor in a shorter time."[59]

In other words, the ratio of necessary labor to surplus labor changes in favor of the bosses, because the amount of labor-time that is necessary for a worker to reproduce her wage will be reduced. If the workers' wages can be reproduced in three hour's time, rather than four hour's, the rate of surplus value will jump from 100 percent (four hours of surplus labor / four hours of necessary labor) to 166 percent (five hours of surplus labor / three hours of necessary labor).

FIGURE 5. RELATIVE SURPLUS VALUE

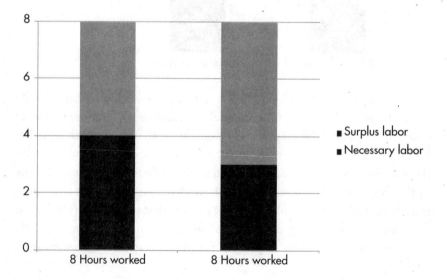

We can see roughly four ways to increase relative surplus value: First, increasing the intensification of labor—that is forcing workers to deliver more value in the same amount of time than they had previously. Marx described this process as a "condensation of labor," or a "closer filling up of the pores of the working day,"[60] more commonly referred to today as speedups and attrition of workers, so that fewer bodies do the work that more employees used to do. As Marx explained: "This compression of a greater mass of labor into a given period now counts for what it really is, namely an increase in the quantity of labor."[61]

In the United States, older workers in the auto industry can remember a time when workers would "work up the line" by moving faster than the belt, and would wind up with some downtime during their shift. Now the belts move at the fastest rate possible so there is no downtime possible. Motions are timed and regulated such that they are in motion fifty-seven seconds in every minute (compare this to forty-five seconds per minute on a traditional Fordist assembly line). The result, explained political science professor Tony Smith, "is an equivalent to hiring an extra 333 workers to work a forty-hour week."[62] This process of intensifying labor was first turned into a science by Frederick Taylor in the late nineteenth century and dubbed "Taylorism" (see sidebar: "A 'Scientific' Obsession").

Since then, the twenty-first century version of the same is often referred to as "lean production": speedups, de-skilling, use of temporary and contract workers, greater management flexibility on hours and tasks, etc. These processes have resulted in "the greatest work intensification in US history," according to Kim Moody, "far surpassing the now quaint norms of Taylorism."[63] Here we see that the value of labor-power (paid out in wages) remains the same, but the time that it takes to reproduce it is lessened. So if you are paid $120 per day, your wage would stay the same, but instead of making $120 worth of value for your boss in four hours, you would make it in, say, three and a half.

Alternatively, a second means of increasing relative surplus value is lowering the value of labor-power—let's say from $120 to $90 a day. In this case, workers employed at the same level of intensity could reproduce this value in three, rather than four hours. This happens if technology in other industries producing necessities like food and clothing create cheaper commodities for workers, and wages are reduced accordingly. For instance, a 75 percent drop in the cost of buying food and other requirements, could lead to wages being cut by 75 percent as well. These costs can also be lessened by reducing the worth and quality of the things that workers need. Thus household items bought from discount stores, cheap shoes, and fast-food dinners increasingly make up what is considered an "acceptable" standard of living.

This is not necessarily a deliberate strategy on the part of the capitalist class, but a convenient by-product of competition. As Marx explained: "When an individual capitalist cheapens shirts, for instance, by increasing the productivity of labor, he by no means necessarily aims to reduce the value of labor-power and shorten necessary labor-time in proportion to this. But he contributes toward increasing the general rate of surplus-value only insofar as he ultimately contributes to this result."[64]

A third means of increasing relative surplus value is the de-skilling of jobs, lowering the amount of education or training necessary, and therefore the value of the labor-power. Consider, for instance, the trend to have home health aides, who have minimal training requirements and are usually paid $7–10 per hour, administer medications, which used to be solely the job of highly trained and well-paid nurses. Or, there are jobs that have become so automated that an afternoon's worth of training is sufficient for their execution. These de-skilled jobs correspond to vastly lower wages, which have the same impact as reducing the pay of current employees.

In fact, a division of labor in the workplace is key to creating efficiency in production, and is also critical to the process of de-skilling and cheapening labor. Charles Babbage, the English mathematician and zealous advocate for a strict division of labor, wrote *On the Economy of Machinery and Manufactures* in 1832. In it, Babbage argued that by dividing crafts into their simplest component parts, each can be devalued to its lowest possible point. Writing about the meatpacking industry, Babbage explained:

> It would be difficult to find another industry where division of labor has been so ingeniously and microscopically worked out. The animal has been surveyed and laid off like a map; and the men have been classified in over thirty specialties and twenty rates of pay, from 16 cents to 50 cents an hour. The 50-cent man is restricted to using the knife on the most delicate parts of the hide (floorman) or to using the ax in splitting the backbone (splitter); and wherever a less-skilled man can be slipped in at 18 cents, 18 ½ cents, 20 cents, 21 cents, 22 ½ cents, 24 cents, 25 cents and so on, a place is made for him and an occupation mapped out. In working on the hide alone there are nine positions, at eight different rates of pay. A 20-cent man pulls off the tail, a 22 ½-cent man pounds off another part where good leather is not found, and the knife of the 40-cent man cuts a different texture and has a different "feel" from that of the 50-cent man.[65]

A final means to increase relative value is to drive wages down below the value of labor-power. In the current age of austerity, the common scenario is that the cost of living (not just food and clothing, but also housing, transportation, and health care) increases, while compensation (usually through cuts to health care and other benefits) is still reduced, forcing wages *below* the actual value of labor-power. The higher the rate of unemployment, the easier it is to push a desperate workforce to accept wages below the cost of living. More often than not, increasing household debt makes up the difference. While recessions are frequently the excuse to drive down living standards, wages don't usually bounce back once bosses start making record profits again.

Each of these routes to increasing surplus value—lengthening the working day, lowering the value of labor-power, lowering the wages paid, and increasing the intensification of labor—yields gains to capitalists. And if they push on multiple fronts at the same time, they can dramatically increase the rate of exploitation.

An additional point, which we will discuss in the next two chapters, is that in the *short-term*, bosses can also raise the rate of exploitation through increases in productivity, by introducing new laborsaving technologies. Using advanced machinery or tools, a single worker can churn out the same commodities in ten or twenty times the speed. Introducing new technologies thus allows capitalists to reduce the unit cost and undersell rivals—but still sell somewhat above value. But this competitive advantage is wiped out when others introduce the same technology. It will have only a temporary effect on profitability, unless, as we noted above, the increases in productivity are in industries that cheapen the goods needed for workers' subsistence, and therefore lower the cost of labor-power in society as a whole. Marx argued:

> New machinery produces relative surplus value, when it is first introduced into an industry not only by directly depreciating the value of labor-power, and by indirectly cheapening the same through cheapening the commodities that enter into its reproduction, thus enabling the capitalist to replace the value of a day's labor-power by a smaller portion of the value of a day's product. During this transitional period, while the use of machinery remains a sort of monopoly, profits are exceptional, and the capitalist endeavors to exploit thoroughly "the sunny time of this his first love" by prolonging the working day as far as possible. The magnitude of the profit gives him an insatiable hunger for yet more profit.[66]

The sunny time of his first love will quickly give way to increasing competition when other capitalists adopt the same means, thus returning to the forefront, yet again, the need to extort more labor from the workers themselves.

CONCLUSION

Surplus-labor is not an invention of capitalism. As Marx argued: "Wherever a part of society possesses the monopoly of the means of production, the worker, free or unfree, must add to the labor-time necessary for his own maintenance an extra quantity of labor-time in order to produce the means of subsistence for the owner of the means of production, whether this proprietor be an Athenian [aristocrat], an Etruscan theocrat, a *civis romanus*, a Norman Baron, an American slave-owner, a Wallachian boyar, a modern landlord or a capitalist."[67]

Previous class societies, too, were predicated on exploitation—the appropriation of a part of the wealth of those who work by a ruling class. A serf, for example, would be required to work for a certain number of days on the lord's land. In this way, the extraction of surplus labor was quite explicit. Modern-day exploitation, however, is disguised by the *appearance* of a fair deal. It seems that workers are paid a fair day's wage for a fair day's work, as the saying goes. But we are not paid for our work, we are paid for our labor-power, and therein lies the rub.

What distinguishes capitalism is the particular (and particularly deceptive!) form in which surplus labor is extracted: the gap between the labor-power's exchange-value, paid out in wages, and the value of the labor that is delivered back to the capitalist. This exploitation of labor by capital is the propellant of class society. It is not newly reinvented each time a worker applies for a job, but is a product of historically ingrained class positions, which continuously repeat and renew themselves. As Marx wrote:

> It is no longer a mere accident that capitalist and worker confront each other in the market as buyer and seller. It is the alternating rhythm of the process itself which throws the worker back onto the market again and again as a seller of his labor-power and continually transforms his own product into a means by which another man can purchase him. In reality, the worker belongs to capital before he has sold himself to the capitalist. His economic bondage is at once mediated through, and concealed by, the periodic renewal of the act by which he sells himself, his change of masters, and the oscillations in the market-price of his labor.[68]

We've gotten a glimpse of what this economic bondage means for the working class. In the next chapter we'll see that capitalists, too, in their own opulent ways, are bound to the economic laws of the system—ones that they clearly benefit from tremendously, but which bind them to a certain modus operandi nonetheless.

A "SCIENTIFIC" OBSESSION

The compulsion to increase the intensity of labor ratcheted up to an obsession in the 1890s with the methods of "scientific management." Frederick Taylor developed the ideas of industrial efficiency first as a manager at Midvale Steel Works and later at Bethlehem Steel. Every task was studied, broken down into individual components, and timed in order to determine the minimal intervals required to accomplish each. The timing and methods of work could then be standardized—whether that be through speeding up the conveyor belt in an auto plant or using keystroke counters to mechanize office jobs.

Scientific management is based on a severe alienation of labor, which assumes that the greatest and most specific level of supervision will yield maximum productivity. So long as workers have any control over the labor process, goes the argument, they will try to thwart their full productive potential. According to Taylor, managers should specify "not only what is to be done but how it is to be done and the exact time allowed for doing it."[69]

Taylor wrote at length about his own experience as a manager at Bethlehem Steel. While studying the physics of loading pig iron, he discovered that a pig iron handler ought to handle between 47 and 48 tons per day, but in fact they averaged 12 ½. To resolve this situation, he set upon buying off the most fit workers and training them to follow second-by-second instruction in order to produce optimal efficiency. These workers were then set as examples and their work-speed imposed as the standard on the shop floor.

Taylor outlined the process by which this was accomplished in his book, *The Principles of Scientific Management.* First they picked out a man who seemed physically capable and who they assumed could be sufficiently convinced to work harder by the promise of a raise: "a little Pennsylvania Dutchman who had been observed to trot back home for a mile or so after his work in the evening about as fresh as he was when he came trotting down to work in the morning."[70] (Imagine the nerve, leaving work still feeling fresh!) Taylor recounted a very patronizing conversation with the man he called "Shmidt," which ended in the following lecture:

> Well, if you are a high-priced man, you will do exactly as this man tells you tomorrow, from morning till night. When he tells you to pick up a pig and walk, you pick it up and you walk, and when he tells you to sit down and rest, you sit down. You do that right straight through the day. And what's more, no back talk. Now a high-priced man does just what he's told to do, and no back talk. Do you understand that? When this man tells you to walk, you walk; when he tells you to sit down, you sit down, and you don't talk back at him. Now you come on to work here tomorrow morning and I'll know before night whether you are really a high-priced man or not.[71]

For the reward of being judged a "high-priced man," Shmidt and eventually others were paid $1.85 a day instead of $1.15, an increase of 60 percent in their wage. In exchange, the workers each loaded 47.5 tons of pig iron on average instead of 12.5, an increase in productivity of 280 percent. Not a bad deal for the bosses. Taylor justified his astonishing condescension toward the workers by explaining that they were too "mentally sluggish" to understand how to efficiently do the work themselves:

> Now one of the very first requirements for a man who is fit to handle pig iron as a regular occupation is that he shall be so stupid and so phlegmatic that he more nearly resembles in his mental make-up the ox than any other type. The man who is mentally alert and intelligent is for this very reason entirely unsuited to what would, for him, be the grinding monotony of work of this character. Therefore the

workman who is best suited to handling pig iron is unable to understand the real science of doing this class of work.[72]

But the real implication of Taylorism is not that workers are too "mentally sluggish" to efficiently work themselves to the bone. Quite the opposite, their own interest would lead them to work as little as possible in order to preserve their health and well-being. This very intelligent sense of self-preservation is in fact the reason that workers need to be supervised to the second. Indeed, more often than not, management observes their employees only to discover that the workers have found ways to shorten the labor-time it takes to perform various functions. They do this in order to have more downtime for themselves, but managers take that knowledge in order to enforce speedups and to steal more surplus labor-time.

Capitalism uses our ingenuity to further immiserate us. Socialism would use every advance to make more time for humans to rest, play, and thrive. This is why Russian Revolutionary Leon Trotsky was onto something when he lauded human laziness as a quality necessary for human progress:

> As a general rule, man strives to avoid labor. Love for work is not at all an inborn characteristic: it is created by economic pressure and social education. One may even say that man is a fairly lazy animal. It is on this quality, in reality, that is founded to a considerable extent all human progress; because if man did not strive to expend his energy economically, did not seek to receive the largest possible quantity of products in return for a small quantity of energy, there would have been no technical development or social culture. It would appear, then, from this point of view that human laziness is a progressive force. Old Antonio Labriola, the Italian Marxist, even used to picture the man of the future as a "happy and lazy genius."[73]

CHAPTER FIVE

THE ACCUMULATION OF CAPITAL

[The capitalist] shares with the miser an absolute drive towards self-enrichment. But what appears in the miser as the mania of an individual is in the capitalist the effect of the social mechanism in which he is merely a cog.

Capital, Volume 1[1]

COMPETE OR GO BUST

"Henry Ford might insist, as he continually did," wrote socialist novelist Upton Sinclair, "that competition was wrong, and that he did not believe in it; but the fact was that he was competing at every moment in his life, and would continue to do so as long as he made motor-cars. In a hundred different plants scattered over the United States, efforts were being made to beat him. In the long run, the successful ones would be those who contrived, by one method or another, to get the most out of a dollar's worth of labor."[2]

Competition is the beating heart of capitalism. It drives production forward and, as we'll see, fuels the dynamism of the system. Individual capitalists may fancy themselves as above the fray. They may want to position themselves as caring capitalists. Or they may rise to heights in their industry that make them appear to be untouchable. But in the end, no capitalist can opt out of competing and none is protected from upstart challengers. Even powerful monopolists—whether Henry Ford or Bill Gates—can't stay ahead of the competition indefinitely.

It was, after all, competition—the need to dominate the automobile market at the expense of any emerging car company—that drove Ford to revolutionize how cars were produced. Mass assembly created the conditions for less labor intensive and therefore cheaper car production. This allowed Ford to sell Model Ts at half the price of other cars, winning the company the dominant position within the new automobile industry.

To understand why competition is central to capitalism, consider again the circuit of capital: M-C-M'. Money (M) is invested in order to create commodities (C), which are then sold for more money than originally outlaid (M'). But the dash between C and M' is always a question mark for the capitalist. It is one thing to produce surplus value; it is another thing to then sell the goods and make an actual profit. In other words, surplus value is *created* in production, but only *realized* in exchange. Will commodities find buyers? The "free" and anonymous market forces capitalists to compete with one another to capture consumers.

M   C   M'

In the previous chapter we saw just how *organized* production under capitalism is, often timed to the second. This level of internal coordination by individual capitalists is a necessary means to staying on top of, or ahead of, socially necessary labor-time. In this chapter we will discuss the very *disorganized* and unplanned process of capitalist exchange faced by capital as a whole. The organization of production, as Engles argued in *Anti-Dühring,* is mirrored by its exact opposite in the anarchy of the market:

> [E]very society resting on commodity production has the peculiarity, that in it the producers have lost the command over their own social relations. Each produces for himself with the means of production which he happens to have, and for his individual exchange requirements. No one knows how much of his article is coming on the market, or how much of it will be wanted; no one knows whether his particular product will meet an actual demand, whether he will be able to cover his costs of production or even be able to sell his commodity at all. Anarchy reigns in social production...
>
> The anarchy of social production made itself evident and became more and more extreme. But the chief instrument with which the capitalistic method of production intensified this anarchy in social production, was the exact opposite of anarchy, namely, the increasing organization of

production, on a social basis, in each individual productive establishment. With this lever, it made an end of the old peaceful stability. Wherever it was introduced in a branch of industry, it brooked no older method of production by its side. Wherever it took possession of handicraft, it annihilated the old handicraft. The field of labor became a battleground... The contradiction between socialized production and capitalistic appropriation is reproduced *as the antagonism between the organization of production in the single factory, and the anarchy of production in society as a whole.*[3]

As we unpack the workings of the market, doing so will shed light on why capitalists are obliged to accumulate evermore capital, invest in mechanization, and continually advance the forces of production. We'll see too the consequences of that ACCUMULATION, which gives rise on the one hand to inventiveness and technological vigor, and on the other hand to their counterparts: monopolies, companies that are "too big to fail," and imperialist instability.

ANARCHY REIGNS

In the idealized version of capitalism touted by mainstream economics, everything that is produced is consumed, and capitalists reap the full benefit of their investments by selling the whole of their product. In reality, they must distribute their profits among a number of other capitalists (see sidebar: "Capitalist Hangers-On"). What's more, selling all—or even most—of their product is far from guaranteed. Each firm must compete for buyers within a market that they do not control. And even if they *could* control the market, they cannot control their competitors.

If every industry were made up of just one company selling goods, then that business would only need to make sure that its commodities were useful to some group of people with the cash to purchase them. Instead several (and sometimes many more) firms compete with each other to reach potential buyers. Each need to command ever-greater market shares in order to survive. If they don't, others will grow at their expense.

Companies can expand their share of the market through branding and marketing or through pricing reductions. Or they can reinvest their capital elsewhere if their current line of business is tapped out (much as phone companies did when they shifted financing from landlines to cellular networks). But they neither make these calculations in collaboration with other capitalists, nor do they know with certainty which direction the market will go.

Their first problem is that markets are anonymous and undefined—even in the days of "big data," which follows potential consumer activity online and offline. No matter how diligently or creepily Facebook tracks your every movement for marketers, companies can only take guesses as to who their potential buyers are, where they can be found, and whether or when they will ultimately decide to pull the trigger to buy. Trying to predict the answers to these questions in order to plan investment and production has driven a boom in "data mining" and marketing analytics.

As *New York Times* journalist Charles Duhigg explained, companies purchase information about "your ethnicity, job history, the magazines you read, if you've ever declared bankruptcy or got divorced, the year you bought (or lost) your house, where you went to college, what kinds of topics you talk about online, whether you prefer certain brands of coffee, paper towels, cereal or applesauce, your political leanings, reading habits, charitable giving and the number of cars you own." Andreas Weigend, former chief scientist at Amazon.com, told Duhigg, "It's like an arms race to hire statisticians nowadays."[4] Yet these and other tools of "demand forecasting" still do not offer a reliable means to predict the size and scope of a market.[5]

Second, no matter how hard analysts try to pin down the spending capacity of their consumer base, markets are constantly changing and their directions are unknown. They contract and expand, new ones are created, old ones collapse. Failing to predict or set the terms of the market in a given industry can drive a once-thriving company out of business.

Automakers, for example, cannot be sure which types of cars will dominate in the coming years. All of them must constantly spend money on research and development of new systems, not knowing whether these investments will help them secure a leading position or will be money down the drain. As Toyota's chief executive complained: "For the last hundred years, gasoline engines have occupied the mainstream, but if you look forward a hundred years, it will not just be gasoline, but diesel, electrics, plug-in hybrids and fuel-cell vehicles. We don't know yet which will be chosen."[6] Or perhaps the terrifying trend to "self-driving" cars will take off. (Thank you, capitalism. What could possibly go wrong?)

Moreover, established car companies are looking over their shoulders at young upstarts like Tesla, which is spending billions of dollars on research and development to create mass-marketable electric cars. If they succeed in automating manufacture to more cheaply produce (and therefore sell) their cars, Tesla could go from obscure upstart to serious competitor in a new field.

Third, each company sets the scope of production independently, with little knowledge of what other firms are planning. In setting production quotas, each corporation's profit is the motive, rather than the industry's overall economic health, let alone social need. The heads of major corporations don't sit together and discuss: "Ok, how many people need our gadgets? . . . So, who's going to make how many? . . . Great! We have a plan!" Even in cases where competitors engage in price collusion in order to team up for greater profits, this collaboration is between a "band of hostile brothers," as Marx called the ruling class, and by necessity any alliance eventually breaks down as the race for market share resumes.

Rather than cooperating, every company angles for greater sales at the expense of their rivals. This competition keeps capitalism in a constant state of motion as businesses hustle to gain efficiencies and push out companies that are not keeping up. Technology must constantly be updated to make cheaper goods. This is why even a corporation like Apple, among the largest corporations in the world, with an estimated value of $1 trillion at the time of this book's writing, can't just coast to stay profitable.[7]

A look at any of Apple's products explains why. The iPod, iPhone, and iPad all came into the market as products that had not previously existed. Apple was able to effectively advertise these products and cultivate an audience of willing buyers, even at high prices. The first generation of iPods were $400–$500, depending on the size of their drive. But in the case of each of these products, other competitors soon entered the market at lower prices, elbowing Apple out of market share and forcing the company to innovate its technologies to create faster, more efficient products at cheaper prices.

So while Apple dominated the early years of the smartphone market, Android's share of mobile browsing has long surpassed Apple's iOS. The price of Android phones (which aren't controlled by a single corporation, and therefore enter more ruthlessly into price wars) has fallen every year since 2011, and are now roughly a third of the average iPhone.[8] The scramble to control the market sets every company on a manic path to produce more and better, faster, cheaper products. In 2015, Apple hustled to get the iPad Pro out before Microsoft's Surface Pro 4 came out—and it needed to prove itself the greater value, that it can do more, and costs less. Of course, by the time you read this book, several newer lines of iPads will have competed with the latest lines of Surfaces or Kindle Fires or an as-of-yet unknown brand.

Though companies spend significant resources on branding and advertising to convince buyers that their products are best, the race to innovate is largely driven by the socially necessary labor-time that it takes to create products. Every company must sell goods at or below the average market price. The more a company gains efficiencies in production by reducing labor-time, the more cheaply they can sell their goods, and the more likely that they will capture buyers by underselling their competitors. Conversely, if a seller has a high cost of production, he will be forced to find ways to lower his costs, or risk going out of business. As Marx explained: "The battle of competition is fought by the cheapening of commodities": that is reducing their value through a reduction in labor-time.[9]

Automation allows a company to generate as much, or more, revenue with fewer workers. This is precisely what Henry Ford did by introducing the moving assembly line. Capitalists are constantly looking to reduce the number of workers they need to employ by greater use of technology, though these changes may have more or less revolutionary effects than Ford's assembly line.

In recent years, for instance, health care providers for the aging have begun to rely on telehealth and patient monitoring technologies to reduce costs of administering care, and of sending doctors or nurses to peoples' homes. Demand for patient monitoring systems, which allow agencies to cut back on the number of hours aides must spend with older adults living at home, has grown dramatically in recent years.[10] "Sensors can be placed around the home," wrote *InformationWeek* reporter Alison Diana, "on doors and windows—as well as in appliances and on the patient. They alert caregivers if the senior misses a meal, doesn't get out of bed, or falls." They can even tell the caregiver if their patient has left the water running too long.[11]

Each company must *at minimum* have enough technological capability to manufacture widgets (or deliver health care services) as quickly as its competitors do. At best, it will innovate *before* its rivals do, thus reducing the cost of production and the prices of its goods. Marked-down prices then translate into greater market share, a higher profit margin, and a dominant position in the industry. The scramble to reduce the cost of production forces capitalists to ceaselessly advance the instruments of production, or be left behind. As Marx and Engels vividly described in the pages of the *Communist Manifesto*:

> The bourgeoisie cannot exist without constantly revolutionizing the instruments of production, and thereby the relations of production, and with them the whole relations of society. Conservation of the old modes of production in unaltered form, was, on the contrary, the first condition of existence for all earlier industrial classes. Constant revolutionizing of production, uninterrupted disturbance of all social conditions, everlasting

uncertainty and agitation distinguish the bourgeois epoch from all earlier ones. All fixed, fast-frozen relations, with their train of ancient and venerable prejudices and opinions, are swept away, all new-formed ones become antiquated before they can ossify. All that is solid melts into air, all that is holy is profaned, and man is at last compelled to face with sober senses his real conditions of life, and his relations with his kind.[12]

CAPITALIST HANGERS-ON

Capitalists must distribute their profits among a number of other capitalists before reinvesting the rest into the next round of production.

Let's say you're in the business of making action figures. Your initial output of M, $10,000, is split into a few components: 1) materials such as rubber, acrylic paints, glue, and so on; 2) sculpting tools and assembly machinery; and 3) labor costs for the designers, engineers, assemblers, and marketers. As we discussed in the previous chapter, the first two components are constant capital. The plastic and other materials pass on their complete value into the final product, while the machinery and tools pass on their value piecemeal through the wear and tear of their use. The final component—labor-power—is variable capital, and reproduces itself, and additionally a surplus value.

At the end of the production cycle, the action figures sell for a total of $15,000. The increased profit reflects the added value of labor that went into converting raw materials into a new product. Within this total, $10,000 replaces the initial investment, but the last $5,000 doesn't all go back to you as extra profit. Presumably, if some or all of the initial outlay of $10,000 was borrowed—either from a bank, or in the form of stocks or other means, at least some of the extra $5,000 will then pay back the interest on those loans, or dividends to shareholders. Other sections of the profits are disbursed to cover real estate costs in the form of rent to a landlord or as a mortgage payment to a bank. In addition, a part of the surplus goes to the state through taxes.

In this way the exploitation of workers must support not only the capitalists that directly employ them, but a whole string of other hangers-on. A capitalist producing action figures is a "productive capitalist" because workers employed by him are producing commodities and surplus value. Other sections of the capitalist class—"unproductive capitalists"—don't directly engage in the production of surplus value, but nonetheless play significant roles in allowing surplus value to be created.

Finance capitalists, for instance, play the role of taking surplus value realized in one part of the system and deploying it to another through loans or direct investments. (The financial system will be discussed further in chapter seven). States create the conditions that allow for production to happen smoothly (police to protect private property, infrastructure that allows for ease of transporting commodities, trade laws that favor domestic business, etc.). And landlords manage properties, in some cases indirectly contributing value to production. Take, for example, Chicago, where there is a high concentration of warehouses stemming from the city's geographic centrality. The ability of companies to stock their goods in these warehouses is central to their ability to then deploy and sell them.

All of these processes facilitate the creation and realization of surplus value, though none produce surplus value in and of themselves.

MOSES AND THE PROPHETS

The disciplining force of socially necessary labor-time propels capitalists to constantly "accumulate"—that is to transform surplus value into further capital. It isn't the case that each capitalist wants to make a greater profit than his neighbor so that he'll feel himself a bigger man. Nor is the drive for profit driven by his insatiable thirst for more luxuries. Rather, he desperately needs to accumulate more capital in order to get hold of the latest, most efficient, laborsaving automation. The bigger the profit of an individual capitalist, the more quickly he'll be able to invest in these technologies, ahead of his competitors. In the words of Dell Computers founder and CEO, Michael Dell, corporations must "grow or die." (See sidebar: "Capitalists Grow or Die.") As Engels explained:

We have seen that the perfectibility of modern machinery, developed to the highest degree, becomes transformed by means of the anarchy of production in society into a compulsory law for the individual industrial capitalist constantly to improve his machinery, constantly to increase its productive power. The bare factual possibility of extending his sphere of production, becomes transformed, for him, into a similar compulsory law. The enormous expansive force of modern industry, in comparison with which that of gases is veritable child's play, appears now before our eyes as a qualitative and quantitative *need* to expand which laughs at all resistance.[13]

In the auto industry, for instance, the average time between redesigns of new models is five years. Automobile technology for electric motors, multispeed automatic transmissions, battery power, and engine power is continually updated to provide "more car for your money." If a car company comes out with a new vehicle that does not significantly improve upon older models, it will spend those years between redesigns losing market share until it can produce a new model.[14]

Marx, therefore, made the point that it is not enough to generate surplus value; it must be reinvested. The part of surplus value that is consumed by capitalists themselves is *revenue*, while the part that is employed as capital is ACCUMULATED. If bosses merely spent their profits on luxuries, production would not expand, and capitalists would not have the means to innovate. "[W]hat does this surplus product consist of?" asked Marx: "Only of things destined to satisfy the needs and desires of the capitalist class, things which consequently enter into the consumption fund of the capitalists? If that were all, the cup of surplus value would be drained to the very dregs, and nothing but simple reproduction would ever take place."[15]

Of course, the ruling class *does* spend an exorbitant amount of money on themselves. Millions of dollars are poured into mansions, yachts, parties, watches, art, and all manner of sundry luxuries. Venture capitalist Marc Bell recently put his Boca Raton mansion up for sale for nearly $25 million, so he could move into larger digs in Miami. Along with a "natural" swimming pool that features waterfalls over sculpted stone, a spa and a basketball court on the property's 1.6 acres, his mansion also includes a "Star Trek" home theatre, which replicates the main bridge of the Starship Enterprise, complete with proper "swooshing" sounds every time the doors open or close.[16]

As a 2018 Oxfam report revealed, the richest forty-two people own the same combined wealth as the world's poorest 3.7 billion. In the US, the wealth of the three richest people equals that of the bottom half of the population. This gap grows by the day. In the economic crisis emerging alongside the COVID-19 pandemic, the rich made a killing. According to the Institute for Policy Studies,

> Between March 18 and April 10, 2020, over 22 million people lost their jobs as the unemployment rate surged toward 15 percent. Over the same three weeks, U.S. billionaire wealth increased by $282 billion, an almost 10 percent gain.[17]

Yet despite their preposterous lifestyles, and the barbarity of the growing inequality between rich and poor, capitalists, too, are like gold-studded cogs in the wheels of the system. As Marx explained: "[C]ompetition subordinates every individual capitalist to the immanent laws of capitalist production, as external and coercive laws. It compels him to keep extending his capital, so as to preserve it, and he can only extend it by means of progressive accumulation."[18] If Ford had contented himself with blowing the profits from the first series of Model Ts on a fancy vacation, rather than investing in new technologies, another company would have been first to innovate car production. Ford would have become a footnote in the history of US capitalism.

History is riddled with such footnotes of companies that fail to innovate and then go under. Consider Blockbuster, once a multibillion-dollar entertainment company, with over 9,000 stores and 60,000 employees. The company took a rather abrupt turn to uselessness and bankruptcy when it failed to stay ahead of streaming technologies. Blockbuster passed up an opportunity to buy a then-small company named Netflix for $50 million in 2000, unaware that most people would be watching their shows and movies through the internet before long. Netflix soon drove Blockbuster out of business.[19]

This is why both Marc Bell and his Star Trek-styled mansion, and Ben Cohen and Jerry Greenfield, founders of Ben and Jerry's "caring capitalism" ice-cream are all disciplined by the same forces of the market, and are all compelled to accumulate, or face bankruptcy. Marc and Ben and Jerry, whatever their personal feelings about capitalism or *Star Trek*, must make enough profit to plow back into further innovation and production. As Marx famously described:

> Accumulate, accumulate! That is Moses and the prophets! 'Industry furnishes the material which saving accumulates.' Therefore, save, save, *i.e.*, reconvert the greatest possible portion of surplus value or surplus-product into capital! Accumulation for the sake of accumulation, production for the sake of production: this was the formula in which classical economics expressed the historical mission of the bourgeoisie in the period of its domination. Not for one instant did it deceive itself over the nature of wealth's birth-pangs.[20]

We can see then that in reality M-C-M' cannot be a linear process with a beginning and end, but a continuous one, which must spiral in growth. When the system is running smoothly, capitalists don't sit on the cash they've made; profits are shoveled back into new rounds of production.[21] Cash from this quarter's auto, health services, or iPhone sales is used to finance next year's models. Each round of production thus proceeds from a more advanced position than the last, built on the larger amount of money—M'—generated by the previous cycle.

FIGURE 6. ROUNDS OF PRODUCTION

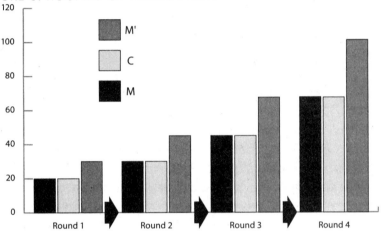

The second round of production, M'-C'-M'', now creates an even greater total. Instead of a $20,000 investment producing value of $30,000, we can now start with $30,000 and end up with $45,000. M-C-M' is really: M-C-M'-C'-M''-C''-M'''-C'''-M'''' in perpetuity. As Marx wrote: "Looked at concretely, accumulation can be resolved into the production of capital on a progressively increasing scale. The cycle of simple reproduction alters its form and, to use Sismondi's expression, changes into a spiral."[22]

This spiraling buildup of wealth brings us back to the definition of capital as the self-expansion of value.[23] On an individual basis, each capitalist is compelled to expand profits and investments or face insolvency. On a *system-wide* basis, this translates to an economy that must grow without bounds. As David Harvey explained: "Just read the press reports on the state of the economy every day, and what are people talking about all the time? Growth! Where's the growth? How are we going to grow? Slow growth defines a recession, and negative growth a depression. One or 2 percent growth (compounded) is not enough, we need at least 3, and only when we reach 4 percent is the economy deemed to be 'healthy.'"[24]

CAPITALISTS GROW OR DIE

For capitalists to increase their market share they must lower prices. And in order to lower prices they need to invest in laborsaving, cost-cutting technologies, which will allow them to produce goods more cheaply than their competitors.

There may be some cases when a corporation may drop their prices, despite not lowering the cost of production, and thus take a temporary hit on their rate of profit for the sake of gaining greater market share. This may be a tempting strategy during periods of recession when markets are saturated with goods that no one is able to buy. A company that is able to lower their prices can force their competitors to pay the consequences of unsold products. Retail companies call this strategy being a "loss leader." They sell a popular good or service below value in order to get people in the door. Then they hope to make up for it by selling other goods, or selling at a higher price once they drive their competitors out of the market.

In the early 2000s, while the United States was going through a mild recession, Dell Computers dealt with diminishing sales of personal computers by dropping their prices below the average selling value. Their strategy was to take a temporary loss to their profit margins in order to sell more computers and grab more market share at the expense of their competitors. Indeed, Dell was able to take advantage of the moment to rise from the number two PC maker in the US to number one and stay there for several years. But ultimately this strategy has to work in tandem with a longer-term strategy to reduce the cost of production. Lower profit margins are not sustainable for any corporation, particularly in the fast-changing computer industry. As soon as another PC maker invests in new laborsaving technology, they will be able to produce faster, better, and cheaper computers.

Dell's key strategy for years had been to lead the charge in developing lean, low-cost production processes. Since the 1990s, Dell used just-in-time manufacturing methods that rely on maintaining only days' worth (and in some cases hours' worth) of inventory, keeping warehouse and delivery costs low, and avoiding the risks and price tag involved with holding on to a backlog of computer parts. This method itself required the investment in extensive, web-based collaborative technologies, which could keep factory managers assessing their inventory by the hour to avoid stoppages in production.

To further reduce costs, Dell invested in their, then new, Topfer Manufacturing Center factory in Austin, Texas, where they increased production by a third while cutting manufacturing space in half. As *Forbes* described it: "Workers already scuttle about in the 200,000-square-foot plant like ants on a hot plate. Gathered in cramped six-person 'cells,' they assemble computers from batches of parts that arrive via a computer-directed conveyor system overhead. . . Workers in the six-person cells now assemble 18 units an hour, double the pace of a couple of years ago."[25]

In part, the drive toward increased productivity comes down to good old-fashioned methods of increasing the rate of exploitation. The teams of workers that fill each "cell" compete with each other to see which line can churn computers out the fastest. "In a blur of synchronized movements," wrote Bill Breen for *Fast Company,* "a veteran builder can piece together a Dell. . . in three minutes."[26] One story that made its rounds at Topfer factory was about a day that CEO and founder Michael Dell himself toured the factory. "A group from one of the packing lines showed him how they'd upped their processing rate from 300 to 350 boxes an hour," Breen reports. "Michael congratulated them, and there were high fives all around. . . But then he issued a challenge: 'How can we improve to 400?'"[27]

And yet, notwithstanding Michael Dell's implorations, workers can only be driven so far. Ultimately, it is investment in laborsaving technology that can make lasting and qualitative leaps in the speed of turnout. To be sure, the main focus of Dell executives' reported "maniacal focus on shaving minutes off assembly time" was in reducing the time needed for "human intervention," i.e. workers' labor on the factory floor. Innovations in hydraulic tools, conveyor belts, tracks, and box-packing robots reportedly decreased the time that workers were involved in production by *half.*

Ultimately, further innovations in the computer industry have rendered personal computers close to obsolete as laptops, tablets, and even smartphones replace their functions. Thus in 2008, in the midst of both a recession and a long-term decline of PCs, Dell's much-touted Topfer plant was closed, showing its eight hundred fast and efficient workers the company's gratitude with pink slips.

ONE CAPITALIST KILLS MANY

Evidence abounds of capitalism's fantastical growth, which has led to corporations of colossal size, along with the accumulation of vast wealth into few hands. In 2016, the world's 500 largest companies generated nearly $30 trillion in revenues and $1.5 trillion in profits, employing 65 million people—more than twice the total workforce of France.[28] These 500 companies generated eight times the amount of revenue as Germany's GDP, and twelve times the combined GDPs of the entire African continent. We noted earlier that Apple was the first company to cross the $1 trillion threshold of net worth. Compare that to the size of US Steel, the largest American corporation a hundred years ago, which was then valued at less than $50 billion (adjusted for inflation).[29] As we'll see, the size of these corporate giants affords them all sorts of benefits, which increase their competitive edge. Large companies have tremendous power in determining pace, pricing, and the establishment of new markets for the industries that they dominate.

Marx identified two key dynamics involved in this scaling up of enterprises: concentration and centralization. CONCENTRATION of capital is the process of an enterprise growing through time, by way of accumulation—the spiraling circuit of capital previously illustrated. He explained:

> Every individual capital is a larger or smaller concentration of means of production, with a corresponding command over a larger or smaller army of workers. Every accumulation becomes the means of new accumulation.

> With the increasing mass of wealth which functions as capital, accumulation increases the concentration of that wealth in the hands of individual capitalists, and thereby widens the basis of production on a large scale and extends the specifically capitalist methods of production.[30]

That is to say: each round of production leaves the capitalist with the ability to invest more in the next cycle. Concentration of capital is thus a historical process, as surplus value accrues over time. Bourgeois economists refer to concentration as "organic growth." Of course, "organic" makes it sound very pleasant and benign! But as we've seen, growth is propelled through exploitation and the theft of our labor.

In Walmart's first decade after opening its initial store in 1962, the chain averaged 3.5 US store openings per year. In its second decade the number jumped to 42.7 and in the third decade it averaged 129.4 yearly openings in the United States. In its fourth decade, openings in the US dropped to 91.6 stores per year (although by then it had started to open stores internationally as well). As a result, in forty-five years Walmart grew from a single store to a chain that had opened 3,176 stores in the United States and became the largest retailer in the world. See Figure 7.

FIGURE 7. WALMART YEARLY AND CUMULATIVE OPENINGS, US, 1962–2005

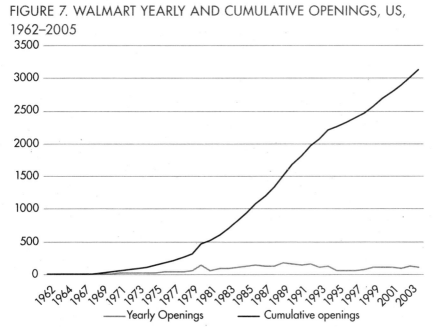

Source: "The Diffusion of Wal-Mart and Economies of Density," *Econometrica* 79, no. 1 (January 2011), 253–302

Not coincidentally, Walmart workers earn an estimated 14.5 percent less than other low-paid retail workers. A full 15 percent of Walmart's Ohio employees are on food stamps, and it should come as no surprise that studies have found that "the entry of Wal-Mart into a county reduces both average and aggregate earnings of retail workers and reduces the share of retail workers with health coverage on the job."[31]

McDonald's, for its part—which has fought tooth and nail against the Fight For $15 [dollars per hour wage] by spying on, threatening, and firing workers engaged in the campaign—grew by nearly 20 percent to 36,899 branches in the last ten years alone.[32] The chain closed more stores than it opened in 2015, for the first year since 1970 (and likely since it became a franchise in 1955). Apparently fast food chains that use more food-like ingredients have finally made a dent in the revenues of the world's biggest burger chain. But its position as fast-food behemoth still remains unchallenged. Similar patterns can be observed among many of the corporate titans that dominate the economic landscape.

Such growth is accelerated by credit and financial structures, which provide a variety of mechanisms for capitalists to pool investments from financiers in order to advance a greater amount of capital, and accumulate further profits. The stock and bond markets, which we'll discuss in chapter seven, are collectively called CAPITAL MARKETS. The sale of stock raises a large amount of cash from stakeholders, who then own fractions of the company and its future profits. Companies can also raise capital by selling bonds. The bonds are a form of debt, which can be issued at set interest rates for a certain number of years. Global capital markets are worth hundreds of trillions of dollars, and their rise has vastly accelerated the process of concentration under capitalism.[33]

The CENTRALIZATION of capital, meanwhile, is the process through which industries come to be dominated by fewer and larger enterprises through consolidation. Centralization "does not mean that simple concentration of the means of production and of the command over labor, which is identical with accumulation," Marx explained. Rather:

> It is concentration of capitals *already formed*, destruction of their individual independence, expropriation of capitalist by capitalist, transformation of many small into few large capitals. This process differs from the first one in this respect, that it only presupposes a change in the distribution of already available and already functioning capital. Its field of action is therefore not limited by the absolute growth of social wealth, or in other words by the

absolute limits of accumulation. Capital grows to a huge mass in a single hand in one place, because it has been lost by many in another place. This is centralization proper, as distinct from accumulation and concentration.[34] [emphasis added]

The end result is a further concentration of capital. But rather than coming about through the creation of new capital, already existing capital shifts hands through debts, mergers, acquisitions, and cutthroat competition. Companies that don't make it face bankruptcy, and can then be bought up on the cheap by their more solvent rivals.

The history of the auto industry in the United States, for example, has seen hundreds of defunct competitors absorbed or put out of business throughout the years to arrive at an industry now dominated by the "big three" automakers.[35] Marx had this kind of story in mind when he wrote: "Capital can grow into powerful masses in a single hand in one place, because in other places it has been withdrawn from many individual hands."[36] Or more simply: "One capitalist always kills many."[37]

The same process is evident in newer industries, particularly the tech sector where start-ups rapidly pop up and then become absorbed by giants like Microsoft, Apple, and Google. Since the late 1980s, Microsoft has acquired more than two hundred small firms and amassed ownership stakes in sixty others. In the same time span, Apple acquired over one hundred.[38] These numbers do not include assets that Microsoft or Apple purchased from bankrupt firms. Property and technology are often sold well below market value, as companies gone bust need cash to satisfy debts and reorganize.[39]

Most dramatically and aggressively, Google transformed itself from a search engine to an online beast. Between 2001 and 2019, the firm completed more than two hundred acquisitions—mostly of small software firms. It now clocks in an average of one acquisition a week, and controls about three-quarters of the market for digital search ads. Acquisitions have been used or integrated into services such as Google Groups, Blogger, Picasa, Google Maps, the Android operating system, Google Docs, YouTube, and a myriad of other products, which puts Google at the center of almost anything you do online. Google is growing past its online home, too, to "driverless cars," artificial intelligence, health care technologies, and other products.[40]

In 2013, Google bought Waze, the navigation app with real-time transportation information, for $1.1 billion. Was this a necessary technological innovation to Google Maps? In fact, they have yet to integrate most of

Waze's technology into Google Maps. More likely, as with many acquisitions, it has more to do with strategic positioning in the market. That is: make sure that you have no competitors who may pose a greater threat down the road.

It is the same principle that spawns several Starbucks stores on one block. There used to be one block in downtown Manhattan where you could sit in one Starbucks, sip your macchiato, and look out at two more. How many more customers could Starbucks possibly hope to attract with three identical cafés facing each other on the same street? But after Starbucks bought out the competition of the smaller independent coffee shops, they eventually sold off that property to other investors. Starbucks would rather lose money on a redundant store than have people walking around town holding cups that advertise another coffee shop.

The number of mergers and acquisitions has hit a fever pitch in recent years. In 2018, companies announced approximately fifty thousand transactions with a total value of $3.8 trillion.[41] Both the number of mergers and acquisitions and their values have set records in the last few years.[42] "America's already huge corporations are combining like nobody's business," Harold Meyerson wrote for the *American Prospect* and the *Washington Post*:

> In recent months, Walgreens bought Rite Aid, uniting two of the nation's three largest drugstore chains; in beerland, Molson Coors is buying Miller; mega-health insurers Aetna and Anthem, respectively, bought mega-health insurers Humana and Cigna; Heinz bought Kraft, good news for those who take ketchup with their cheese; and American Airlines completed its absorption of US Airways, reducing the number of major US airlines to four, which now control 70 percent of the air travel market. On Wall Street, the five biggest commercial banks hold nearly half of the nation's bank assets; in 1990, the five biggest held just 10 percent.[43]

As it does for the process of concentration, credit works as a powerful lever for centralization. First, as a means by which companies and other investors can pool capital. Second, companies often borrow massive amounts in order to buy out their competitors, or bring smaller firms into their folds. Such has recently been the case in China, where companies and investors feared slowing growth, leading to a surge of debt-fueled acquisitions in the quest for more revenue. Large companies with good banking relationships, explained the *Financial Times*, "can spend heavily overseas as a way to diversify away from their dwindling earnings at home."[44]

As Marx wrote: "In its first stages, [the credit] system furtively creeps in as the humble assistant of accumulation, drawing into the hands of individual or associated capitalists by invisible threads the money resources, which lie scattered in larger or smaller amounts over the surface of society; but it soon becomes a new and terrible weapon in the battle of competition and is finally transformed into an enormous social mechanism for the centralization of capitals."[45] Thus credit is first a tool for the simple concentration of capital, but is then wielded by those large companies that have greatest access to it as a means to bludgeon their weaker competitors.

SIZE MATTERS

Concentration and centralization are not merely by-products of accumulation, or the "organic growth" of companies gaining compound profits. Centralization, aided by credit and financial structures, transforms the speed and scale at which the economic landscape is revolutionized in the "twinkling of an eye." Marx's eloquent description of this process is worth quoting at length:

> Centralization supplements the work of accumulation by enabling industrial capitalists to extend the scale of their operations. Whether this latter result is the consequence of accumulation or centralization, whether centralization is accomplished by the violent method of annexation—where certain capitals become such preponderant centers of attraction for others that they shatter the individual cohesion of the latter and then draw the separate fragments to themselves—or whether the fusion of a number of capitals already formed or in process of formation takes place by the smoother process of organizing joint-stock companies—the economic effect remains the same. Everywhere the increased scale of industrial establishments is the starting point for a more comprehensive organization of the collective labor of many people, for a broader development of their material motive forces, i.e., for the progressive transformation of isolated processes of production, carried on by customary methods, into socially combined and scientifically arranged processes of production.
>
> But accumulation, the gradual increase of capital by reproduction as it passes from the circular to the spiral form, is clearly a very slow procedure compared with centralization, which needs only to change the quantitative groupings of the constituent parts of social capital. The world would still be without railways if it had had to wait until accumulation had got a few individual capitals far enough to be adequate for the construction of a railway. Centralization, however, accomplished this in the twinkling of an eye.[46]

What is more, both concentration and centralization feed back into the competitive struggle by creating further advantages for the corporations that most quickly succeed in gaining the largest size. Marx argued:

> The battle of competition is fought by the cheapening of commodities . . . and this depends in turn on the scale of production. Therefore, the larger capitals beat the smaller. It will further be remembered that, with the development of the capitalist mode of production, there is an increase in the minimum amount of individual capital necessary to carry on a business under its normal conditions. . . [Competition] ends in the ruin of many small capitalists, whose capitals partly pass into the hands of their conquerors, and partly vanish completely.[47]

Marx is making the point that large corporations can most easily cheapen the cost of production, and therefore the cost of goods. For this reason, the minimum capital for running a business at all increases over time.

There are several reasons why the size afforded to corporate giants allows them to put a great distance between themselves and their competitors. First, on a basic level, large numbers of workers are more efficient than individual or small groups of laborers. Organizing work collectively creates the advantage of simultaneous work. Whereas an individual craftsman would have to perform one task at a time, putting down her tools and picking up a new set in between each operation, setting herself to another piece of production, simultaneous work limits interruptions in the labor process. As Marx explained with one example, "Twelve masons, in their collective working day of 144 hours, make much more progress with the building than one mason could make working for 12 days, or 144 hours. The reason for this is that a body of men working together have hands and eyes both in front and behind, and can be said to be to a certain extent omnipresent. The various parts of the product come to fruition simultaneously."[48]

In a factory setting, one of the best-known examples of the revolutionary impact of simultaneous work is that of automobile production. Cars, we saw, became popular consumer commodities once they could be mass-produced and therefore sold more cheaply. A single worker could build a car. It might take days or even weeks.[49] It could be done. But when work is collectivized, cars can be produced in minutes. Thus at the start of the twentieth century, auto production shifted away from a system in which a group of workmen overseen by a skilled craftsman built the automobile at a stationary site. Every piece of the car was brought in, welded, assembled, installed, painted, and so on. Needless to say, this was an incredibly time-consuming process.

Each coat of paint took upwards of twelve hours to dry. A great deal of running back and forth to piece together the car was involved, so much so that in many cases several workers were dedicated exclusively to retrieving parts. And every person involved in assembling the car had to learn and remember dozens of tasks and every component part.[50]

Conveyor-based assembly lines and a tight division of labor changed the face of the auto industry. By 1920, 85 percent of autoworkers were unskilled or semiskilled workers, and within a few years, production time necessary to produce the Ford Model T went down from twelve hours per car to ninety minutes per car.[51] Cars were therefore much easier to produce in great numbers and low cost, and sales shot up from the thousands to the millions within a matter of years.

Along with collectivization of labor, the exploited workforce has to be effectively *supervised* for maximum efficiency. There's no greater danger to efficiency than a large, alienated group of workers laboring together. Their interests naturally lead to sabotage, slowdowns, or—heaven forbid—organizing efforts! The market treats workers as individuals—necessary inputs for production— and, as was discussed in the previous chapter, reduces our mental and physical capabilities to their barest and most alienated forms. But once in the workplace, workers are thrown together into similar conditions and often in close enough proximity to each other that we can organize. As business historian Norman Gras wrote in *Industrial Evolution*: "It was purely for the purposes of discipline, so that the workers could be effectively controlled under the supervision of the foreman. Under one roof, or within a narrow compass, they could be started to work at sunrise and kept going till sunset, barring periods of rest and refreshment. And under penalty of loss of all employment they could be kept going almost all throughout the year."[52]

Second, larger companies develop what mainstream economists call ECONOMIES OF SCALE—cost advantages gained through operational efficiencies and economic leverages. As output grows, the average cost of producing each unit falls. How does this work? Once a company pays for factory or office space, for storage, and for delivery and transportation costs, the difference between producing ten times the amount of goods does not result in ten times the cost in inputs, since the core expenses have already been paid for in the main.

An article in the *Economist* laid out the following example: "It might cost $3,000 to produce 100 copies of a magazine but only $4,000 to produce 1,000 copies. The average cost in this case has fallen from $30 to $4 a copy because the main elements of cost in producing a magazine (editorial and design) are unrelated to the number of magazines produced."[53] Similarly, if you were to build a factory with ten times the productive capacity, the additional electric wiring and piping would not require a significant amount of additional labor or materials. Or if you were to ship one thousand books this would not be ten times more expensive as shipping one hundred, since the operating crew size for ships and planes does not increase in proportion to capacity. Some costs, like advertising, don't increase at all no matter how many units of a good are being advertised. A billboard on the highway or an ad on the subway cost the same for a small or a large company.

Costs also drop as production scales up because large technological investments are spread out over a greater number of units of output. A printing company must invest in high-grade printers for fast, high-quality printing. But a printing company that produces ten thousand pages a day will recoup the cost of these printers much more slowly than one that produces a million pages.[54] Other sources of cost efficiencies have to do with leverages that large companies have over smaller companies, including the ability to purchase raw materials in bulk or forcing distributors to sell goods more cheaply. Small firms depend on large corporations, but the reverse is not true. Walmart is notorious for ruthlessly driving down prices with its suppliers in its efforts to lower costs. But its distribution reach is unparalleled. Walmart's more than sixty thousand suppliers have no choice but to play ball, even if it means minimal profits in return.[55]

A final aspect of economies of scale lies with corporate access to credit. Obtaining lower interest rates from banks and having the ability to utilize a range of financial instruments affords economic advantages. Bigger companies can more easily secure credit to drive investments and expansion, and then carry great amounts of debt for long periods of time, taking advantage of low interest rates. They can also circumvent banks altogether through bond markets. A paper from the Federal Reserve Bank of New York explained: "Small firms tend to rely more on credit obtained through intermediaries, such as banks, [incurring greater fees] while larger firms have more varied sources of financing, such as direct credit, including the issuance of equity, corporate bonds, and commercial paper."[56]

Third, during periods of shrinking markets, large companies can more easily weather the storm, and even find "opportunities" to make gains at the expense of smaller, weaker companies going bust. They can carry a large debt load for longer periods of time and can keep the spigot of credit going through more diverse means, which allows large corporations to wait out a recession, and keep payroll and bills paid despite absorbing losses to profitability. This is why, as the *Financial Times* noted, the crisis of US oil companies between 2014 and 2016, brought about by a precipitous drop in prices, impacted some more than others. "Some companies, though, are more stressed than others. It is no coincidence that the four companies that sold bonds in the first quarter were some of the largest and most secure in the sector."[57]

At the same time, big companies can afford to close down the least profitable wings of production and still keep money flowing. As Marx wrote: "The larger size of his capital compensates him for the smaller profits, and he can even bear temporary losses until the smaller capitalist is ruined and he finds himself freed from this competition. In this way, he accumulates the small capitalist's profits."[58] This plays out on an international scale, as big multinationals use their global reach to cushion the impact of recessions at their home bases, and "diversify" their investments to take advantage of any part of the global economy that is growing. McDonald's and Starbucks, for instance, saw hundreds of closed stores and declining revenue in 2009, but rebounded largely based on strong sales outside the US.[59]

Large size will also afford these companies the option of offering customers discounts and bargains, securing whatever remains of a recession's shrinking consumer base and driving smaller companies out of the market altogether. Finally, outsized companies can use their greater capital to buy up failed companies, or the excess equipment and goods that they leave behind, on the cheap. In this way, using a bargain-priced means of production, they can further lower their own production costs and increase their rates of profit. Thus capitalism's crises often destroy smaller businesses and further strengthen larger players.

From a capitalist's perspective, such efficiency is irresistible. Workplaces and even cities themselves are transformed through ever-greater concentration and centralization of wealth, producing the largest factories the world has ever known. (See sidebar: "Mega Capitalism.") The largest among them, a Boeing assembly plant in Everett, Washington, sprawls over four million square feet, the size of about seventy football fields. Amazon's distribution center also clocks in at over a not-too-shabby million square feet.[60] Here, fast moving conveyor belts and scuttling robots move products across a sci-fi-looking landscape, along with several hundred very unlucky employees, paid about $11 an hour, *if* they have full-time status. Amazon has been known to quietly get rid of injured workers at their warehouses, station ambulances outside their doors to treat heatstroked employees, and, in one case, even hire a neo-Nazi security firm at its German warehouse to watch and abuse the predominantly immigrant workforce there.[61]

MEGA CAPITALISM

Alongside giant corporations, concentration and centralization have given rise to colossal cities. Global capitalism requires ever-greater numbers of workers living and laboring in dense urban areas. These conditions have given rise to urban explosions reminiscent of the enclosures and early birth pangs of capitalism. Rural peasants and workers driven from their land have continued to feed ongoing industrialization.

The majority of the world's population now lives in urban areas, and are increasingly concentrated in very large cities.[62] United Nations projections to 2025 suggest that the future list of "megacities" (cities with populations of over ten million) will include a growth of African, Asian, and Latin American cities from Lima to Tianjin. The World Economic Forum reports: "In 1960, the only city in sub-Saharan Africa with a population of over 1 million people was Johannesburg. Ten years later, there were four. By 2010, that number had skyrocketed to 33 cities. It is estimated that by 2050, 70% of the world's population will be living in urban areas."[63]

Some of the most explosive of these urban eruptions can be found in China, where the number of people living in cities has nearly tripled between 1990 and 2018, adding approximately 527 million people to the ranks of the working class.[64] As of 2017, China is home to fifteen of the world's forty-seven megacities.

Among the most widely known is Shenzhen, often referred to as "a city without history," for its seemingly overnight conversion from a small fishing village of scarcely three thousand people to a city of approximately thirteen million and counting.[65] But Shenzhen does, of course, have a history. Its path to urbanization began in 1979 with economic "modernization policies" driven by Deng Xiaoping. The city was established as one of Deng's "Special Economic Zones," which functioned as experimental grounds for market capitalism, dubbed by the Chinese government in Orwellian doublespeak as "socialism with Chinese characteristics."

It has since become one of the world's largest cities, and among the leading manufacturing bases in the world. Its frenzied growth has created a demographic that is almost wholly made up of migrants. And the extreme density of its population has led to the sprouting of massive skyscraper apartment buildings and "urban villages," where basketball courts are turned to night markets with food stalls, and parking garages function as elementary schools for unregistered children of migrants.[66]

Shenzhen is the epicenter of Apple's production in China, and the site of one of the notorious Foxconn plants, which make iPhones, iPads, and other iGadgets. Apple employs almost half a million workers in Shenzhen, many of them living in the plant's barracks in cramped rooms with triple-decked bunks. In 2010 the plant made national headlines after fourteen suicides took place within the year. Despite Steve Jobs's assertion that the plant was "pretty nice" and "not a sweatshop," a Fair Labor Association audit in 2012 found that employees typically work more than sixty hours a week and almost half had witnessed accidents at work. Other reports found incidences of child labor, guards beating workers, and new recruits drilled along military lines.

The British newspaper, *Daily Mail*, went undercover at Shenzhen's Foxconn plant where they reported dystopian work conditions alongside disturbing suicide prevention practices. These include forcing all Foxconn employees to sign documents that they will not take their own lives, the installation of ten-foot-high wire fences on the roofs and fifteen-foot-wide nets at the base of all buildings, along with the enlistment of hundreds of monks and social workers to the plant. "Workers who fail to respond to the chanting monks or the entreaties of social workers," reports the *Mail*, "are secretly shipped to Shenzhen Mental Health Centre, a private facility where there are several wards crammed with Foxconn employees."[67]

Employees are kept under tight watch and fined for things such as having long nails or talking to coworkers. But their morale is surely lifted by the daily playing of the national anthem over the loudspeakers: "Arise, arise, arise, millions of hearts with one mind." The public address system, explains the *Mail*, "relays propaganda, such as how many products have been made; how a new basketball court has been built for the workers; and why workers should 'value efficiency every minute, every second.'" Workers meanwhile wear jackets bearing slogans such as: "Together everyone achieves more."[68]

All the morale boosts in the world could not help Yan Li, twenty-seven, who collapsed and died from exhaustion. "Yan collapsed having worked continuously for 34 hours," reported the *Mail*. "He was on the night shift for a month and had worked overtime every night, according to his wife. Speaking on condition of anonymity, one line manager told us that there is constant pressure among all workers. 'We must meet the quota every day at the maximum quality,' said the man. 'There are several layers of management with the pressure coming from above.'"[69]

Nine hundred miles northwest of Shenzen, Chongqing City's population grows by four thousand people each week. There, migration is largely driven by the displacement of people by the Three Gorges Dam, the largest infrastructure project in the world. "Some of these new residents took jobs at local manufacturing plants and moved into instant skyscrapers," wrote blogger Alissa Walker, "as other residents continue to farm the land between them as they have for centuries. . . The building boom is unprecedented. . . Chongqing is home to some of the largest bridges in the world, the scale of which is needed simply to get the people from one side of the city to another."[70]

Driving these developments is the international scramble to find low-wage "flexible" workers, such as those supplied by China's huge rural population. He Pengyuan, a manager at a

Beijing-based courier company, explained it simply to the *Financial Times*. Not one of the workers he supervises is actually from Beijing. "We had two people from Beijing last year but they quit; they couldn't handle the workload," he said. "People from the city are too soft and spoiled. . . . China's rural labor force is a huge army that keeps advancing. They come to the cities and keep the cost of labor relatively low."[71]

The *Financial Times* described the conditions underlying this profitability:

> The jobs come with a frightening human toll. Most couriers say they are grateful for a job in the city, but they describe long hours, months away from their families and hard labor in a city to which they will never properly belong. "I hope my son remembers who I am," says Chen Bing, a ZTO courier who hails from neighboring Hebel province. He says he is only able to return home to his wife and child once every three months due to the workload. . . During peak time, work starts at 7 a.m., and doesn't end until midnight.[72]

The despotic conditions of unregulated capital faced by ZTO couriers, Foxconn employees, just as those endured by undocumented workers in New York's or Los Angeles' garment districts,[73] recall the devastation of laborers described by Marx and Engels in the early stages of the Industrial Revolution:

> [W]ithin the capitalist system, all methods for raising the social productivity of labor are put into effect at the cost of the individual worker. . . they distort the worker into a fragment of a man, they degrade him to the level of an appendage of a machine, they destroy the actual content of his labor by turning it into a torment; they alienate for him the intellectual potentialities of the labor process in the same proportion as science is incorporated in it as an independent power; they deform the conditions under which he works, subject him during the labor process to a despotism the more hateful for its meanness; they transform his life-time into working-time, and drag his wife and child beneath the wheels of the juggernaut of capital.[74]

COMPETITION AND MONOPOLY

Though concentration and centralization are outcomes of the competitive struggle, they feed back into the process of accumulation to breed its opposite: monopolies. A MONOPOLY is a lone company that dominates its market (for instance Saudi Aramco, the state-owned Saudi oil and gas company), and an OLIGOPOLY is a market dominated by a handful of companies (for instance Big Pharma or the auto industry). Pure monopolies are rare, but monopolistic tendencies and practices abound. As ever-larger companies use increased clout to drive out competitors, these processes transform a market of many competitive firms into one dominated by handfuls of powerful corporate behemoths, able to take advantage of their preeminent positions. In the words of journalist Matt Stoller:

> Giant companies are operating as "cartels," engaging in illegal conspiracies among themselves to divide up their turf. As a result, they have been able to fix the price of almost everything in the economy: antibiotics and other life-saving medication, fees on credit card transactions, essential commodities like cell-phone batteries and electric cables and auto parts, the rates companies pay to exchange foreign currency, even the interest rates on the municipal bonds that cities and towns rely on to build schools and libraries and nursing homes. A single price-fixing scandal by the world's largest banks—fixing the global interest rates known as LIBOR—involved more than *$500 trillion* in financial instruments.[75]

One of America's earliest and most powerful monopolies, Standard Oil, dominated 90 percent of oil production in the United States in the early twentieth century. Standard Oil's founder, John D. Rockefeller, utilized secret pacts to gain preferential shipping rates on American railroads, and bought up smaller companies at rock-bottom prices once they had been ruined by the uneven treatment. Standard Oil gained enough momentum to acquire fifty-three refineries, keeping the most efficient and closing down the rest. "Thanks to its new economies of scale," explained *Money and Power* author Howard Means, "Standard Oil could cut the cost of refining oil by two-thirds, from 1.5 cents a gallon to .5 cents a gallon," further fueling its soaring market share.[76]

Standard Oil would soon team up with General Motors and Firestone Tires to literally derail public transit systems in the United States. In the 1920s, electric trolleys were common in cities across the country, and only one in ten people owned cars. GM received funding from Standard Oil and others to buy National City Lines, a bus company, which—with this funding—came to control bus systems in forty-five cities. These busses were meant to eliminate the need for trolley tracks that had been embedded in the roads. Alfred Sloan, GM's president at the time, said, "We've got 90 percent of the market out there that we can. . . turn into automobile users. If we can eliminate the rail alternatives, we will create a new market for our cars."[77] Once the national bus company replaced rail, they would let the business run itself into the ground, and make way for individual cars.

One of the most infamous modern-day monopolies is the biotech agricultural company Monsanto. The company specializes in environmentally toxic, genetically modified crops and seeds, and utilizes patents to dominate seed markets. In India, 95 percent of cottonseed is controlled by Monsanto, as Indian companies have been locked into joint ventures and licensing arrangements for the last couple of decades. Every patented seed is the "intellectual property" of Monsanto, entitling them to royalties, thereby raising the costs of seeds. Perhaps most shockingly, these patented seeds have come to include "gene use restriction technology"—seeds that will not produce viable offspring seeds. In this way farmers are forced into buying new seeds every year, rather than harvesting them out of the previous year's crops. The swelling of Indian farmers' debt—along with increasing farmer suicides— are a product of what Indian environmentalist and ecofeminist Vandana Shiva has dubbed Monsanto's "seeds of suicide."[78]

Monopolization clearly has a very distorting impact on the purportedly "free market" principles touted by mainstream economists and ideologues. As former Secretary of Labor Robert Reich put it, "those with the most economic power have been able to use it to alter. . . the rules of the market to meet their needs."[79] The impulse to do so is not reserved for the ultra-greedy or malicious, but is simply an outgrowth of the so-called free market itself. This is why a 2014 Goldman Sachs report basked in what they called "dreams of oligopoly":

> There is a natural pull toward consolidation among mature or maturing industries. An oligopolistic market structure can turn a cut-throat commodity industry into a highly profitable one. Oligopolistic markets are powerful because they simultaneously satisfy multiple critical components of sustainable competitive advantage—a smaller set of relevant peers faces lower competitive intensity, greater stickiness and pricing power with customers due to reduced choice, scale cost benefits including stronger leverage over suppliers, and higher barriers to new entrants all at once.[80]

Of course, "pricing power" is just a euphemism for price gouging. By limiting consumer choices, Goldman analysts gleefully explain, oligopolies have created conditions in which they can get away with almost anything (because, as consumers, we're "stuck" to these limited choices). The inflation of prices way past the value of goods and services turns nearly every arena of our lives into a nightmare.

The airline oligopoly—in which just four airlines control 80 percent of seats on airplanes—employs a strategy that can only be understood as "calculated misery," as journalist Tim Wu dubbed it. This includes the practice of "dynamic pricing" where prices change in real time, as demand increases. By their own admission, they will charge as much as they can get away with, as much as customers are desperate enough to pay. The cynicism of this approach came to light after a deadly Amtrak train crash in 2015 drove many fearful train riders into the hands of the airline industry, who waited with $1,000-plus airline tickets for flights across the Northeast.

And this is to say nothing of the seemingly unending growth of extra fees that airlines have added for such privileges as bringing a bag along with you on your flight, the ability to choose a seat ahead of time, or to guarantee having a seat at all in the likely event that the airline overbooks. (This is a lesson David Dao found out the hard way one day when he was dragged off his United Airlines flight, bloodied, kicking and screaming, for refusing to give up his paid-for seat.[81]) Ostensibly, many of these fees were added to help airlines contend with higher fuel prices, but when the price of oil tanked, the extra fees remained, while the airlines quietly pocketed billions of dollars in fees. Soon we'll be asked to pay for cushions on our chairs and the right to use oxygen masks.[82]

Among the most devastating effects of price gouging is the impact that it has on our medications. The pharmaceutical companies—or, Big Pharma—are largely to blame. According to the World Health Organization, "The global pharmaceuticals market is worth $300 billion a year, a figure expected to rise to $400 billion within three years. The 10 largest drugs companies control more than one-third of this market, several with sales of more than US$10 billion a year and profit margins of about 30%."[83]

The biggest of Big Pharma—Johnson & Johnson, Pfizer, Merck & Co., and others—are certainly responsible for skyrocketing pharmaceutical costs, as well as a growing epidemic of addictions to pain medication and psychiatric drugs.[84] But "small pharma," too, including many of the ones charged with producing ostensibly cheaper "generic" drugs, have gotten in on the game by creating monopoly conditions through acquisitions and patent manipulations. Companies find a drug for which there is little market competition, buy out the firm that produces it, and immediately raise the prices. In this way, even smaller companies can mimic monopolistic strategies by cornering markets for particular drugs.

This was exactly what Martin Shkreli and Turing Pharmaceuticals did in acquiring and then jacking up by 5,000 percent the price of Daraprim. As *Business Insider* pointed out, "For drugs like Daraprim, for which only about 8,000 prescriptions are filled a year, it simply isn't worth it for other companies to try to come up with generic alternatives. This allows for a price monopoly in which the drug manufacturer can set virtually any price it wants."[85] Thus the price of one Daraprim tablet—used mostly by HIV/AIDS and cancer patients to battle parasitic infections—shot up overnight from $13.50 to $750. Shkreli defended the move on the same grounds that many pharma executives and apologists do, saying the superprofits are necessary to fund further research and development. This is a patent lie. Pharmaceutical companies spend, at most, 15–20 percent of their revenues on research and development. And those companies that have most aggressively pursued the acquisition and price-hike game spend much less.

Take Valeant Pharmaceuticals, which until recently was considered a "star performer" among companies of its size. Valeant's "business model" is to use colossal amounts of debt to fund a string of acquisitions. "After an acquisition," explained the *Financial Times,* "Valeant usually lifts prices and slashes research and development." The company spends a mere 3 percent of its revenues on developing new drugs. Meanwhile, in 2015 alone, it raised prices for fifty-six drugs (that's 81 percent of its portfolio) totaling a 66 percent price rise overall. And so, for instance, Borna Heyman's out-of-pocket expenses for battling Wilson's disease, reported the *Financial Times,* went from $510 a year in 2010, to $12,000 a year in 2014.[86]

This is the irony of the ideology of the "free market." Corporations gain in size, or corner a market, precisely so that they *don't* have to compete to make the best or most affordable product. In the US, monopolistic activities are further entrenched by patent laws, which allow drug manufacturers to remain the sole makers of patented drugs for twenty years (and can easily game the patent system to extend past this point). Both Democrats and Republicans have maintained a system in which the government has no ability to negotiate or regulate the price of drugs. As Peter Bach, director of Memorial Sloan Kettering's Center for Health Policy and Outcomes, explained, pharmaceutical companies charge high prices simply "because they can. We have no rational system in the US for managing prices of drugs."[87]

Many other countries around the world—both rich and poor—have practices in place that help to keep prices of medicines down. The United Kingdom's National Health Service, for instance, negotiates nationwide drug prices. By negotiating on behalf of the entire country, they exert "bulk buying power." If pharmaceuticals were to charge too high a price, they would simply be left off the nation's formulary.[88] American insurance plans and hospitals (not that we should pity them either!) are each obliged to pay whatever prices are set in an unregulated market. Even Medicare, which covers over forty million people, is legislatively barred from negotiating drug prices. Instead, we pay whatever the drug companies ask for, and pray that the "invisible hand" of the market leads to more competitive prices. The system's ideologues promise us that the free market will deliver an efficient health-care system, just as it will peace on earth and a greener world. Yet the workings of the market lead to the exact opposite: the tyranny of corporate behemoths at the expense of all living things. (See sidebar: "Can the 'Free Market' Save the Planet?")

The state plays its part, too, in shielding monopolistic companies deemed "too big to fail" from the ravages of a competitive, "free" market. After the 2008 economic crisis, as we'll see in chapter seven, megabanks in the United States, each holding billions of dollars' worth of assets, were rescued with an enormous taxpayer-funded bailout. As Petrino DiLeo explained: "The Treasury Department and Federal Reserve Bank have doled out an incredible $16 trillion in assistance to financial institutions and corporations in the US and around the world . . . Through the various mechanisms, Citigroup borrowed $2.5 trillion, Morgan Stanley took $2 trillion, Merrill Lynch received $1.9 trillion, and Bank of America got $1.3 trillion."[89]

Once a company or a financial institution is so big, it is not just the sheer size of its collapse that poses a problem. Massive corporations are deeply interconnected with a vast web of industrial, service, and financial institutions, such that the collapse of one mega-institution threatens the stability of the whole system. Bankruptcies, ostensibly part of the free market's ability to regulate and weed out inefficiencies, pose too great a risk. Take China's "zombie" companies (so-called for logging in at least three years' worth of losses). They collectively hold over a trillion dollars in debt. If they are allowed to go bust, the financial sector will go into shock. And this is to say nothing of the impact that several million laid-off steel and coal workers will have on the rest of the economy.

Thus both the incentive to innovate and the penalty for abuse are ruled out, leaving even the ruling-class mouthpiece, the *Financial Times*, to complain:

> The problem of 'too big to fail' has made society—more precisely, the taxpayer—hostage to the survival of individual financial institutions. . . The rules of the game should be clear. Those who succeed are free to take the profits (after taxation); those who make losses have to bear the consequences, with bankruptcy as the ultimate sanction. Thus 'too big to fail' not only undermines a fundamental principle of market economies but also a principle of societies in which individuals are responsible for their actions.[90]

But what the likes of the *Financial Times* will not admit is that the tendency for "too big" companies is not an aberration, but the result of market fundamentals functioning as they should through the processes of concentration and centralization.

Of course, capitalism still maintains its dynamism through the constant jostling for market positioning by large and small companies. In some cases, a newer business, not so deeply entrenched in outmoded methods, could come out ahead. Thus a dozen years ago Bill Ford (of that "family-owned business," Ford Motor Company) could say of the new auto company, Tesla, that it had little chance of staying alive. As the *Financial Times* explained, Ford assumed that "the complexity of the global supply chain and international regulation requirements made it all but impossible to launch an important new carmaker from scratch."[91] A decade later, the "Big Three" American automakers are mired in over-supplied markets and old technologies. It is yet to be determined what kind of long-term success Tesla will fare, but no doubt, the established auto industry is nervous. Other "disruptive" companies exist in every field, from Uber and Airbnb, to internet-based homecare agencies and furniture stores that challenge the dominance of conventional brick and mortar enterprises.

If this were not the case, we would see the economy increasingly dominated by fewer and fewer companies, until one day we found ourselves with a single McGoogleAzon Corporation that ran everything from our dishwashers to our morning commutes. Instead, competition continues, but within a context of ever-greater economic players, which make the shifts, rivalries, and bankruptcies all the more volatile. As Russian revolutionary V.I. Lenin wrote, "At the same time monopoly, which has grown out of free competition, does not abolish the latter, but exists over it and alongside of it, and thereby gives rise to a number of very acute, intense antagonisms, friction and conflicts."[92]

IMPERIALISM: THE HIGHEST STAGE OF CAPITALISM

A final point about the implications of concentration and centralization can only be briefly touched on here. Lenin and fellow revolutionary Nikolai Bukharin argued that the concentration and centralization of capital had developed to such a point that large monopolies are able to wield great economic and political control within their states of origin.[93] So much so, they noted, that the interests (and in many cases the institutions) of capital and the state become fused. States, in turn, come to play an increasingly active role in managing the long-term corporate interests of its national ruling class, both at home and abroad.

It's easy to see the many ways that national governments look out for corporate interests through economic means. The US government, for instance, heavily subsidizes the grains and oil-seed companies through supplements to agribusinesses if prices fall below a certain limit. Loan programs also commit taxpayer dollars to financing and underwriting corporate debt if prices drop. In this way US companies can have a leg up, relative to other global competitors. Monsanto's seeds of suicide, for instance, dominate international markets in large part because the company uses farm subsidies to undercut the prices of their competitors. The company has received over $1 billion in federal loans since 2000, along with millions of dollars in grants and subsidies.[94]

The Chinese government, for its part, took a different tack in responding to a global steel glut in 2016. They vowed to aggressively restructure their steel industry by drawing back lending to inefficient mills, and at the same time safeguard the country's large "national champions." Smaller and less profitable companies without extra financing would thus be pushed out of an oversupplied market. Meanwhile the government would prop up its larger firms and make them more efficient and competitive with the rest of the world's steel producers, also struggling with a glut of supply and dropping prices.

Internationally, each state will go to bat for its corporate base at home with trade agreements, political maneuvering, and—when necessary—the threat of military force. As free market hack Thomas Friedman once declared: "The hidden hand of the market will never work without a hidden fist."[95] Greater and smaller tensions play out daily across the globe: whether the United States Treasury Secretary warns that he would "deter US investment in Europe" following a European Union (EU) tax-evasion claim against Apple, or the EU imposes import duties on Chinese steel. Trade wars across the globe position states to line up behind their respective business classes. The line between economic and military tensions can be thin. Thus trade wars between the United States and China around steel and aluminum tariffs or patent laws go hand-in-hand with low-grade military disputes over naval control in the South China Sea, rich in oil reserves and important waterways. Of course, this line has grown thinner and thinner under the Trump presidency, which has ramped up China bashing in both word and deed, and led to an increase of anti-Asian racism in this country.

At the same time that monopolies become increasingly wedded to the protection that their home states afford, the mass scale of production necessitates the breaking down of national boundaries for trade and investment. As Marx and Engels wrote: "The need of a constantly expanding market for its products chases the bourgeoisie over the whole surface of the globe. It must nestle everywhere, settle everywhere, establish connections everywhere."[96] Corporations are thus just as dependent on their states to beat down barriers to foreign markets as they are on governments creating a corporate-friendly environment at home. States help capital access markets, financing, and production across borders in an increasingly globalized economy.

National competition therefore spills over into international, geopolitical competition. Both of these tendencies—melded interests with the state, and a need for access to international production and markets—lead to military rivalries for territory and power.

SOCIALISM AND GROWTH?

Marx and Engels have been widely misinterpreted on the question of growth. They did celebrate the productive capacity of capitalism and saw it as laying the basis for a world of abundance that could make socialism possible. One famous passage from the Communist Manifesto reads:

The bourgeoisie, during its rule of scarce one hundred years, has created more massive and more colossal productive forces than have all preceding generations together. Subjugation of nature's forces to man, machinery, application of chemistry to industry and agriculture, steam navigation, railways, electric telegraphs, clearing of whole continents for cultivation, canalization of rivers, whole populations conjured out of the ground—what earlier century had even a presentiment that such productive forces slumbered in the lap of social labor?[97]

But Marx and Engels's seeming appreciation of the productive forces of capital had more to do with the future possibilities embedded within them, and nothing to do with the destructive manner in which they currently manifest. The subjugation of nature to man, they noted in many of their writings, has deadly effects, not just to the natural world around us, but to humankind, which is itself a part of nature. As Engels wrote: "Thus at every step we are reminded that we by no means rule over nature like a conqueror over a foreign people, like someone standing outside nature—but that we, with flesh, blood and brain, belong to nature, and exist in its midst, and that all our mastery of it consists in the fact that we have the advantage over all other creatures of being able to learn its laws and apply them correctly."[98]

Marx and Engels were very much *against* the destruction and degradation wrought by capitalism's endless growth of commodities. At the same time, they understood that these same forces have created the conditions for a new society. "The development of the productive forces of social labor is capital's historic mission and justification," they wrote. "For that very reason, it unwittingly creates the material conditions for a higher form of production."[99] Socialism would advance the development of society's productive capacity. But the production of use-values that do not have *exchange-values* would lead to a very different dynamic.

Rather than the compulsion to produce more and more stuff in order to accumulate more and more profits, the purpose of production in a socialist society would be use, rather than profit. Human need would therefore drive decision-making, and would compel advances in technology and research for more efficient and sustainable production. Capital relies on "planned obsolescence" of goods made with nondurable and shoddy materials, or "upgrades" in designs, which render our expensive technology useless within a year or two. This is one of the many ways that we are continually induced to buy more. Socialized production, on the other hand, would allow us to develop methods that produce durable and ecologically sustainable goods. Simultaneously, we could cut necessary labor-power to *increase* our free time and unleash the creative potential of human beings unencumbered by dreadfully long work weeks.

Many things can and should stop being produced immediately—like military arms, and advertisements. Others ought to be drastically reduced as quickly as possible, including cars and plastics. A socialist society would therefore need to tackle planning a system of public transportation that ends the need for cars. Beyond that, a future society will have to take up complex questions in facilitating the satisfaction of human need without destroying the earth that we live on. For instance, how do we want to organize food production? Research indicates that multi-crop, rotating agriculture, which is significantly more sustainable for the soil, can also produce more crops than the common methods of corporate farming.

Discussion of a future socialist society is beyond the scope of this book, but the key point to emphasize here is that capitalism forces us into a spiral of accumulation for the sake of accumulation. Planned development to improve the quality of life for the vast majority of humanity on the basis of sustainable production and planning is its polar opposite. That is the vision of a socialist society. From there, wrote Marx, "the private property of particular individuals in the earth will appear just as absurd as the private property of one man in other men. Even an entire society, a nation, or all simultaneously existing societies taken together, are not owners of the earth. They are simply its possessors, its beneficiaries, and have to bequeath it in an improved state to succeeding generations, as *boni patres familias* [good heads of the household]."[100]

CONCLUSION

Competition forces the capitalist class to constantly transform and advance the forces of production. "All that is solid melts into air," Marx and Engels had written. In one sense they recognized that ever-revolutionizing the means of production creates possibilities that could not have been imagined centuries, or in some cases years earlier. But Marx and Engels argued that great contradictions are embedded within these "advances": the immiseration of the working class, the destruction of the land, the concentration of greater wealth and power into fewer hands. (See sidebar: "Socialism and Growth?") The ideologues of capitalism never tire of celebrating the so-called "invisible hand" of the market and its supposed ability to determine how to allocate social resources. Yet rather than a "free market" of unadulterated competition, we've seen that competition also leads to its opposite in the form of monopolies and companies that are "too big to fail."

In the next chapter we will delve further into the contradictions of capital accumulation. Contradictions that not only undermine human and social need, but ultimately the system's profitability. Even by capitalism's own terms, the system periodically breaks down and fails. The very same forces that drive its vitality—competition, the pursuit of surplus value, and the continual expansion of production—also erect barriers to its ability to effectively function.

CAN THE "FREE MARKET" SAVE THE PLANET?

"The market knows best." Competition, we're told, will bring us a more "sustainable capitalism." We're expected to believe this despite the fact that the drive towards accumulation and the domination of corporate giants has ensured that aggressive, unrestrained cost cutting has brought us to the brink of planetary annihilation. The free market ideology of "green capitalism" rests on two main arguments. One—demand, which is increasingly driven by more environmental consciousness, will create a supply of clean technologies and products. And two—the market can be "incentivized" to compel corporations to do the right thing.

So, for example, if consumers of cars want to live in a breathable world, they will create a demand for fuel-efficient, clean-emissions, and electric cars. The greater demand will then drive production toward these technologies, and those automakers who are ahead of the curve in upgrading will be the first to corner this new market. In one sense, something like this does happen. The market for "environmentally friendly cars" is getting bigger. Toyota's fuel-efficient Prius competes with Chevrolet's electric Volt, while Tesla's electric cars made a flashy entrance into the market. But there are gaping holes in this philosophy.

First, consumers don't drive production, profits do. Whatever makes the quickest buck will either be deployed to *create* a market, or to *manipulate* an existing need.

The shameless flagrancy of the corporate elite did not have a "cleaner" face than Volkswagen, who promised that their "clean diesel" cars emit 90 percent fewer emissions than standard diesel. Their ads declared: "Green has never felt so good!" and compared driving their "clean diesel" cars to riding a bicycle. But Volkswagen was compelled first and foremost to cut corners in producing its "clean diesel" cars, and they found it cheapest to install software that could cheat emissions tests, which would reduce emissions only during an inspection! The cars would otherwise emit forty times the allowable amount. Perhaps they meant that *other* green. Their profits have never felt so good.

Diesel emissions cause severe respiratory problems, leading, according to the *Financial Times*, to approximately fifty-two thousand premature deaths in the United Kingdom every year.[101] But more important for VW and other car manufacturers is that the cost of using emissions reducing technology averages to about $1500 or more per car. Skirting these costs, and hoping to get away with it, is much cheaper. Why produce diesel cars to begin with? The production capacity has long been invested in. To walk away from it would be to throw away billions of dollars.

Second, as Volkswagen's "Green has never felt so good" ads have proven, the concept of "green" or "sustainable" or "clean" technology is completely robbed of any real meaning in order to generate revenues, and fast. The same can be said of "organic" foods, and other consumer-placating concepts, around which massively profitable industries have arisen. Even in a best-case scenario, where customers aren't downright cheated and lied to, the confines of the debate regarding these "solutions" are so narrow that they will never confront the scale of the crisis. How low have we sunk that only certain foods are labeled "organic" in the first place? And why are we producing greater numbers and more varieties of cars instead of investing in public transportation and infrastructure? The profiteering of auto companies is the first priority. Our public health needs and the long-term viability of the planet are not in the ranking. This brings us back to our basic framework: Capitalism is not designed to meet human need; it is designed to generate profit. This means not only robbing workers of our humanity and life, but also the soil, the air, the planet.

What then about the strategy to incentivize corporations to be more environmentally sustainable? Here the assumption is that even if the drive to accumulate is at odds with ecological considerations, we can at least exploit capitalists' interests to our (and the planet's) benefit. The best-known example of this is cap and trade, touted by mainstream environmental groups such as the Environmental Defense Fund, The Nature Conservancy, Audubon, and others. Cap and trade is an emissions trading system which first caps the maximum amount of emissions allowable for each corporate entity, and then authorizes companies that are polluting above the quota to buy "credits" for greater emissions from those companies that are "under-polluting," so to speak. In this way, the theory goes, it would be more profitable to reduce emissions below the quota and generate income by selling credits on the cap and trade market. And it would cost polluting companies more money to have to buy pollution-enabling credits.

There are many problems with this scheme. The first is, again, scale. If we are to reduce carbon levels in the atmosphere to 350 parts per million that scientists agree is necessary for our survival, the United States, for one, will have to reduce our carbon emissions by 80 percent. This requires a tremendous shift in the whole way our economy runs. Our factories, cars, and major transportation of goods via ships and trucks run on carbon-emitting gases. Providing extra incentive to chip away at the emissions of these same toxic entities is a distraction comparable to rearranging the deck chairs of the Titanic.

The other problem is that the large companies that dominate our economy can afford to buy extra credits in order to continue business as usual. Why are they given the option to buy their way out of capped emissions? The Clean Air Act, passed in 1963, long ago defined carbon as a pollutant that can be regulated by the state. Yet the government continues to subsidize the politically connected fuel industry at twice the rate of renewables. Lastly, these programs, which are written by the likes of ex-Enron executives and bankers at Goldman Sachs, are set up to benefit businesses and financial institutions. Thus countless loopholes for free permit giveaways and easy-to-access credits for companies that barely have to show emissions reductions only act to incentivize cheating the system.

Most importantly, both consumerism and market incentives fly in the face of the need to *regulate* corporations, whose interests are fundamentally at odds with ecological, health, and workplace demands. If we understand that capitalists are driven through mutual competition toward frenzied accumulation and the maximization of profits, then we know that capitalists do not have any interest in slowing down their own production with cleaner and less-hazardous methods, any more so than they have an interest in raising their workers' living standards and sharing out profits. The "market cures all" mantra is a way to counter any steps toward regulation.

The American Petroleum Institute, for its part, jumped to claim that emissions are already dropping due to the introduction of new technologies, and therefore government intervention is not necessary. And yet they gave lie to this claim when they *also* argued that any new regulations "could put the shale revolution at risk," by raising costs and diverting investment from further production.[102] Cost is the real concern, not an interference with the "natural" process of gradually decreasing emissions.

In reality, capitalism views the earth merely as a source of raw materials and a sinkhole for dumping waste. As Marx put it, under capitalism, "nature becomes purely an object for humankind, purely a matter of utility; ceases to be recognized as a power for itself; the theoretical discovery of its autonomous laws appears merely as a ruse so as to subjugate it under human needs, whether as an object of consumption or as a means of production."[103] Capitalists must think only of short-term profits in the scramble to stay ahead of competitors, and not the long-term impacts of their actions.

We can see how this plays out all too clearly in relation to the life-or-death issue of global warming. After decades of hand-wringing, the major world powers cannot produce a climate change agreement with any bite. Is it incompetence or a lack of scientific evidence? Neither. No country can risk restraining the toxic emissions of its own domestic capitalists, while other nations continue to push ahead and make quicker, dirtier profits. Capitalists, and their representatives in government, never forgo short-term economic benefits, because to do so would mean falling behind in the unceasing race to produce more for less.

As climate activist Chris Williams explained, for over two decades, no agreement "has been reached that would move the world toward the 80 percent reduction in greenhouse gas emissions that many scientists believe is necessary to avoid destabilizing the planetary climate system. Instead, atmospheric levels of carbon dioxide, the most common greenhouse gas, have increased every year and recently surpassed thresholds not seen since three million years ago."[104]

The reason that governments around the world obstruct emissions agreements is not only to provide a short-term favor to the corporate elite, but also for broader geopolitical gain. Think of the benefits to the US ruling class of the climate-crushing "shale revolution," which utilizes "extreme extraction" techniques to extract oil from previously unyielding shale rocks. The US now plays a dominant role in the international energy market; the American elite is no longer beholden to Organization of the Petroleum Exporting Countries (OPEC), or politically hostile nations like Venezuela. The greater their share of the market, the greater their control of production pacing and prices. This dramatic geopolitical turn has made for a devastating blow to the planet.

Finally, the requirement for ever-greater material and energy in order to keep expanding production puts capitalism profoundly and irrevocably at odds with a sustainable planet. According to a study by the National Academy of Sciences, the world economy exceeded the earth's regenerative capacity in 1980, by 1999 had gone beyond it by as much as 20 percent, and by 2009 the gap had grown to 30 percent.[105] No country, government, or corporation can opt out of growth, and therefore cannot afford to opt out of exploiting the cheapest possible energy sources.

Bolivia's Evo Morales, a former coca farmer and union organizer, and the country's first indigenous president, came to power in 2006 following a wave of struggles against foreign extraction of resources, privatization, and economic polarization. His continued popularity has largely hung on his ability to bring more people out of poverty than has been achieved anywhere else in the region. But economic growth within the capitalist model cannot come without grave environmental costs, particularly in developing nations, whose economies have long been impeded by exploitative and colonial abuses from the US and other superpowers.

And so despite the fact that Morales has put forward radical critiques of capitalism and climate change, "the establishment of government programs to alleviate poverty," wrote Chris Williams and Marcella Olivera, have rested "on an expanded and intensified exploitation of the country's natural resources, principally from fossil fuel production, mining, and the growth of large-scale, mono-crop agriculture and manufacturing."[106] Morales's government has opened seven of Bolivia's twenty-two protected areas for hydrocarbon exploration. And mining exports have quadrupled from $1 billion in 2006 to $4 billion in 2014.[107]

Bolivia's extractive strategy is largely responsible for the drying up of Lake Poopó, which in 1986 was a vast lake of 3100 square kilometers, and today "has shrunk to 5 square km, leaving just a few puddles on a cracked lake bed pockmarked by dead *vicunas* and abandoned fishing boats." About half of the 750 Uru-Munto familes that depended on the lake for their sustenance have had to migrate to the cities looking for work. "There used to be plenty of water that provided us with everything we water people could possibly need," explained Felix Condori, mayor of the Uro-Munto village Llapallapani. "Now there is no food to eat; the water is gone so the fish and birds are gone. That's why our people are leaving and we face extinction."[108]

Marx and Engels seem to have predicted today's world when they wrote: "Modern bourgeois society, with its relations of production, of exchange and of property, a society that has conjured up such gigantic means of production and of exchange, is like the sorcerer who is no longer able to control the powers of the nether world whom he has called up by his spells."[109]

CHAPTER SIX

CAPITALIST CRISIS

In these crises, there breaks out an epidemic that in all earlier epochs would have seemed an absurdity—the epidemic of over-production. Society suddenly finds itself put back into a state of momentary barbarism; it appears as if a famine, a universal war of devastation, had cut off the supply of every means of subsistence; industry and commerce seem to be destroyed; and why? Because there is too much civilization, too much means of subsistence, too much industry, too much commerce. . . And how does the bourgeoisie get over these crises? On the one hand by enforced destruction of a mass of productive forces; on the other by the conquest of new markets, and by the more thorough exploitation of the old ones. That is to say, by paving the way for more extensive and more destructive crises, and by diminishing the means whereby crises are prevented.

—*The Communist Manifesto*[1]

A DISTURBED BALANCE

We've discussed capitalism's dynamic drive to accumulate, but that is only half the story. If capitalism were simply a "growth engine" then we would see continuous expansion. But in reality, periods of growth give way, in Marx's words, to momentary barbarism when capitalism goes into crisis. Profitability slows, businesses shutter, debts used to fuel the expansion can no longer be paid. "The chain of payment obligations," as Marx wrote, suddenly breaks "in a hundred places."[2] The system seems to have gone into a state of shock. "All this," continued Marx, "therefore leads to violent and acute crises, sudden forcible devaluations, an actual stagnation and disruption in the reproduction process, and hence to an actual decline in reproduction."[3]

We said that competition is capitalism's beating heart. Profits are its lifeblood. Without them, capital crashes. A breakdown in profitability—whether in a single corporation, or more widely spread out through society—is not an abstract mathematical problem. It takes a punishing toll on people's lives and leads to staggering levels of devastation.

What became known as the Great Recession from 2007 to 2009 left in its wake more than nine million foreclosed on US homes. (A decade later only a third of those that lost their homes were reported "likely to become homeowners again.")[4] Unemployment figures, which always underestimate true unemployment,[5] hit 10 percent in 2009, and job growth has since depended on low-wage, temporary work. Meanwhile, banks were bailed out to the tune of trillions, as working-class people were left drowning in debt. A decade after the recession, student loans topped $1.3 trillion, an increase of 120 percent since 2008.[6]

Among readers' stories collected by the *Nation* during the Great Recession, Joseph, a twenty-nine-year-old veteran of the Iraq War, explained that he graduated college in 2007. In the two years that followed he held two jobs lasting for a total of five months. "I currently am living in my parents' basement," Joseph wrote, "where I have to share time on the PS3 [PlayStation 3] with my 55-year-old also unemployed father."[7]

Joshua, another recent college graduate wrote: "A year and a half ago, I was on cloud nine . . . the very first of my entire immediate and extended family to go to college . . . That was then. After hundreds of applications and job fairs alike, I was not even given the opportunity for an interview, let alone a full-time job." Saddled with $65,000 in student loans, and working a part-time job with no benefits, he reported, "I have no health insurance, have high blood pressure, and have to decide whether or not I can afford my medicine or not. I have battled a sickness for the past 2 months, long enough to sacrifice food to save up and go to a clinic. I was diagnosed with walking pneumonia. This is no way to live."[8] Of course, for every Joseph and Josh, there are hundreds of thousands more.

Many regions in the world reckoned with even deeper recessions or depressions, and in some cases, entire countries faced bankruptcy. Workers across the globe were forced to pay the price. In Greece, a quarter of the population remained unemployed for several years, and youth unemployment hit double that rate. Greek workers—along with those in Jamaica, Spain, Ireland, Brazil, Puerto Rico, and other countries—faced crippling austerity measures in order to "service the public debt" of the state.[9]

Despite the widespread turmoil and suffering caused by the financial meltdown, the recession that followed, and the limping "recovery" since, mainstream economists were largely caught flatfooted as to its causes. In the midst of the crisis, former chairman of the Federal Reserve and humble "rock star of economics" Alan Greenspan said he was "in shocked disbelief"—eventually coming to the conclusion that the crisis was precipitated by an inexplicable "once in a century credit tsunami."[10] Economist Eugene Fama, considered the "father of the efficient market hypothesis" (essentially the idea that markets are fully democratic and always lead to the "correct" economic outcomes), said: "We don't know what causes recessions. I'm not a macroeconomist, so I don't feel bad about that! We've never known. Debates go on to this day about what caused the Great Depression. Economics is not very good at explaining swings in economic activity."[11] (See sidebar: "Why Mainstream Economists Get It Wrong.")

For Marxists, understanding the system's propensity to break down is central to our analysis of capitalism, as well as the potential for its revolutionary overthrow. We've seen that at its best, a "healthy" capitalist economy depends on exploitation, poverty, oppression, and environmental destruction in order to function. But even this "health" gives rise to contradictions, which are only resolved through crises. As Marx put it: "Crises are never more than momentary, violent solutions for the existing contradictions, violent eruptions that reestablish the disturbed balance for the time being."[12]

Mainstream economic analysis starts and ends at the surface of the economy—price fluctuations, monetary policy, and financial markets. But Marxists argue that crises originate at the system's core and are not imposed on the system from outside. Capitalism's own process of accumulation—the very thing that drives it forward—also undermines it from within. As Marxist sociologist Simon Clarke explained, "For Marx crises were not exceptional periods in which a normal, uncontradictory, pattern of accumulation breaks down, but the most dramatic expression of the inherently contradictory foundations of accumulation."[13] Understanding capitalist crisis is central to the theory and politics of revolutionary Marxism. The volatility and destruction brought upon by endemic, periodic crises make capitalism a fundamentally precarious system, and at the same time open the way toward class struggle and the potential for revolution.

Below, we will outline in broad brushstrokes the contradictions embedded within the process of capital accumulation. With these contradictions in mind, we'll then describe the form that crises often take under capitalism. Finally, the chapter ends by taking up longer-term tendencies that may contribute to periodic crises, but also play a role in undermining the stability and integrity of the system as a whole.

WHY MAINSTREAM ECONOMISTS GET IT WRONG

Despite the regular occurrence of disruptive crises throughout the history of capitalism, bourgeois economics by and large denies that crises are intrinsic to the system. The market self-corrects, and crises are aberrations, exceptional departures from the norm. With every boom, amnesia sets in about the devastation wrought by the previous recession, and apologists for capitalism claim that the boom-and bust-cycle have been overcome. Yet when the boom goes bust, economists and mainstream commentators are dumbfounded, grappling for particular and exceptional explanations of what went wrong. As Simon Clarke put it:

> The crisis of the early nineteen nineties was the result of the incautious lending of the nineteen eighties. The crisis of the early nineteen eighties was the result of excessive state spending in the late nineteen seventies. The crisis of the mid nineteen seventies was the result of the oil price hike and the inflationary financing of the Vietnam War . . . the crisis of the nineteen thirties was the result of inappropriate banking policies . . . Every crisis has a different cause, all of which boil down to human failure, none of which are attributed to the capitalist system itself.[14]

"After two hundred years of repeating this nonsense," Clarke continued, "one would have expected that the economists would have begun to smell a rat. The economists' explanation of crises is as if a scientist were to deny that the recurrence of the seasons was a natural phenomenon, attributing the return of spring each year to the whim of a supernatural force."[15]

Mainstream economists were largely at a loss to explain the financial meltdown of 2007 to 2008 and the recession that followed. Eugene Fama insisted that there was no crisis in the housing or credit markets because markets are fully democratic and driven by rational economic actors, and thus always lead to the "correct" outcomes.

Another school of thought, known as chaos and behavioral theory, attributes movements in the economy to "animal spirits."[16] Unlike Fama's theory, economic players are here assumed to be driven not by rational behavior, but by animalistic impulses, which can fly out of control and have the potential to create massive fluctuations and disruptions in the system. These animal spirits include things like overconfidence and corruption. (Characteristics which, incidentally, animals are not known to exhibit.) In the 1990s, Alan Greenspan added to the lexicon "irrational exuberance."[17]

Then there are popular weather pattern explanations, which go back to neoclassical economist William Jevons who hypothesized that the number of sunspots help create a business cycle.[18] Many contemporary versions of this exist, including a paper by two American economists called "Good Day Sunshine: Stock Returns and the Weather," which studied sunniness and cloud patters at twenty-six cities around the world for fifteen years to find that sunny days often translated to better stock trading patterns.[19]

Beyond poking fun at economists, the question remains as to why their theories fail to properly analyze—or in many cases recognize—the occurrence of economic crises in the system. One of the most important foundations of bourgeois economics is known as "Say's Law," which originated with the classical economist Jean-Baptiste Say. Say's Law argues that supply and demand exist in equilibrium. There may be occasional disruptions to that symmetry, but the market eventually evens them out. Say's assumption is that supply always creates an equal demand because every time a capitalist produces and sells a commodity,

he then turns around and uses that money to buy someone else's product. In *A Treatise on Political Economy*, Say
argued:

> It is worthwhile to remark, that a product is no sooner cre-
> ated, than it, from that instant, affords a market for other
> products to the full extent of its own value. When the pro-
> ducer has put the finishing hand to his product, he is most
> anxious to sell it immediately, lest its value should diminish
> in his hands. Nor is he less anxious to dispose of the money
> he may get for it; for the value of money is also perishable.
> But the only way of getting rid of money is in the purchase
> of some product or other. Thus the mere circumstance of
> creation of one product immediately opens a vent for other
> products.[20]

That is to say, the prospect of the value of commodities and
money declining over time compels producers to both sell
and buy as quickly as possible. In reality the purpose of money is to *not* be perishable. As we discussed in chapter three,
money can be used to hold on to value over time. Its value
may go up or down.[21] And capitalists often sit on the profits
they've made—or use it to pay back their debts—if it doesn't
look like investment will turn out a profit.

Say's Law is predicated on the assumption that goods
will be sold, thus creating the funds that can then be used
to purchase other commodities. But this is not the case. As
Engels put it: "The economist comes along with his lovely
theory of demand and supply, proves to you that 'one can
never produce too much,' and practice replies with trade
crises, which reappear as regularly as the comets."[22]

Thus while profits recovered after the financial meltdown
of 2008, investment in real production did not materialize
for some years. Despite massive infusions of taxpayer money to banks, auto companies, and other corporations via
government bailouts, capitalists by and large saw an excess
capacity of goods and decided to hold on to cash rather
than spend it. Before 2008, about 40 percent of investment
in the US was going toward construction in housing. But
for years after the crisis, no one invested in building more

houses because there was an oversupply.[23] Jump ahead a decade and profits have recovered but investment has not.[24] As Marxist economist Doug Henwood explained, instead, "they've been shipping out gobs of money to their share-holders—an average of $1.2 trillion a year since 2015."[25]

This is what Marx had in mind when responding to Say's Law, he wrote: "Nothing can be more foolish than the dogma that because every sale is a purchase, and every purchase a sale, the circulation of commodities necessarily implies an equilibrium between sales and purchase. If this means that the number of actual sales accomplished is equal to the number of purchases, it is a flat tautology. But its real intention is to show that every seller brings his own buyer to the market with him." Nothing of the kind, answered Marx: "No one can sell unless someone else purchases. But no one directly *needs* to purchase because he has just sold."[26] [emphasis added.]

As we discussed previously, the separation of the man-ufacture of goods from their direct consumption through an intermediary stop of sale on the market leaves open the po-tential for a breakdown in the conversion of the production of goods to their realization in sales. "Circulation," contin-ued Marx,

> bursts through all the temporal, spatial and personal barri-ers imposed by the direct exchange of products, and it does this by splitting up. . . into the two antithetical segments of sale and purchase. . . If the assertion of their external in-dependence proceeds to a certain critical point, their unity violently makes itself felt by producing—a crisis.[27]

One of the critiques against Say's law to emerge *with-in* mainstream economics was developed and popularized by John Maynard Keynes.[28] Keynes accepted many of the basic assumptions of the neoclassical school, but he recog-nized that the real world often reveals disequilibrium be-tween supply and demand, and that this can produce great crises and ruptures within the system. Keynes conceptual-ized capitalism as a system for the distribution and consump-tion of goods—thus focusing on effective demand. Along with his contemporary counterparts—people like Paul Krugman, Joseph Stiglitz, and Jeffrey Sachs—Keynes argued for state intervention and government spending as a way to create jobs and increase workers' ability to spend and consume, thereby returning supply and demand to a state of equilibrium.

Although Keynesian economists offer an explanation of crises as inherent to the system, ultimately, since Keynes did not see growth or profits as essential to the system, he assumed regulation could provide a means to reassert the harmony of capitalism. But capitalism is not a system of distribution and consumption; it is a system of profit maximization. There are times where it is quite logical for capitalists, from their perspective, not to expand production, and even to prefer recessions and economic "shock therapies"[29] when it is in the interest of capital as a whole.

Keynes's ideas remained within the framework of helping capitalism to run more smoothly, and have in any case largely been pushed to the sidelines in mainstream economic discussions. Crises—even ones as big as the Great Recession—are once again seen as aberrations. Ultimately, whether one considers crises to be caused by external shocks (like Greenspan's credit tsunami), or by a lack of effective demand caused by improper management (such as would be argued by Keynes), in either case, they are seen as departures from an otherwise healthy system.

Whatever the different theories and explanations (or in many cases non-explanations) of crises advanced by bourgeois economics, their method begins with analyzing surface data in the form of prices, and from there conclusions are drawn about market performance and profits. It logically follows then that economic crises are understood to originate from the surface of the system: monetary policy, issues of credit, and financial markets, rather than from their roots in production and capital accumulation. As Marx eloquently summarized in *Theories of Surplus Value*:

> The constant recurrence of crises has in fact reduced the rigmarole of Say and others to a phraseology which is now

only used in times of prosperity but is cast aside in times of crises. In the crises of the world market, the contradictions and antagonisms of bourgeois production are strikingly revealed. Instead of investigating the nature of the conflicting elements which erupt in the catastrophe, the apologists content themselves with denying the catastrophe itself and insisting, in the face of their regular and periodic recurrence, that if production were carried on according to the textbooks, crises would never occur. Thus the apologetics consist in the falsification of the simplest economic relations, and particularly in clinging to the concept of unity in the face of contradiction.[30]

THE CONTRADICTIONS OF ACCUMULATION

First and foremost, we know that capital accumulation is driven not by needs but by profits—that is, not by the *creation of use-values*, but by the *realization of exchange-value*. It is not enough for capital to be employed in order to produce commodities (M-C), but those commodities must then be converted to profit (C-M'). As Marxist Duncan Foley put it: "The production and distribution of use-values is an incidental by-product of this pursuit of value."[31]

Were it the case that the construction of housing was driven by people's needs to have proper shelter, it wouldn't be that difficult for society to determine how many houses are required, and then to employ the workers necessary to build them. But the homebuilding and real estate industries have no interest in building homes to shelter people who cannot pay for them. Marx explained:

> It should never be forgotten that the production of this surplus value— and the transformation of a proportion of it back into capital, or accumulation, forms an integral part of surplus value—is the immediate purpose and the determining motive of capitalist production. Capitalist production, therefore, should never be depicted as something that it is not, i.e., as production whose immediate purpose is consumption.[32]

Rather than needs, investment in construction is driven by market prices and profits. And there is no guarantee that the houses built—no matter how desperately needed—will be profitably sold.

The creation of surplus value through the exploitation of labor, and the realization of surplus value in exchange are two different actions. Capitalism first separates the production of goods from their consumption through an intermediary stop of sale in exchange for money. These processes therefore occur at different times and places, and the time lag separating them is precisely what leaves open the potential for a breakdown in the conversion of the manufacture of goods to their realization in sales.

Second, because capitalists must continually expand production on pain of extinction, any limitations to expansion are seen simply as barriers to be overcome. This drive to produce, accumulate, and reinvest is done without system-wide planning, and with little regard to the limits of the market. Production and consumption are, in Marx's words, "not only separate in time and space, they are also separate in theory." As we'll discuss below, the laws that govern each are distinct and often conflicting. Marx explained: "The former is restricted only by the society's productive forces, the latter by the proportionality between the different branches of production and by the society's power of consumption. And this is determined... within a given framework of antagonistic conditions of distribution, which reduce the consumption of the vast majority of society to a minimum level."[33]

In previous societies, supply and demand were more or less in proportion because supply was determined by demand. "It was demand that dominated supply, preceded it. Production followed close on the heels of consumption. [Now] large-scale industry, forced by the very instruments at its disposal to produce at an ever-increasing scale, can no longer wait for demand. Production precedes consumption, supply compels demand."[34]

Recall our discussion of Ford's assembly line in chapter five. In the 1910s, Ford revolutionized car manufacture by vastly reducing the amount of time required to make each car. Prices for the new Model Ts were half of those of their predecessors. It was not a sudden desire for cars that produced this innovation. Rather the innovation was motivated by the need to push out competitors through cheaper prices. Once prices were reduced, cars became accessible to masses of people, thereby *creating* a new market and thus greater demand.

Third, advances in productivity necessitate ever-increasing investment in laborsaving technologies. As these technologies squeeze out the number of workers employed relative to machines, we'll see below how the part of capital that produces surplus value (labor) diminishes relative to capital invested in the means of production. While individual capitalists gain in the short-term by increasing productivity, the long-term implications of this compulsion create instability in the system.

Finally, all of these contradictions are further exacerbated by the slow speed at which market conditions are evaluated and at which production quotas can be adjusted accordingly. Changes in demand are only signaled through fluctuations in prices and profits. But these fluctuations themselves only happen once imbalances in production and exchange have already developed beyond a certain point. Capitalists necessarily respond after the fact, and do so slowly, as large-scale investments can't simply be erected and destroyed overnight.

POVERTY AMID PLENTY

We've seen that competition forces each capitalist to "accumulate for accumulation's sake." Every industry does not collectively take stock of the need (and, more importantly for capital, the ability to pay) for the goods that they produce. Rather, each company is concerned with expanding *their individual share* of the market. In order to do so they must drive down prices through increases in productivity. Marx wrote: "The market . . . must be continually extended, so that its relationships and the conditions governing them assume ever more the form of a natural law independent of the producers and become ever more uncontrollable."[35]

The extension of the scale of production must, of course, lead to a greater volume of goods. If Ford were to cut the prices of automobiles in half but still sell the same number of cars that had been sold before, it would result in half as much money earned in sales! Instead, Ford could gain market share by cutting prices in half, while doubling (or tripling) the number of cars produced. This way the company is assured a greater costumer-base and greater profits. Otherwise, what would be the point of gains in productivity?

As Simon Clarke wrote: "The result of these efforts is that the capitalists throw an increasing mass of commodities onto the market. However, this increase in production has not been motivated by a desire to meet expanding demand, but by a desire to increase the production of surplus value."[36] This compulsion creates a tendency for capitalists to overproduce—for production to run ahead of demand, often way beyond what the market can absorb.

Any limits that consumptive demand imposes on the expansion of capital are seen as obstacles to overcome. Capitalists never take these conditions as given, but rather confront these challenges by means of further increases to productivity, the intensification of labor, and conquering new markets. In other words, capital confronts the limits of the market by producing even more. As Marx argued:

> When considering the production process we saw that the whole aim of capitalist production is appropriation of the greatest possible amount of surplus-labor, in other words, the realization of the greatest possible amount of immediate labor-time with the given capital, be it through the prolongation of the labor-day or the reduction of the necessary labor-time, through the development of the productive power of labor by means of co-operation, division of labor, machinery etc., in short, large-scale production, i.e., mass production. It is thus in the nature of capitalist production, to produce without regard to the limits of the market.[37]

Or as Engels put more succinctly: The expansion of production "laughs at all resistance."[38]

One outcome of this tendency is that while the forces of production seem to know no bounds, the ability of workers to *buy* increasing masses of goods that we ourselves have created, is limited. Our wages sadly do not have the same expanding quality as capital; quite the contrary, they are under constant pressure to be reduced. Thus demand for consumer goods can have a hard time keeping up with supply. In Marx's words: "since capital's purpose is not the satisfaction of needs but the production of profit . . . there must be a constant tension between the restricted dimensions of consumption on the capitalist basis, and a production that is constantly striving to overcome these immanent barriers."[39]

Yet, in and of itself, this dynamic is not enough to throw the system into crisis because capitalists don't just produce commodities for workers to consume. (See sidebar: "The Problem with Theories of 'Underconsumption.'") They also produce luxury goods for the rich, and more importantly, raw materials and means of production for *other* productive capitalists. The key commodities that drive our economy are indeed oil, steel, and other goods necessary to fuel production. These markets keep expanding as long as money is being made and investment continues to move forward. "When we consider the accumulation process as a whole," wrote Clarke, "it is clear that the expansion of production in one branch of production expands the market for another, so that the 'balanced growth' of production remains a formal possibility."[40]

Nevertheless, this expansion happens unevenly and in an unplanned way. Every industry is susceptible to a variety of natural, technical, or social limits to manufacture and exchange. Raw materials, for instance, make up a good deal of production costs for industries. Consider the consequences of a contracting supply of natural gasses. This will increase the price of oil as an input to production. (On the other hand, new advances in oil extraction processes will cheapen the inputs). Weather conditions too—and increasingly global warming—can have drastic impacts on crops, such as corn, grain, or cotton, which are central to many branches of production. A sharp rise in the price of cotton due to drought conditions will impact the production of goods that require cotton as a raw material—from textiles, to livestock feed, to food products.

Unexpected changes in the limits or affordability of production inputs can give way to certain branches of production producing far beyond the limits of the market, while other branches may fall short of producing enough to meet growing demands. These asymmetries across branches of industries, often referred to by Marxists as "disproportionalities," can easily lead to an overproduction of goods in one or another branch of production, relative to the supply needs of other connected industries. If this happens in a key industry (say auto or oil, as opposed to lollipop production), the interdependence of capital makes it easy to see how OVERPRODUCTION can become generalized across the economy.

Marx used the example of Calico, a type of cotton, to make the point in *Theories of Surplus Value*. A glut in the calico industry would hamper the ability of a weaver to sell his goods at their value. Argued Marx:

> This disturbance first affects his workers. Thus they are now to a smaller extent, or not at all, consumers of his commodity—cotton cloth—and of other commodities which entered into their consumption. It is true, that they need cotton cloth, but they cannot buy it because they have not the means, and they have not the means because they cannot continue to produce and they cannot continue to produce because too much has been produced, too much cotton cloth is already on the market. [Referring to David Ricardo's argument for why the market will naturally fix any imbalances:] Neither Ricardo's advice "to increase their production," nor his alternative "to produce something else" can help them. They now form a part of the temporary surplus population, of the surplus production of workers [i.e. the unemployed], in this case of cotton producers, because there is a surplus production of cotton fabrics on the market.[41]

But apart from these workers, Marx went on to explain, an interruption in the weaving of calico hits those businesses (and likewise their workers) who have any connection to the production of cotton: agricultural workers that grow cotton, engineers of spindles and looms, iron and coal producers, and so on.

> Reproduction in all these spheres would also be impeded because the re-production of cotton cloth is a condition for their own reproduction. This would happen even if they had not *over-produced* in their own spheres, that is to say, had not produced beyond the limit set and justified by the cotton industry when it was working smoothly . . . They are now, all of a sudden, *relatively* over-produced, because the means with which to buy them and therefore the demand for them, have contracted.
>
> If over-production has taken place not only in cotton, but also in linen, silk and woolen fabrics, then it can be understood how over-pro-duction in these few, but leading articles, calls forth a more or less general (*relative*) over-production on the whole market. On the one hand there is a superabundance of all the means of reproduction and a superabundance of all kinds of unsold commodities on the market. On the other hand bank-rupt capitalists and destitute, starving workers.[42]

A more modern-day example of oil makes the same point. If refineries sit idle because there is an overproduction of oil, the workers are laid off, and the creditors, who financed the investment, are dragged down as well. But as future oil extraction and refining projects are pulled back, so too are demand for the raw materials (steel, concrete, plastics, electricity, etc.) and engineer-ing necessary for the production of oil rigs, pipelines, and so on. The con-struction business, and service and retail companies, which had benefitted from the springing up of oil boomtowns, suffer as well. (See sidebar: "Over-production; The Case of Oil.") In this way what may begin as overproduction in just one or a couple of industries, can spread and become a more general crisis in the system.

A generalized "crisis of overproduction" leads to absurd and tragic con-clusions. Previous societies suffered from crises of scarcity when plagues, famine, or wars destroyed the ability of society to adequately produce ne-cessities for the majority of people. Yet economic crises under capitalism are not the result of too few goods, but of too few *profits*. In other words, as we've said, capital is not concerned with the consumption of use-values, but with the production of exchange-value and the realization of profits through its sale. As Ernest Mandel put it: "Pre-capitalist crisis is a crisis of *under-produc-tion of use-values*. . . A capitalist crisis, however, is a crisis of *overproduction of exchange-values*."[43]

As a result, we see an overproduction not of things that are *needed*, but an overproduction of what can be *profitably sold*—whether these are tangible goods, or (as we'll discuss in the next chapter) complicated financial cock-tails. This is what mainstream economists refer to as "effective demand."

Effective because there are dollars behind the need for this or that good. So, for instance, a "surplus" of housing is part of what led to the recession that began in 2008. But this is not because there isn't a need for homes! It's just that people don't have the *money to buy* those homes. Marx wrote:

> It is not that too many means of subsistence are produced in relation to the existing population. On the contrary. Too little is produced to satisfy the mass of the population in an adequate and humane way. . . Secondly, not enough means of production are produced to allow the whole potential working population to work under the most productive conditions. . . It is not that too much wealth is produced. But from time to time, too much wealth is produced in its capitalist, antagonistic forms.[44]

From here proceeds a downward spiral in which profits tank, businesses and creditors go bust, and workers lose their jobs.

THE PROBLEM WITH THEORIES OF "UNDERCONSUMPTION"

Theories based on "underconsumption" argue that the working class is paid too little in the form of wages, and therefore workers' demand cannot keep up with a continually expanding supply. Underconsumption sounds like it should be the other side of the overproduction coin, and some of Marx's writing, taken in isolation, has been interpreted to make this point. In *Theories of Surplus Value*, for instance, he argued:

> Over-production is specifically conditioned by the general law of the production of capital: to produce to the limit set by the productive forces, that is to say, to exploit the maximum amount of labor with the given amount of capital, without any consideration for the actual limits of the market or the needs backed by the ability to pay; and this is carried out through continuous expansion of reproduction and accumulation, and therefore constant reconversion of revenue into capital, while on the other hand, the mass of the producers remain tied to the average level of needs, and must remain tied to it according to the nature of capitalist production.[45]

That is to say, capitalist production tends to accumulate and expand, while workers' consumptive abilities are constrained by capital's hunger for maximum exploitation. Therefore, it would seem supply would always exceed demand.

Yet if it were the case that capitalism depended on workers' consumption to survive, it would not only be prone to crises, it would fail to function at all. The fact that many commodities remain out of reach for much of the working class is a constant feature of life under capitalism, during booms and busts alike. As an article in *Socialist Voice* put it: "If underconsumption were the cause of crises, then crisis would not be cyclical but permanent."[46]

The logical implication of theories of underconsumption is that capitalists could be convinced to follow their own self-interest and invest in jobs and higher pay so that workers could purchase more goods and keep supply and demand in equilibrium. But in actuality many crises arise just when workers' wages are at a high point and unemployment is at a low. As Marx argued:

> It is pure tautology to say that crises are provoked by a lack of effective demand or effective consumption. . . The fact that commodities are unsaleable means no more than that no effective buyers have been found for them. . . If the attempt is made to give this tautology the semblance of greater profundity, by the statement that the working class receives too small a portion of its own product, and that the evil would be remedied if it received a bigger share, i.e., if its wages rose, we need only note that crises are always prepared by a period in which wages generally rise, and the working class actually does receive a greater share in the part of the annual product destined for consumption. From the standpoint of these advocates of sound and "simple" (!) common sense, such periods should rather avert the crisis. It thus appears that capitalist production involves certain conditions independent of people's good or bad intentions, which permit the relative prosperity of the working class only temporarily, and moreover always as a harbinger of crisis.[47]

In fact, Marx was clear that capitalists are compelled to produce *not* because of the demands of consumption, but because of the drive to appropriate surplus value. That surplus value in turn is used to accumulate further capital. Profits therefore enter back into the production process, employing additional labor and means of production. So long as there are outlets for profitable investment to be made, these will provide a demand for manufacturing equipment, software, and other means of production. In a nutshell, capitalists do not just produce commodities meant for working-class (or middle-class or capitalist) consumption, but also the means of production.

WHAT GOES BOOM. . .

To see how crises unfold, let's start with a "healthy" economy in which profits are strong and capitalists readily expand production, invest in new technologies, and employ more workers. Times are good for business, and some sections of the working class will likely see a rise in living standards (though many workers—disproportionately people of color, immigrants, women—will just as surely be left behind). We're usually told at this point that good times are here to stay and crises are a thing of the past.

A low level of unemployment gives workers greater bargaining power to demand higher wages. These workers are in turn more likely to buy goods and services. And *productive* goods—the means of production—are in high demand as well, as businesses eager to get in on rising profits invest in more machinery, technology, and raw materials. Because investment is expanding quickly, *demand for such goods typically outstrips supply*. Companies which produce the means of production race to keep up with demand, and to capture as much of the expanding market's share as possible.

Businesses hustle to produce more, knowing that it is likely that their goods will find buyers. And those firms that invest most quickly in labor-saving technology will be able produce goods most cheaply. Since markets are undersaturated, and since they were among the first to cheapen the cost of production, they won't need to fight hard for buyers. Instead of reflecting lower production costs in reduced prices for consumers, they can pocket the difference between the manufacturing expenditures and average sale prices. Thus they will enjoy "superprofits" while their competitors, using older means of production, maintain average profitability. And, as we've said, these cheaper costs of production will also compel the manufacture of a greater *mass* of goods.

Every industry in which investment rises will spur demand in other related industries. The housing market will drive a need for construction, which in turn will spur demand for wood, cement, and other raw materials, as well as household appliances and goods. The newly employed construction workers and service employees at Bed Bath & Beyond, Target, and others, will also fuel the purchase of other consumer goods.

Demand for new means of production in nearly every industry rises. Yet the expansion is never rapid enough to satisfy capital's needs. This is because the more developed capitalism is, the more production depends on complex equipment and technologies. In the past if you wanted to produce more shirts, you just needed to acquire more handlooms, but now increased production necessitates investment in technologies that require a longer period of time to construct. It is thus impossible for the system to quickly adjust to new levels of demand. As a young Bolshevik economist, Pavel Maksakovsky, wrote:

> Whatever capitalism's capacity for significant expansion might be, it is not able "suddenly" to satisfy the massive demand that results from moral wear of existing equipment [the need to update technology/machinery]. As a result, the available supply of commodities lags behind the growing demand, and the tendency towards "equilibrium" comes to a halt. It is not possible to "rectify" production speedily as the disruptions occur. On the contrary, the further the expansion develops, the more aggregate supply lags behind demand, and the greater is the detachment of market prices from values.[48]

In other words, at this point in the cycle, the limits of the market have not yet been reached. Quite the contrary, growing demand and lagging supply during the expansion has the added effect of driving up prices. Capitalists facing a growing market can get away with charging more, and in this way the cost of goods can become increasingly detached from base values. This, in turn, creates a greater incentive to invest: there's more money to be made! Add to this perfect storm of expansion the force of financial speculation (which we'll discuss in the next chapter) and prices can fly way off kilter.

But there are two problems brewing within this storm. The first, as we've said, is that expansion is driven by the need to maximize profits, not by "effective demand." But a lack of demand eventually asserts itself, whether capitalists like it or not. If no one buys the goods, surplus value is produced but not realized.

This leads to a second problem. As Maksakovsky's quote above implies, there is a time lag between a market's saturation point and its reflection in prices and a further lag in the adjustment of production quotas after prices drop. Market prices are capitalists' only guide to reading demand. Richard

Day, a professor of political economy at University of Toronto, explained: "The cyclical movement necessarily arises from the fact that *today's prices*, leaving aside speculation, are merely a 'snapshot' of the consequences of *past actions*. Even more irrational is the fact that today's prices, in determining *today's investments*, also determine *tomorrow's production*."[49]

Overproduction of goods in branches of industry that are tied to consumer goods very clearly run up against the limits of the market. As we've noted, since working-class income will never expand at the same pace as the growth of production, the gap between production and consumption will eventually make itself known. But the further the industry is from consumer demands, the more easily does expansion run amuck. Those branches of industry that produce the necessary materials for other industries engage in a self-arming frenzy: corporations supply each other with goods for production, great profits are realized, in turn leading to even greater demand, and evermore production. The longer the period of time that it takes to build and deliver machinery, the greater the degree to which production can expand without hitting up against the limitations of the market.

"The growth of consumer demand," wrote Maksakovsky, "can be compared to throwing a stone into the water, causing ripples to spread continuously outward. The further the ripples spread, the further removed from consumption are the production branches that are affected."[50]

. . . MUST GO BUST

Alas, the fever pitch of expansion eventually oversaturates the market. Too many goods have been produced to be able to sell at the exaggerated prices produced by the boom, or even at their value. Profits begin to tumble. Marx wrote:

> Crises are usually preceded by a general inflation in prices of all articles of capitalist production. All of them therefore participate in the subsequent crash and at their former prices they cause a glut in the market. The market can absorb a larger volume of commodities at falling prices, at prices which have fallen below their cost-prices, than it could absorb at their former prices. The excess of commodities is always relative; in other words, it is an excess at particular prices. The prices at which the commodities are then absorbed are ruinous for the producer or merchant.[51]

That is to say, the inflation of prices hits a point at which they threaten effective demand, much as rising real estate prices during the housing boom of the mid-2000s gave way to foreclosures and plummeting demand.[52] Once they do, the low prices at which excess supply must be sold off devastate the profits of business. Yet even at this point, competition exerts itself more strongly and capitalists are slow to pull back on their investments. As the pressures of overproduction squeeze industry, competition between the capitalists of that field increases and the compulsion to expand the production of surplus value enforces itself. A timid approach is anathema to capital. As Argentinian Marxist Claudio Katz put it: "The law of rising profits prevented them from adopting a conservative attitude in the proper moment. . . What seems rational after the explosion is discarded beforehand so as to not lose opportunities for profit."[53]

There are several reasons why capitalists do not draw down production levels once the market is saturated. In part, as we've said, they don't know exactly when this happens. Once they do, they can't adjust production levels immediately. Economists William Foster and Waddill Catchings explained it this way: "When this point comes, few men are aware of the fact, because the volume of commodities offered for sale does not indicate either the large volume in the making of the invisible supply in the hands of the speculators. . . on account of the time it takes to produce commodities and get them into the shops, the markets do not feel the full effects of maximum productivity until months after that stage has been reached. Production, therefore, continues at a high rate; and the volume of commodities coming upon the market, as a result of loans previously made, continues to increase."[54]

The lack of effective means to read the market and to correct production quotas accordingly aren't the only reasons that capitalists don't draw down production. During the boom, prices rise fantastically, responding to increasing demand and lagging supply. When prices fall just as dramatically, no player is willing to leave the table and give up market shares to their rivals. Instead they must jockey for their cut of a dwindling market and wait for their competitors to give ground. This dynamic plays out all the more so because during the boom, corporations invested heavily in new machinery and technologies. Letting these new investments go unused means losing more profit. Because the value of machinery depreciates over time, even if businesses resume production in the future, the value that the machines will pass on to the goods produced will have been diminished.

Lastly, those capitalists using more advanced methods of production achieved superprofits during the boom. Once the market is saturated, they can lower their price to increase market share and still maintain profitability.

These capitalists are likely to *expand* production further in order to capitalize as rapidly as possibly on market opportunities while they still exist. Even those capitalists whose production methods are lagging behind are likely to try whatever it takes—cut wages, intensify production, close down less profitable wings—in order to weather the storm while giving up as little market share as possible. Never content to let profitability dry up, capitalists keep pushing the market further, delve deeper into the pockets of credit, and intensify exploitation. "Capitalist production," wrote Marx, "seeks continually to overcome these immanent barriers, but overcomes them only by means which again place these barriers in its way and on a more formidable scale."[55]

Thus the necessary "adjustments" in levels of production take months or years to take place. As they do, they will wreak havoc on countless lives in their wake. Eventually a crisis of overproduction appears to be a can that can no longer be kicked down the road. A glutted market drives down prices and capitalists must try to get rid of their commodities. The diminishing returns on their investments finally lead to a pulling back on investment, and a downward spiral begins. Just as the overproduction of goods in one or more key industries can spill over to other related industries, so too does a retreat in one branch have a ripple effect on other industries.

If auto factories draw down production, the demand for rubber and steel that goes into making cars also drops. Workers at auto, rubber, and steel factories, among others, are laid off and this limits their ability to buy more cars and other commodities. Thus discussing the future of diesel cars, for instance, the *Financial Times* warned of the "cascading effect" for parts suppliers and slackening demand for wires, door handles, air conditioners, and plastic components. "Any prolonged slump," the article continued, "would rebound around the interconnected web of European car parts manufacturers, damaging economies, exports and outputs across the European Union."[56]

Now, rather than a self-arming frenzy of investments, production and financing will stiffen. Factories go idle. Capitalists sit on cash. While mainstream economists insist that supply must always equal demand because for every sale there is a purchase, and for every purchase a sale, reality proves otherwise. Capitalists and bankers tend to hoard money during crises, rather than invest. As Marx put it: "during crises—*after* the moment of panic—during the standstill of industry, money is immobilized in the hands of bankers, billbrokers [speculators], etc."[57] Just at the moment where it is most needed, credit dries up. Industrial and financial capitalists alike refuse to invest in production, which means less labor and less constant capital is employed, thereby spreading and intensifying the crisis.

State governments, as we'll discuss in the next chapter, may step in to make cheap credit available, but investors still won't bite. There is no incentive to do so, as long as a glut of goods is making it impossible to sell at a profit. In the wake of the Great Recession, for instance, a worldwide overcapacity of steel led to more than 20 percent of steel factories and capacity sitting unused. There's not enough demand for steel to motivate capitalists to invest in production, even if the factories and equipment are on the ready and cheap credit is made available to them.

OVERPRODUCTION: THE CASE OF OIL

Between 2004 and 2013, annual spending by the eighteen largest oil companies in the world quadrupled from $90 billion to $356 billion.[58] In the US, oil boomtowns sprang up seemingly overnight. The *Financial Times* reported that in North Dakota, "drilling rigs doubled from May to December 2009, from 35 to 75, and then doubled again to 173 by the end of 2010. The sleepy rural town of Williston, residents say, 'went crazy.'"[59] The town's population more than doubled:

> The roads were jammed with trucks and Ford pickups. You might have to wait in line for 90 minutes to get your hair cut at Walmart, or for two hours to get a table at one of the town's handful of restaurants. Rents for single-bedroom homes were the highest in the country, according to a survey for *Apartment Guide* last year, at $2,394 per month; more than in the metropolitan areas of New York or San Francisco.
>
> Businesses catering to the predominantly male oilfield workforce, including bars, strip clubs and tattoo parlors, did roaring trade. Boomtown Babes, a bright pink hut in a hotel car park, opened with women in vests selling "the Bakken's breast coffee," charging more than $7 for a large double-shot latte. . .
>
> Williston's infrastructure scrambled to keep up. There are new and half-built homes all around the city and plans for a $500m mall development, expansion of the water treatment system and a new airport.

"We're playing SimCity in real life," says Jeff Zarling of Dawa Solutions, a local web design and marketing firm. "We had to build everything."[60]

Oil production shot up from an average of 5.4 million barrels per day in 2009, to 9.4 million six years later. At its peak, it sold for $107 per barrel. Yet by mid-2014, a glut of crude oil forced prices down by about 70 percent to below $30 a barrel. This glut was the result of increased supply due to the technological innovations involved in extracting shale oil, as well as depressed demand due to weak economic growth in much of the world.[61] "The price fall," continued the *Times,* "has been like a bucket of cold water in the face for Williston and other oil boomtowns, waking them up from the frenzy of the past half-decade to a more sober reality."[62]

The "market indicators" professed by bourgeois economists to keep supply even with demand and prices in check, completely failed. Two years after the drop in prices, oil production kept on churning. An optimistic analyst at the Swedish bank, SEB, told the *Financial Times* in March 2016, "there is a rebalancing on the way," but, he admitted, "we are still running a surplus and stocks are building as far as we can see."[63]

In part, production levels can't quickly adjust down because high levels of technology and fixed capital necessary for production cannot be abandoned without the company and its investors taking a financial bath. Despite a drop in oil production, new projects in the Gulf of Mexico and Canada, for example, which were commissioned during the oil boom, just came online several years past the fall in prices.[64] And so the necessary pullback in supply simply cannot happen fast enough.

But there is another critical reason why supply keeps rushing forward. As we noted, competition forces capitalists to continue to fight for increased market share (or at least not give up their existing sales), for fear of abdicating greater share to their rivals. None of the oil-producing players want to be the first to fold. And this is even more exaggerated because oil is such a politically potent commodity.

Major oil-producing countries in OPEC met in April 2016 to try to come to an agreement to "freeze" output to their current levels. This was a laughable goal to begin with, since current levels were already at record highs. In the end, they couldn't even agree to this, because Iran—having slowed production while under sanctions—was only then catching up to *old* output levels and didn't want to stop ramping up production. Saudi Arabia, for its part, would rather sell oil on the cheap than let its rival, Iran, regain market share. And so "OPEC members," reported the *New York Times*, were "unable to agree on production cuts to manage the market. Instead, most members pumped oil at full capacity, trying to maximize revenues in the face of falling prices."[65]

To be sure, some countries, like Saudi Arabia and Russia, can continue to pump out oil with little regard to how far prices drop, since their reserves are more easily accessible and only cost $3–5 per barrel to extract. In comparison to other oil-producing countries with more strained economies, they have some state resources to rely on to persist through the crisis and wait for others to fail. At the same time, in the United States, falling prices are much more quickly putting companies out of business. Here shale oil, despite the technological "advances" (fracking and horizontal drilling) used for its extraction, is still a lot more expensive to dig up. Even companies like Royal Dutch Shell, large enough to weather the storm, suffered major losses. Happily, for the rest of the planet, Shell altogether abandoned its exploration of the Arctic for drilling, despite a $7 billion, nine-year investment.

Of course, even this news is bittersweet, as capitalism always makes workers pay for hits to profitability. Thus the *New York Times* reported: "Earnings are down for companies that made record profits in recent years, leading them to decommission more than two-thirds of their rigs and sharply cut investment in exploration and production. Scores of companies have gone bankrupt and an estimated 250,000 oil workers have lost their jobs."[66]

As prices crashed, the oil industry was left to reckon with a three-trillion-dollar mountain of debt following its borrowing binge during the boom. "The North American shale boom of the past decade," explained the *Financial Times*, "was driven by real technological progress but also a rapid accumulation of debt. Now the boom has gone but the debt remains, and it will hang over the sector for many years to come."[67]

Thus in early 2016, as oil prices bottomed out, Eagle Ford Shale was selling its trucks, trailers, and earthmovers at rock-bottom prices at a machinery auction in San Antonio. A flatbed truck for moving drilling rigs, usually worth about $400,000, was sold for $65,000. And mobile sand containers used for fracking, worth about $275,000 new were going for $17,000 a pop. Terry Dickerson, the Machinery Auctioneers founder, recounted to the *Financial Times* that many of the sellers were disappointed with the prices they got. "I feel like a funeral director. I'm the one that has to tell them the bad news." This kind of "fire sale" in San Antonio, reports the *Times*, "is just a small part of the worldwide value destruction caused by the oil decline. From Calgary to Queensland, oil and gas businesses are scrambling to sell assets, often at greatly reduced prices, to pay back the debts incurred to buy them."[68]

The nature of the boom and bust cycle is that the crisis in the oil industry does not remain forever. Rather it was in large part resolved on the backs of bankrupt companies, laid-off workers, and hollowed out boomtowns.[69] And those who have survived the bust figured out ways to boost productivity and cut costs in order to maintain profitability at a far-lower selling point per barrel. "When oil prices fell, the industry scrambled to adjust," the *New York Times* reported. "It initially relied on tried-and-true tactics: cutting jobs and investment. But then companies realized they had to go further, starting a far-reaching reworking of their businesses to embrace new technologies and construction methods to stretch each dollar just a little more. The result has been drastically lower operating costs and higher cash flows. Learning to live in a weaker oil price environment gives them an upside if prices firm up."[70]

Two years after the funeral-like machinery auctions in San Antonio, the *Financial Times* reported that once again at CERAWeek, the energy industry's annual jamboree, the mood had "perked up enormously from the gloom of 2016 and last year's tentative optimism. This year the smiles were broader and the drinks parties more crowded[sic]. Attendance was up 15–20 percent from last year. The improvement even extended to the quality of the food," which participants described as "rich" and "exotic." And yet, the article continued, "the general sense of relief is undercut by unease about the renewed boom in the US shale oil industry. Soaring US crude production raises the threat of renewed oversupply in world markets and another slump in prices."[71]

And so, as Marx said, "we go 'round the whole circle once again."[72]

OVERACCUMULATION OF CAPITAL

Finally, this brings us to a problem of OVERACCUMULATION. Too much supply of goods is one thing. This will eventually (if belatedly) be dealt with by reducing production to allow time for excess inventories to sell off. An additional and deeper problem arises as capitalists draw down production, leaving unused capacity in the form of factories, machinery, buildings, and other "fixed capital" (capital that is relatively *fixed* in place—land, buildings, large machinery). They cannot put all of their capital into motion, and this serves as a huge financial drain on their books. Thus as fixed capital remains unengaged and goods build up in warehouses, debt grows and prices continue to fall.

For this reason, crisis inevitably involves a large-scale liquidation of capital. Sometimes this means physical destruction—through wars, or wholesale dumping of goods—but also, as Marx pointed out, letting factories idle can also destroy capital:

> In so far as the reproduction process is checked and the labor-process is restricted or in some instances is completely stopped, *real* capital is destroyed. Machinery which is not used is not capital. Labor which is not exploited is equivalent to lost production. Raw material which lies unused is

no capital. Buildings (also newly built machinery) which are either unused or remain unfinished, commodities which rot in warehouses—all this is destruction of capital. All this means that the process of reproduction is checked and that the *existing* means of production are not really used as means of production, are not put into operation. Thus their use-value and their exchange-value go to the devil.[73]

Think of Detroit since its abandonment by the auto industry in the 1950s and 60s and you get an idea of what Marx means by destruction of capital. An unused factory is no longer capital. Only when labor is employed can a factory or machinery be engaged to produce value, and therefore amount to capital.

Of course, sometimes certain industries are allowed to limp along through state intervention, extending and exacerbating the overaccumulation of capital by not letting inefficient companies go bust. Consider the case of steel, which has experienced a colossal level of overcapacity for at least a decade since the Great Recession. Globally, the industry produces 35 percent more steel than can find effective demand. Yet production has not "adjusted" accordingly. The popular, politically opportunistic (and often laden with nationalist, racist rhetoric) explanation is to blame China. But it is capitalism's own inherent tendencies (only most successful in China at present), which have led to this phenomenal global glut. A Duke University report, sponsored by American steel manufacturers and titled "Overcapacity in Steel: China's Role in a Global Problem," unwittingly makes this point. It's worth quoting at length:

> In theory, overcapacity ought to be a short-term phenomenon. When demand and prices fall, profit-maximizing firms should reduce production and idle capacity. If the situation persists, firms will seek to permanently reduce capacity because the costs of maintaining capacity, notably maintaining furnaces and rolling facilities, decrease profits. Firms not maximizing profits will exit the market, while more efficient producers will capture market share, effectively eliminating excess capacity in the industry.
>
> In practice, however, economic downturns cause overcapacity because capacity is price insensitive in the short-term; that is, the physical plant has limited, if any, ability to rapidly reduce its total capacity in response to changes in price. High exit barriers in the steel industry prevent rapid adjustments to capacity. The costs of reducing capacity include the dismantling and demolition of mills, environmental clean-up and remediation, and legacy pension or other labor-related costs. Expectations about increases in future demand and the cyclical nature of the industry also limit the incentives of steel producers to reduce plant capacity in the face of economic downturns. Many countries seek to preserve steelmaking capacity during economic downturns in order to mitigate increases in

unemployment. Public subsidies or tax rebates are rationalized as preserving a strategic industry and reducing the effects of social problems caused by unemployment. Therefore, many steel producers find that the marginal cost of reducing capacity exceeds the marginal benefit, and prefer to continue production at lower levels to cover fixed costs, while either holding inventory or shipping the excess tonnage to spot markets where it is sold at lower prices. The result is overcapacity.[74]

An auto factory may be able to lay off workers and stop buying steel and rubber, thereby scaling back their costs. But they can't simply take down entire standing factories and equipment and regain their costs. So, for instance, *Automotive News Europe* reported in 2013 that Europe's 160 car plants were operating below 70 percent of their capacity. The other 30 percent is simply lost profitability.[75] While in the US, GM began plans to close five plants in 2018, while admitting that the four remaining plants still operate at less than half capacity.[76] Fewer goods are produced and less profit is made on the same base of previously invested capital. This is a recipe for an industry to limp along.

RESTORING PROFITABILITY

Finally, the destruction of capital lays the basis for recovery. As weaker capitals go bust, those corporations that remained solvent through the crisis inherit a looser market, which has been abandoned by failing competitors. At the same time, falling prices during the recession have also devalued the means of production. The overproduction of machinery, software, and raw material has made them cheaper to buy. A weakened working class, meanwhile, will accept lower wages rather than risk joining the growing ranks of the unemployed. As Marx explained: "Stagnation in production makes part of the working class idle and hence places the employed workers in conditions where they have to accept a fall in wages, even beneath the average; an operation that has exactly the same effect for capital as if relative or absolute surplus value has been increased while wages remained at the average."[77]

In addition to these "natural" devaluations in the cost of constant and variable capital, the remaining companies also benefit from the bankruptcies of other corporations. Those surviving capitalists can buy raw materials and machinery from bankrupted companies at bargain prices, thus further reducing the cost of constant capital. All this adds up to lower costs for inputs and therefore reduced costs of production. The capitalists that have managed to ride out the storm can make up for their losses and then some.

In this way, crises are resolved through the competitive struggle. Overproduction gives way to the devaluation of capital, the destruction of productive capacity, and mass layoffs. A "restructuring" of the economy, as the talking heads dryly call it, involves mergers and acquisitions, buyouts, and the sale of assets at fire-sale prices. The process happens unevenly, with one capitalist gaining ground at the other's expense. Economists Robert Wade and Frank Veneroso explained: "Financial crises have always caused transfers of ownership and power to those who keep their own assets intact and who are in a position to create credit... One recalls the statement attributed to [US robber baron] Andrew Mellon: 'In a depression, assets return to their rightful owners'"[78]

Marx described it like this:

> How then is this conflict to be resolved? How are the relations corresponding to a "healthy" movement of capitalist production to be restored? ... It involves this, that capital should lie idle, or even, in part, be destroyed ... although this loss is by no means uniformly distributed amongst all the particular individual capitalists ... the distribution being decided instead by a competitive struggle in which the loss is divided very unevenly and in very different forms according to the particular advantages or positions that have already been won, in such a way that one capital lies idle, another is destroyed, a third experiences only relative loss or simply a temporary devaluation, and so on.[79]

Now if remaining capitalists are to recover profitability in a context of falling prices, they are compelled to raise productivity and lower their cost of production. To do so they must invest in laborsaving technology. This then starts the process of accumulation up again, and brings us back to where we started at the beginning of the cycle as the economy begins to once again expand.

"And so," wrote Marx, "we go round the whole circle once again. One part of the capital that was devalued by the cessation of its function now regains its old value. And apart from that, with expanded conditions of production, a wider market and increased productivity, the same cycle of errors is pursued once more."[80] Depression will again give way to an expansion, which will inevitably culminate in overproduction, leading to a crisis, a depression, "and so on, until reaching," as Maksakovsky put it, "capitalist 'infinity.'"[81]

Marx's analysis of the crisis of overproduction disproves the conventional wisdom that tells us that supply and demand exist more or less in equilibrium, and that the market knows best. More importantly, it shows that crises are not special or outside occurrences, arising from exceptional circumstances, but rather are just the most dramatic (and damaging) expressions of contradictions inherent to capitalism. These contradictions culminate in violent disruptions of working people's lives. For capitalists, politicians, and economists, a crisis is a drop in profitability, but from a human perspective, it is the devastation wrought on families who lose their homes and workers who lose their jobs, and the vulnerability it creates among children, the elderly, and people with disabilities, robbed of their social safety nets.

The Marxist understanding of the inevitability of crisis, and what's more, its origins at the heart of the process of accumulation, make its regulation and reform akin to a Band-Aid on a gaping wound. Crises instead show the possibility and the necessity, certainly of class struggle, and ultimately of revolution. "Within the ruling class themselves, the foreboding is emerging that the present society is no solid crystal," wrote Marx, "but an organism capable of change, and is constantly engaged in a process of change."[82]

A FALLING RATE OF PROFITABILITY

We've seen that the very process of capital accumulation leads to crises, which play out in a boom-bust cycle. It also has a longer-term destabilizing effect on the system. The origin of these troubles is based on what Marx referred to as the ORGANIC COMPOSITION OF CAPITAL—the ratio in which capitalists invest in constant capital relative to variable capital. As we've discussed in previous chapters, constant capital is money invested in materials and equipment, and variable capital is invested in labor-power. Why is the ratio between these types of investment so important?

Marx observed that over time, the organic composition of capital rises, as fewer workers are required to wield more technology in production. So, for instance, in the preindustrial days of textile production, individuals spun and weaved in their homes utilizing a single loom. A single weaver to a single loom would imply a 1:1 ratio of machinery to labor-power.[83] The invention of the power loom in the early nineteenth century automated the process such that a child could operate six looms at once. Today a weaver is expected to run up to thirty looms simultaneously, and is trained to ensure that no machine should stop running for more than a minute. Each loom produces around three thousand meters a week.[84]

You can find similar trajectories in nearly every industry. Early print houses required journeyman printers who prepared ink and sheets of paper, compositors who set type for printing, and pressmen who each manually worked a press. Today, web-based printing orders are highly automated. One company boasted that a print run of hundreds of sheets requires as little as sixty seconds of labor.[85] Meanwhile, the most complex printers now print 3-D models, and do so much faster and with fewer employees than were needed to produce newspapers even a century ago.[86] Examples dominate every industry, from agriculture, to electronics, to fast food.

This is because the capitalist class, in Marx's words, "cannot exist without constantly revolutionizing the instruments of production."[87] As we saw in the previous chapter, in order to stay competitive, every company must innovate, and this impulse propels technological vitality across industries. But the problem for capitalists is that no firm can privately hold on to their advances. Whichever company is first to pioneer new methods can undersell its competitors by producing goods more cheaply. But once the faster mode of production becomes the standard throughout the industry, then the average amount of *socially necessary labor-time* required to make the commodities drops, and prices fall accordingly to reflect this fact.

You can see how this plays out with computers. Huge, clunky, and much less powerful computers used to be more expensive because a lot more labor went into producing them. Now the technology that is used to make computers has vastly reduced production time. Your smartphone can do more than the old clunkers used to do, and for less cost.[88] The reduced necessary labor-time that goes into producing them is reflected in cheaper value and therefore cheaper prices.

Laborsaving technologies, by definition, squeeze out the number of workers employed relative to machinery. As we discussed in previous chapters, labor creates new value for capitalists, while investment in machinery and raw materials doesn't. Constant capital simply embodies and passes on the existing value of previous generations of labor. Essentially, you can't squeeze extra value out of a piece of machinery: you get what you pay for. So, when the organic composition of capital rises, the part of the investment that generates *new, added* value drops. The surplus value per unit of capital falls. This whole process leads to what Marx calls "the law of the TENDENCY FOR THE RATE OF PROFIT TO FALL."

For the sake of numerical ease, let's use a made-up company, BigBucks Printing, to follow the path of this process. BigBucks Printing runs three traditional lithographic presses, which each produce two thousand sheets an hour. Their twenty print press operators and technicians each earn $50,000 per year and split daytime and nighttime shifts such that they can run the presses 24/7. This allows BigBucks to maximize the time that the presses are running, and produce a total of 144,000 sheets a day. If the going rate was 10¢ per sheet, they would produce a daily value of $14,400 (or approximately $5.3 million per year).

BigBucks purchased each of their printers for $5 million. Anticipating a ten-year life for this equipment, every printer would then pass on $500,000 of value into the products per year, over the course of ten years. Myriad costs beyond labor and printers are associated with printing—ink, paper, rent, advertising, executive pay, research and development, just to name a few. In order to keep the numbers simple, we'll lump these costs together, since they won't impact the changes we are trying to understand.

Our very simplified annual budget might look something like this:

Labor-power (v)	*20 workers x $50,000*	$1,000,000
Printing presses (c)	*3 printers x $500,000 per year*	$1,500,000
Rent, materials, other machinery (c)	*Combined costs*	$1,500,000
Total		**$4,000,000**

BigBucks' annual spending therefore comes out to $4 million. And the annual revenue we said is approximately $5.3 million. Once BigBucks pays back its expenses, this nets a profit of $1.3 million. Thus:

- Surplus value (s) = $1.3 million

- Constant capital (c) = $3 million

- Variable capital (v) = $1 million

In chapter four we defined the rate of surplus value, which measures the rate at which workers are exploited to produce surplus value. It is measured as s/v: surplus value to variable capital. In this case $1.3 million /$1 million equals a rate of surplus value of 130 percent. Yet the rate that capitalists are truly concerned about is the rate of profit, which is measured by the amount of surplus value, divided by the total investment: labor, machinery, and raw material. This formula is summed up as s/(v+c). In this case $1.3 million /$4 million equals a 33 percent rate of profit.

But a few years after purchasing the three lithographic printers, a tight and shrinking market for print magazines puts a squeeze on BigBucks' profits, sending their corporate managers to Miami for a lavish, soul-searching retreat, where they ultimately come to the conclusion that they must replace the old presses for the latest top-of-the-line digital printers.[89] They cost twice as much, $10 million a pop, but produce 30 percent more sheets per day. (If we assume again that the life of the new printers is ten years, each printer will pass on $1 million in value per year.) What's more they require only half the labor-time to run them. So their new annual budget looks like this:

Labor-power (v)	10 workers x $50,000	$500,000
Printing presses (c)	3 printers x $1,000,000 per year	$3,000,000
Rent, materials, other machinery (c)	*Combined costs*	$1,500,000
Total		**$5,000,000**

Ten pink slips later, they now produce 187,200 sheets a day (30 percent more than before). At the same going rate of 10¢ per sheet, they would produce a daily value of $18,720 (or approximately $6.8 million per year). Their annual net profit will be $1.8 million. The rate of surplus value therefore jumps to $1.8 million/$500,000, or 360 percent. And the rate of profit also rises to $1.8/$5 million: from 33 percent to about 36 percent. This good news sends BigBucks bigwigs back to Miami for some pool parties on yachts, floating cocktail bars, manicured fire pits, and gourmet s'mores. Profitability is up!

Assuming BigBucks was among the first to get the new top-of-the-line print-ers, there's no reason that they would have to lower their prices. If most printing companies are using the old technology, the socially necessary labor-time for printing is set by the old, rather than the new, technology. But this positioning gives BigBucks some wiggle room in a competitive market. They *could* reduce their prices from the standard 10¢ per sheet, to 9¢ per sheet to grab more market share, and still make out with a wide profit margin of $1.1 million.

But following BigBucks' success, it's not long before other competitors decide to invest in their own advanced presses. And once BigBucks is no lon-ger the single user of this technology, they lose the luxury of setting prices. In fact, other print presses will likely try to sell their products as cheaply as pos-sible in order to regain their share of a shrinking market. Thus the standard socially necessary labor-time drops to the pace set by the new digital presses. Across the industry, companies are printing more in less time. Eventually, the fact that printers can produce 30 percent more goods using half of the labor-time is reflected in cheaper prices—say 8 cents per sheet.

At the end of this process the competitors are back on a level playing field. Workers across the industry are more productive—they can print more sheets per hour. But each company is left with having to make a much greater investment in constant capital than they had before, relative to the surplus value that their workers produce. The cost of production has increased, owing to the new, more expensive technology that is now the standard, and prices have dropped to reflect these productivity increases.

How does this impact the rate of profit? Let's go back to the last iteration of BigBucks's budget. The cost of variable and constant capital remains $5 million. But at 8¢ per sheet, the 187,200 sheets a day produces a daily value of $14,976 (or approximately $5.5 million per year). Surplus value has therefore dropped down to about $500,000; the rate of surplus value is ($500,000/$500,000) or 100 percent; the rate of profit is ($500,000/$5 million) or 10 percent.

FIGURE 8. BIGBUCKS PRINTING: STAGES OF PROFITABILITY

	M	C	M'	Rate of Profit: s/(v+c)
Stage 1	v = $1,000,000 c = $3,000,000 TOTAL = $4 million	144,000 sheets per day $14,400 value per day TOTAL = $5.3 million per year	v = $1,000,000 c = $3,000,000 s = $1,300,000 TOTAL = $5.3 million	$1.3 million /$4 million = 33% rate of profit
Stage 2	v = $500,000 c = $4,500,000 TOTAL = $5 million	187,200 sheets a day $18,720 value per day TOTAL = $6.8 million per year	v = $500,000 c = $4,500,000 s = $1,800,000 TOTAL = $6.8 million	$1.8million /$5 million =36% rate of profit
Stage 3	v = $500,000 c = $4,500,000 TOTAL = $5 million	187,200 sheets a day $14,976 value per day TOTAL = $5.5 million per year	v = $500,000 c = $4,500,000 s = $500,000 TOTAL = $5.5 million	$.5 million /$5 million =10% rate of profit

Of course BigBucks, and their competitors as well, will try to answer with speed-ups and salary cuts, but the overall trend is toward a slackening rate of profit.

Marx summarized the process like this:

> [E]very new method of production of this kind makes commodities cheaper. At first, therefore, [the capitalist] can sell them above their price of production, perhaps above their value. He pockets the difference between their costs of production and the market price of the other commodities, which are produced at higher production costs. This is possible because the average socially necessary labor-time required to produce these latter commodities is greater than the labor-time required with the new method of production. His production procedure is ahead of the social average. But competition makes the new procedure universal and subjects it to the general law. A fall in the rate then ensues—first perhaps in this sphere of production, and subsequently equalized with the others—a fall that is completely independent of the capitalists' will.[90]

In short: an ever-greater proportion of capitalists' investments go to machinery and technology rather than increasing the size of the workforce. (The workforce may very well expand, but not at the same pace as the growth in machinery.) While individual companies may enjoy a short-term bump in profits, these benefits prove disastrous for the capitalist class as a whole. Once again, the short-term impetus of capital runs up against the long-term health of the system.

The process of accumulation therefore tends to *increase the rate of surplus value* through advances in productivity, but at the same time, it raises the organic composition of capital, and consequently *lowers the rate of profit*. As Marx wrote:

> The tendential fall in the rate of profit is linked with a tendential rise in the rate of surplus value, i.e. in the level of exploitation of labor... The profit rate does not fall because labor becomes less productive but rather because it becomes more productive. The rise in the rate of surplus value and the fall in the rate of profit are simply particular forms that express the growing productivity of labor in capitalist terms.[91]

These two tendencies—increases in the rate of exploitation and decreases in the rate of profit—go on together, but in such a way that the former does not keep up with the latter. Rising levels of capital investment (and with them the organic composition of capital) have no natural limits, while increasing the rate of exploitation most certainly does. No matter how much the bosses push, the working day cannot be "infinitely extended" past twenty-four hours. Nor can capitalists lower our wages to zero. Further, the more capitalism develops its productive forces, and the more machinery is employed in production relative to labor, the smaller the impact of rising exploitation, as the ratio of necessary to surplus labor take up a smaller piece of the overall capital investment. Surplus labor may rise "but in an ever smaller relation to development of the productive force."[92]

SYSTEM FAILURE

Marx understood that this process occurs in the whole of the economy, not just in particular industries. Even in the most stubbornly labor-intensive industries, the *tendency* still exists to develop higher rates of productivity through the introduction of machinery, thereby increasing the organic composition of capital. Indeed, today almost every industry uses computers to coordinate its accounting, shipping, and supply chain.[93]

More importantly, declining profitability generalizes across the system because a mature capitalist economy develops an "average rate of profit" throughout the economy. In volume 3 of *Capital*, Marx explained that all industries—regardless of their individual organic composition of capital—have an average rate of profit. If this were not the case, capital-intensive industries with higher organic compositions would disappear, because no one would invest in businesses that yield lower profit margins. The equalization of a rate of profit across industries develops through the effects of supply and demand. Let's pause here for a moment to see how this works.

If, for instance, the auto industry is generating rates of profit of 4 percent while the biotech industry is generating rates of profit of 8 percent, capitalists will want to invest less in auto and more in biotech. The ultimate result of this—less auto production and more biotech investment—will affect the profit rates in both industries in opposite directions. The increased supply of biotechnology will flood the market, forcing companies to reduce their prices in order to gain customers. In other words, increased supply will eventually drive down their prices, and therefore profitability. At the same time, drawing back the scale of auto production will decrease the supply of cars, eventually allowing for prices—and therefore profit rates—to rise.

In this way, increased competition and investment drive down the rate of profit in one industry while the other industry may "cool down" and its profits grow. Thus rising profit rates in low-profit industries and falling rates in high-profit ones leads to an equalization of the rate of profit for the economy as a whole as capitalists chase the best rate of return across the economy.[94]

With an average rate of profit in effect across the economy, the tendency of rate of profit to fall operates not only in those industries where the organic composition of capital rises precipitously, but in all industries.

COUNTERVAILING TENDENCIES

This seems like a pretty big glitch in the matrix, and one could assume that capitalism ought to have ground to a halt long ago. Profits are, as we said, the lifeblood of capitalism. And if the rate of profit keeps dropping until it reaches zero, the system will undoubtedly shut down. As Marx put it:

> If we consider the enormous development in the productive powers of social labor over the last thirty [now 180!] years alone. . . and particularly if we consider the enormous mass of fixed capital involved in the overall process of social production. . . then instead of. . . the problem of explaining the fall in the profit rate, we have the opposite problem of explaining why this fall is not greater or faster. Counteracting influences must be at work, checking and cancelling the effect of the general law and giving it simply the character of a tendency, which is why we have described the fall in the general rate of profit as a tendential fall.[95]

There are two main reasons why the tendency of falling profitability has not already dealt a deathblow to the system. One reason is that while the *rate* of profits may drop, so long as it stays above zero percent, the *mass* of profits does not necessarily have to fall. A declining rate of profit can (and often does) occur alongside a rise in the mass of profits. Tracking the rate of profit tells us the amount of profits reaped relative to investment in labor and technology. If capitalists are able to grow the *mass* of products and therefore the *mass* of profits, they can compensate for this drop and keep cash flowing.

Nevertheless, were the rate of profit to continually fall, eventually hitting zero, capitalists would not gain from their investments. M-C-M' would become M-C-M, a waste of time. But this brings us to the second point, which is that the drop in the rate of profits is a *tendency* and not a *certainty*. Marx argued that capitalism was plagued by the "law of the tendency for the rate of profit to fall" rather than "law of the rate of profit to fall." This phrase may be linguistically clunky, but it's more accurate nonetheless.

Writing in *Capital*, volume 3, he explained: "The same causes that bring about a fall in the general rate of profit provoke countereffects that inhibit this fall, delay it, and in part, even paralyze it. These do not annul the law, but they weaken its effect. If this were not the case, it would not be the fall in the general rate of profit that is incomprehensible, but rather the relative slowness of this fall. The law operates therefore simply as a tendency, whose effect is decisive only under certain particular circumstances and over long periods."[96]

What are these countereffects? First, capitalists can make up for a drop in profitability through good old-fashioned exploitation. Never willing to let their profits slide, capitalists always respond to diminished returns by increasing exploitation. Thus we see the many variations of attacks on the working class, which raise the rate of surplus value through means other than laborsaving technology. Teachers in New York City are asked to work a longer day without compensation. Children are employed in sweatshops in Los Angeles at superexploited wages. Immigrants in Chicago are picked up at parking lots and work all day for well below a minimum wage. Union wages in Wisconsin are shattered through right-to-work laws that break the power of unions. Workers at an Austin-based computer factory are sped up, their every move timed to the second. And so, for these reasons, the "rationalization" of work pioneered by Frederick Taylor, which we discussed in chapter four, has become the standard of how labor-power is organized.

Where corporations are unable to increase the rate of exploitation by intensifying the labor process, they can also move overseas, or to right-to-work states, to find cheaper labor, and thus postpone the need to invest in technology. Historically, capitalism has known no human bounds in its quest to offset falling profit rates. Slavery, concentration camps, and European colonies have all been used to prop up profitability.

A second countervailing tendency has to do with the value of constant capital itself. While businesses make ever-greater investments in machinery and raw materials, the price of each of these technologies may decline over time through, as we discussed in chapter four, their MORAL DEPRECI-ATION. That is, the machines become less valuable before their value *physically* deteriorates when they are superseded by faster machines. Increases in productivity in industries that manufacture the means of production lead to decreasing values of these inputs as well. So, for instance, while printing companies need to buy more advanced presses, the value of these presses will drop, as new technology decreases the amount of labor-time necessary for their manufacture. (If BigBucks Printing spent $10 million per printer in 2015, by 2020 these same printers may cost their competitor RetroPrint only $8 million a pop.)[97] The rate that the value of technology drops may not always keep up with the rate at which new technology needs to be procured (for instance, if you need twice as many printers, but the price of printers doesn't drop in half). But overall, the rate at which investment in constant capital rises is at least stunted by this countervailing tendency.

Other factors, as well, can neutralize or lessen the tendency for the rate of profit to fall. An expansion of markets through colonialism and the globalization of trade, for instance, can increase the rate of sales and create a higher TURNOVER RATE OF CAPITAL. The turnover rate measures the time that elapses between the investment of capital toward the production process, and when the produced goods are sold. The faster the speed at which invested capital becomes realized, the more rounds of production can happen within a given span of time, and the more profit can be made.[98]

The strength of these countervailing tendencies ensures that falling profitability is a *tendency* rather than an absolute law. Instead of plummeting towards a 0 percent rate of return, the downward pressure on profits manifests itself over a long period of time and not in a linear trajectory. So long as there is the prospect of a positive rate of profit, capitalists will invest, and capital will remain in circulation.

A REAL DRAG

For these reasons, rather than producing regular economic crises, the tendency for the rate of profit to fall creates a long-term drag on capitalism.[99] Both the downward pressures on profits, and the desperate attempts to counteract it, work to destabilize the system. First, workers are disposed of and replaced by more machinery, creating higher unemployment—or "surplus population"—as Marx called it.[100] Those workers who remain on the job are forced to work harder and harder as bosses drive up the rate of exploitation. As the mass of profits grow, class relations become increasingly polarized.

Second, a fall in the rate of profit brings about a competitive struggle among capitalists to drive out the least efficient and the smallest capitalists. Larger companies can use economies of scale, monopoly positions, and access to cheap credit to ride out the crisis and beat out lesser companies. The weeding out of smaller capitalists drives the system toward greater concentration and centralization. Marx explained:

Concentration grows at the same time [as the profit rate falls], since beyond certain limits a large capital with a lower rate of profit accumulates more quickly than a small capital with a higher rate of profit. . . The mass of small fragmented capitals are thereby forced onto adventurous paths: speculation, credit swindles, share swindles, crises. The so-called plethora of that capital is always basically reducible to a plethora of that capital for which the fall in the profit rate is not outweighed by its mass. . . [101]

Third, as the quote from Marx hints at, dropping profitability in industrial production encourages speculation in nonproductive, financial products, which we will discuss further in the next chapter. As the 2007 to 2008 economic meltdown showed, the casino of finance capital can lead to dramatic explosions. Finally, capitalists are compelled to invest in production in countries where the rate of profit is higher, while simultaneously expanding markets across the globe. These economic imperatives are backed by the barrel of a gun. Aggressive economic globalization spills into imperialist missions, threatening the stability of global capital.

The significance and effect of the tendency for the rate of profit to fall, and its role within a broader theory of crisis, is the topic of long-standing and deep debates among Marxists. But at a minimum, it's clear that any falls in the rate of profit make the system more prone to crises. As Simon Clarke argued, Marx did not identify the tendency for the rate of profit to fall as a "privileged cause for crises," but it nevertheless "plays the role of a factor which makes crises more likely, primarily because it leads to an intensification of the competitive struggle between capitalists."[102]

Marx certainly attached great importance to the tendency for the rate of profit to fall. It points to a fundamental contradiction at the heart of capitalism: the drive toward maximizing profitability is undermined *by its own process* of accumulation. Marx explained that the rate of profit "is the spur to capitalist production," and thus:

[A] fall in this rate slows down the formation of new, independent capitals and thus appears as a threat to the development of the capitalist production process; it promotes overproduction, speculation and crises, and leads to the existence of excess capital alongside a surplus population. Thus economists like Ricardo, who take the capitalist mode of production as an absolute, feel here that this mode of production creates a barrier for itself and seeks the source of this barrier not in production but rather in nature (in the theory of rent). The important thing in their horror at the falling rate of profit is the feeling that the capitalist mode of production comes up against a barrier to the development of the productive forces which has nothing to do with production of wealth as such; but this characteristic barrier in fact testifies to the restrictiveness and the solely historical and transitory character of the capitalist mode of production; it bears witness that this is not an absolute mode of production for the production of wealth but actually comes into conflict at a certain stage with the latter's further development.[103]

In short: "The *true barrier* of capitalist production, is *capital itself.*"[104]

CONCLUSION

The highly contested role of the tendency for the rate of profit to fall in part owes itself to the fact that Marx did not outline a systematic theory of crisis in any one place. Instead, pieces of the theory exist scattered in notes and in a few chapters of *Capital*, volumes 1 and 3, and in *Theories of Surplus Value* (sometimes referred to as volume 4 of *Capital*.) Of those writings, only volume 1 of *Capital* was written and completed by Marx himself, during his lifetime. For this reason (as well as the complexity of the issues), Marxists have differed in which aspects of Marx's writing—falling profitability, overproduction (or in some cases, underproduction), disproportionality among branches, the role of credit—are emphasized, and how these pieces fit together.[105]

Yet whatever the cause of each particular crisis, all express the contradiction between the limitless development of the forces of production and the subordination of that production to the realization of surplus value. But crisis is not only the product of these contradictions; it is also—for capital—the solution. The devaluation and destruction of capital can wipe out excess capacity, and also restore falling profit rates through the cheapening of the means of production. This "solution" violently restores profitability on the backs of working people. And what's more, it is always temporary. Thus capitalism jolts back and forth through booms and busts. It is characterized, in the words of Ernest Mandel, by a "rhythm of development—*uneven, unsteady*, proceeding by leaps which are followed by periods of stagnation and retreat."[106]

Nevertheless, whatever the scale and fury of economic crises, none automatically translate to revolution or the end of capitalism. As Russian revolutionary Leon Trotsky put it, "There is no crisis which can be, by itself, fatal to capitalism."[107] Rather, crises create objective conditions, which make struggle, and ultimately the overthrow of capitalism, *possible*. But this depends on the subjective element—the confidence, organization, and politics of the working class. These are topics that lay outside the scope of this book, but the final word will be left here to Trotsky, who went on to explain:

The oscillations of the business cycle only create a situation in which it will be easier, or more difficult, for the proletariat to overthrow capitalism. The transition from a bourgeois society to a socialist society presupposes the activity of living men who are the makers of their own history... The crises of capitalism are not numbered, nor is it indicated in advance which one of these will be the "last." But our entire epoch and, above all, the present crisis imperiously command the proletariat: "Seize power!" If, however, the party of the working class, in spite of favorable conditions, reveals itself incapable of leading the proletariat to the seizure of power, the life of society will continue necessarily upon capitalist foundations—until a new crisis, a new war, perhaps until the complete disintegration of European civilization.

CHAPTER SEVEN

CREDIT AND FINANCIALIZATION

> If the credit system appears as the principal lever of over-production and excessive speculation in commerce, this is simply because the reproduction process, which is elastic by nature, is now forced to its most extreme limit.
>
> —*Capital, Volume 3*[1]

SWINDLERS AND CHEATERS

We've seen that the very process of accumulation comes into conflict with the system's own goal of profit making. Capitalism simultaneously bursts through the barriers set in front of it, and in so doing erects new barriers, which threaten its stability and integrity down the line. An additional element must be added in order to understand how these contradictions play out, and that is the role of credit and finance. Although the size and complexity of today's financial markets have grown tremendously since Marx's day, his writings on finance capital—in his words, "an entire system of swindling and cheating"[2]—provide a framework for breaking down this mystifying component of today's economy.

In this final chapter we'll discusses why credit is necessary to the daily functions of capitalism and outline some of the specific roles that it plays. From there we'll see how finance has evolved to occupy a greater and more absurd stature in today's economy. And we'll take an important detour along the way to explain the roots of the Great Recession of 2007 to 2009, not only because its impact has shaped the state of the world economy for years and perhaps decades to come, but also because no other example more clearly illustrates the way that a crisis of overproduction is exacerbated by the role of credit and finance.

Credit expands capitalists' abilities to invest in production. It also increases consumers' buying power. But these very functions, to hasten and extend production and consumption, also contribute to the system's contradictions and downturns by intensifying the processes of overproduction and falling profitability. As Marx explained: "The credit system hence accelerates the material development of the productive forces and the creation of the world market... At the same time, credit accelerates the violent outbreaks of this contradiction, crises, and with these the elements of dissolution of the old mode of production."[3]

A MOUNTAIN OF DEBT

Simply put credit is capital lent out in a variety of forms—from direct loans and cash advances, to stocks and bonds, to mortgages. Capitalism relies on mountains of debt. Every day, corporations borrow large sums of capital to conduct business. So much so that in recent years, the average amount of debt carried by companies is greater than their actual earnings. Typically measured as a debt-to-EBITDA (earnings before interest, tax, depreciation, and amortization) ratio, a 2019 S&P report found that companies' median debt load is 3.2 times their EBITDA.[4]

Global debt has hit an all-time high of $253 trillion in 2019.[5] That is more than three times the total value of the world's annual economic output.[6] The amount works out to approximately $30,000 for every man, woman, and child on the face of the planet. This gigantic debt pile is divided amongst non-financial companies, which hold the largest share ($68 trillion), followed by governments ($63 trillion), financial institutions ($58 trillion), and households ($44 trillion).[7]

Why capital needs debt to function is easy to see. We defined M–C–M' as the circuit of capital. But these stages don't take place in a linear succession. Companies must "grow or die," and therefore stay in constant motion. Production is ongoing, as is the attempt to sell finished goods. So too then is the need for credit. If companies waited until all their goods were sold before investing in the next round of manufacture, production would happen in fits and starts. Given how integrated the economy is, this would cause the system to stall out. The sheer volume of investment that capitalists need to make is massive, and individuals or corporations typically don't have enough on reserve themselves to make this happen on the scale and in the speed with which they need to invest. Capitalists must therefore regularly borrow funds to cover the basic costs of reproduction.

FICTITIOUS CAPITAL

Finance capital—the sector of the economy singularly devoted to lending money—has thus always been a necessary component of capitalism. For as long as large-scale corporations have existed, so to has the issuance and centralization of loans in the form of credits and shares. The Dutch and English East India Companies issued shares in the early seventeeth century, and stock exchanges existed loosely in seventeeth-century Amsterdam and eighteenth-century London. Present-day stock exchanges like the London Stock Exchange and the New York Stock Exchange emerged at the beginning of the nineteenth century, alongside of modern corporations. The synchronicity of the histories of financial and industrial capital is not coincidental. Neither can exist without the other. Corporations depend on investments to fund their growth, while investors bank on shares of companies' profits, granted through interest payments or dividends.

As we know, capitalists invest money to buy materials, equipment, infrastructure, and labor-power. Workers engage in a production process in which we are exploited, our unpaid labor turned into surplus value for capitalists. But a section of capitalists take an alternate route.

Banks and other financial capitalists are capitalists that do not invest in their own production of goods or services, but rather *enable* production to take place by loaning their funds to *other* capitalists. In return, financial capitalists are paid back what they loan plus more than a little extra—in the form of interest. These payments come out of the productive capitalists' realized profits. In a sense, productive capitalists must share out their profits because they need finance in order to operate. As Marx explained: "The part of the profit paid to the owner is called interest, which is just another name, or special term, for a part of the profit given up by capital in the process of functioning to the owner of the capital, instead of putting it into its own pocket."[8]

While M–C–M' represents the basic circuit of productive capital, from a financial capitalists' standpoint, the process seems to be M–M'. Money is turned into more money through the mechanisms of loans and interest. But what actually occurs is an extension of our previous formula. Rather than

M–C–M', what we have is: M1–(M–C–M')–M1'. Here M1 is a portion of the total capital (M) invested that is borrowed from a bank. And at the end of the circuit, the M1' is returned to the bank in the form of loan payments plus interest. It is a share of the M' generated by the productive capitalist.

$$M1 \quad (\quad M \quad - \quad C \quad - \quad M' \quad) \quad M1'$$

Put in monetary terms, a capitalist may have $20 million in cash on hand to invest. He borrows $80 million from a bank to expand production. Let's assume a rate of profit of 5 percent and a rate of interest of 5 percent.

The values would be:

M1 = $80 million

M = $100 million

($20 million of cash plus the $80 million borrowed from a bank)

M' = $105 million (5 percent rate of profit)

M1' = $84 million

($80 million in the loan + $4 million in 5 percent interest)

The bank has turned $80 million into $84 million. While the capitalist, after paying off his loan, has turned $20 million of cash into $21 million. In this model, both productive and financial capitalists have an identical profit rate. What drives capitalists to borrow heavily, however, is an attempt to invest where their profit rates are higher than their interest costs. This can raise their returns above and beyond what they would have otherwise realized with their own cash. But when their bets go bad, they are saddled with a large amount of debt.

Marx explained the relationship between the creation of value and credit as that of FICTITIOUS CAPITAL. Fictitious capital is not real, existing capital, but *claims* on future capital. The value of debts extended—whether through direct loans, stocks and bonds, mortgages, or more complex derivatives, which we'll discuss later in the chapter—are fictitious because their *current* values are based on an assumption of the creation of *future* values and therefore repayment of the loans.[9]

In a simple extension of credit, let's say you lend your roommate $100 to cover the rent in the beginning of the month. You are then entitled to $100 from her at mid-month, when she gets her paycheck. But your right to this future $100 is "fictitious" in that it is based on the anticipation of a forthcoming paycheck. If your roommate should lose her job, or keep the job but need to spend her next paycheck on an unexpected health crisis, or if she's just a flake and blows it on slot machines—that $100 will never materialize.

On a larger scale, corporations may invest extra funds in other companies by lending capital or issuing credit. If, for instance, an auto company cannot profitably employ its capital to produce more cars (i.e. there is not effective demand to sell cars at a profit), it might invest some of its revenue in a growing biotech company instead. Thus *idle* capital—profits that have outgrown a corporation's internal investment needs—is converted into *active* capital, by investing in another corporation's production. This movement of capital is also what leads to a process we touched upon briefly in the last chapter, in which the rate of profit adjusts across the economy. (See sidebar: "Equalizing Profit Rates.")

With the development of the banking system, issuing credits and mediating investments among capitalists became the specialized function of the banks. As Marx explained:

> To put it in general terms, the business of banking consists. . . in concentrating money capital for loan in large masses in the bank's hands, so that, instead of the individual lender of money, it is the bankers as representatives of all lenders of money who confront the industrial and commercial capitalists. They become the general managers of money capital. . . A bank represents on the one hand a centralization of money capital, of the lenders, and on the other hand a centralization of the borrowers.[10]

One of the foremost early theoreticians of finance capital was Austrian Marxist Rudolf Hilferding. Writing in 1910, at the dawn of modern finance, he described the process: "Special institutions are required for this purpose. The collection and clearance of credit instruments is a task performed by the banks." Bills of credit can only function, he explained, to the extent that they can be guaranteed. There must be, he continued: "certainty that they will be redeemed; that is if their security as a medium of circulation and means of payment is publicly recognized. This, too, is one of the tasks for the banks. Banks perform both functions by buying bills [of credit]. In so doing, the banker becomes a guarantor of credit and substitutes his own bank credit for commercial craft in so far as he issues a bank note in place of industrial and commercial bills."[11]

Imagine the alternative. You go to buy a $300,000 home, and you arrive at the homeowner's door with a briefcase of $50,000 in cash and a note that you swear to god, you will pay back the rest. Banks play a necessary mediating role by guaranteeing that loan. They run you through credit checks, debt and income assessments, an assortment of hoops, and ultimately hold the legal power to take your possessions should you fail to pay up. With this small and gracious favor, they take on the risk of holding your debt—along with the significant economic benefit of collecting on your interest payments, likely for the rest of your life.

The same is true for the millions of loans that corporations count on daily in order to stay afloat. In facilitating and centralizing credit (be it corporate or consumer debt), banks play a "social" role of moving money through the economy. Finance capital ensures that money that would otherwise be sitting in a cash reserve is put into circulation. As *Financial Times* columnist Gillian Tett put it in her book *Fool's Gold:* "Money is the lifeblood of the economy, and unless it circulates readily, the essential economic activities go into the equivalent of cardiac arrest."[12]

Thus finance capital draws investment from individual or private holders, combines and depersonalizes it, and then extends it for use in the production process. As Hilferding explained, in order for sums of money to become useable capital, the following conditions need to be in place: "(1) The individual sums must be collected until, through centralization, they are sufficiently large to be used in production; (2) they must be made available to the right people; and (3) they must be available for use at the right time." In short, banks have "taken charge of the conversion of idle capital into active money capital by assembling, concentrating, and distributing it."[13]

As Doug Henwood explained, "The transformation of a future stream of dividend of interest payments into an easily tradeable capital asset is the founding principle of all financial markets . . . This enables a whole class to own an economy's productive assets, rather than being bound to a specific property as they once were."[14] Of course this role is a "social" one not in the sense that it improves the health and sustainability of any society, but in the sense that it increases the pace of capitalist accumulation. . . (at great social cost).

Financial capitalists, for their part, don't take on the risks associated with these tasks for nothing. They charge interest to make the extension of credit worthwhile. A bank provides a loan at a certain rate of interest to a corporation assuming the corporation will stay in business, maintain profitability, and pay back the loan plus interest. Likewise, a credit card company will assume that you will eternally pay back the interest on the debt that you owe. In this sense, credit extended is capital that may come to be but does not yet exist. (If it never comes into being, only then does the "fictitious" nature of that capital become plain to see, as it did when trillions of dollars disappeared from the stock market during the Great Recession.)

There's a deeper reason, too, why extending credit creates fictitious capital. Banks are only required to only keep about 3 cents per dollar on hand in cash. This means that for every hundred dollars you deposit to your bank, they can lend out $97 of it. Once that $97 winds up in another bank account, another $94.09 (97 percent) can be lent out again. In this way more money is generated than banks have actual liquidity (cash) to return, should depositors want to withdraw it all. As Marx argued:

> With the development of interest-bearing capital and the credit system, all capital seems to be duplicated, and at some point triplicated, by the various ways in which the same capital, or even the same claim [on a debt], appears in various hands in different guises. The greater part of this "money-capital" is purely fictitious. With the exception of the reserve fund, deposits are never more than credits with the banker, and never exist as real deposits.[15]

Lastly, an additional layer of fiction is embedded within what are known as "capital markets"—the issuing and trading of stocks and bonds. Along with direct loans from banks, businesses can borrow money by issuing bonds, or they can raise more cash by selling shares of their company in the form of stocks. BONDS are publicly traded debt. Essentially a company is borrowing from public markets by issuing certificates that it agrees to repay at a set time, with a set amount of interest.[16] STOCKS on the other hand, are claims to the total value of a company (its assets minus its debts, or "equity"). Each *share* is a claim to a fraction of the company's worth.

Like all forms of credit, the value of stocks and bonds are based on the assumption that the corporation issuing them will remain profitable and will be able to return the funds advanced (in the case of bonds) or pay out dividends from their profits (in the case of stocks). While bonds accrue interest rates that are agreed upon ahead of time, the value of stocks are only theoretically tied to a company's total equity. The stock market functions like an auction in which the "value" of stocks are estimated by buyers and sellers many times during the day based on their confidence in *future* streams of profits. Share prices are recorded every time a sale of the stock takes place, and thus fluctuate constantly as individual buyers and sellers agree to the terms of their trades.

The buying and selling of stocks and bonds in and of itself constitutes a titanic amount of economic activity with billions or trillions of dollars coming into existence (if markets rise) or disappearing (if markets fall) on a daily basis. The convoluted nature of these processes does not mean that fictitious capital is devoid of any substance or worth. But assigning a value to credit based on future expectations of growth creates the conditions for wild speculation. Moreover, as we'll see below, when claims on a future value are packaged up and used as collateral for further investments (i.e. your bank takes the money you owe, and sells that debt in exchange for a second investment), or is used to create derivative financial products, suddenly a whole façade has been erected in which exchanges can be made, and losses and profits booked, apart from real activity in the productive economy.

EQUALIZING PROFIT RATES

The financial system is the infrastructure through which money can move from one part of an economy (for example, auto manufacturing) to another (say, biotech). Through this process a rate of profit becomes generalized across the economy because of the effects of supply and demand.

As we said in the last chapter, auto manufacturers facing declining car sales may choose to take some of their profits and withhold further investments in the auto industry. They can take that capital and put it in a bank. They can invest it in the stock market. They can invest in a private fund. Regardless of the form it takes, the net result is the same. The capital is withdrawn from the auto industry and placed at the disposal of other capitalists either directly (through the form of direct investment or purchase of a stock or bond) or indirectly (placed in a bank where the deposit becomes the basis for loans). The capital is routed to an industry where the expected rate of return is higher.

The process represents two sides of the same coin. It is a reduction of investment in an industry where the profit rate is low and the increase in an industry where the profit rate is higher. And as we said previously, the result is a "cool down" of the automobile market, leading to rebounding of profit rates, and a "heating up" of biotech, or another industry, driving down profit rates there. As capitalists move their capital from less profitable industries to more profitable ones, profit rates equalize across the economy as a whole.

It's very difficult to simply shut down an auto plant and convert production toward biotech. It would require massive capital outlays, time, and expertise to build new factories and compete with existing firms. But credit mechanisms are one way in which capital can be redeployed quickly, and for capitalists to gain a share of the profits in a high-profit industry, without starting up new companies from scratch. The financial system allows for that process to take place in a matter of hours rather than years.

GREASING THE WHEELS

The primary role of credit is to speed up and expand both production and consumption. In our previous example a capitalist with $20 million in capital borrowed $80 million from a bank. In this way accumulation can take place at a much more accelerated pace. In chapter five, we discussed Marx's writing about the concentration and centralization of capital. He wrote: "The world would still be without railways if it had had to wait until accumulation had got a few individual capitals far enough to be adequate for the construction of a railway. Centralization, however, accomplished this in the twinkling of an eye, by means of joint-stock companies [a company whose stock is owned jointly by the shareholders]."[17]

Corporate debt is another means toward centralization. It expands a capitalists' ability to invest way beyond what would otherwise be possible with its available deposits, by using other capitals. In this case investment increased fivefold through the use of debt. Credit likewise maintains continuity in production by enabling capitalists to begin the next round of production before the sale of the previous round of production has finished.

Consumers rely on credit as well. If working-class people had to wait until we had saved up enough money to buy a new home in total or enroll our children in college, these things would always be out of reach. It's very likely that many of us would only gain the benefits of a college education and keg parties in the later years of our lives, if at all. Industries such as auto and construction that produce higher-cost goods would certainly go out of business. This is why every major auto company also has its own financing wing. In order to assure that potential buyers have enough credit to purchase their cars, GM, Ford, and Chrysler created GM Financial, Ford Credit Services, and Chrysler Capital.

As credit inflates the "buying power" of consumers, it necessarily speeds up the rate at which goods are bought. This increases the turnover rate of capital—how quickly the production of surplus value turns into the realization of surplus value, and then is reinvested into production. If it takes a full year for an automaker to make and sell ten thousand cars, this will limit the profits it collects. However, if it can do so in three months' time instead, it can turnover ten thousand cars four times in a given year, and quadruple its profits. In this way, credit greases the wheels of every aspect of production and circulation. German revolutionary Rosa Luxemburg explained this same process over a hundred years ago, in her famous pamphlet, *Reform or Revolution*. "Credit eliminates the remaining rigidity of capitalist relationships. It introduces everywhere the greatest elasticity possible. It renders all capitalist forces extensible."[18]

Of course, it's not just high-priced items that need financing to grease the wheels of circulation. As the cost of living rises and wages do not, debt has filled the gap. In the decade since the Great Recession, medical costs have increased 34 percent and food prices by 22 percent. A survey conducted by the nonprofit Dēmos in 2012 found that 40 percent of low- and middle-income households reported using credit cards to pay for basic living expenses such as groceries, gas, or utilities, because they did not have enough money in their checking or savings accounts.[19] This number has surely risen since, along with the average credit card debt per household. See Figure 9. Young people in the US are under $1.3 trillion of student debt. No wonder: the cost of college has gone up over 1120 percent between 1978 and 2012.[20] A 2017 study by Kaiser Family Foundation found that 37 percent of households have increased credit card debt to pay for medical bills and are racking up hundreds of dollars in *interest* payments on medical expenses alone.[21]

FIGURE 9. AVERAGE HOUSEHOLD CREDIT CARD DEBT

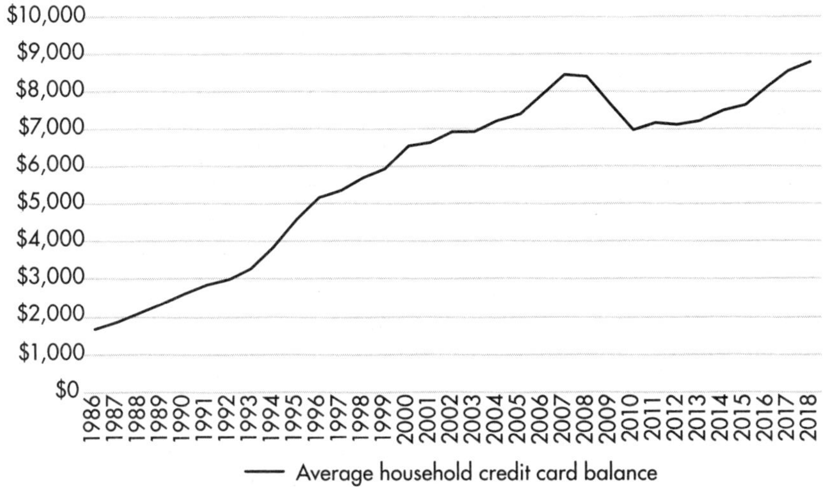

— Average household credit card balance

Source: Wallet Hub: "Credit Card Debt Study: Trends & Insights"

In short, working-class households have become increasingly dependent on credit card, student, and mortgage loans because incomes have declined or stagnated for the last several decades. Workers have been paid below the value of labor-power (that is, the amount of money that it costs to reproduce themselves and their families); to make up for it, the vast majority have gone into debt to survive. In the process, they—and their debts—have become deeply enmeshed in financial markets, as we'll see later.[22]

CREDIT'S SPECULATIVE ROLE

Greasing the wheels of the economy has an added effect of exaggerating capitalism's proclivity toward speculation.

As long as there have been markets, there have been speculative bubbles: trading of commodities at vastly inflated prices. The Dutch Tulip Mania in the 1600s is one particularly ludicrous, oft-quoted example. At the peak of Tulip Mania, in March 1637, some single-tulip bulbs sold for more than 10 times the annual income of a skilled craftsman, and bulbs were trading hands as many as 10 times a day. In the last 20 years, there have been a series of bubbles in various assets, all of which eventually popped with disastrous results: the Asian financial crisis in the late 1990s was driven by a collapse in real estate and currency prices. In the late 1990s and early 2000s a substantial bubble in technology stocks grew and then burst. Preceding the Great Recession, many countries experienced dramatic bubbles in residential and commercial real estate.

In a sense, all investment is speculative. Capitalists are never guaranteed a profit when they invest in anything. But the availability of large pools of credit allows financiers to engage in far riskier behavior than they would otherwise take part in were they using their own capital, and with larger volume. The riskier the behavior, in fact, the greater the potential payout, in the form of higher interest rates. As Marx argued, "a large part of the social capital is employed by people who do not own it and who consequently tackle things quite differently than the owner, who anxiously weighs the limitations of his private capital in so far as he handles it himself."[23]

Rather than profiting off the growing value of expanded production, investors buy or sell assets based on the expected direction of price movements. These assets may have little identifiable substance, such as complex financial cocktails discussed subsequently, but their "value" is driven by the expectation that they will sell at a higher price down the road to someone else. As economics professor Gerald Friedman explained in the pages of *Dollars & Sense:* "Unlike tangible commodities whose price should reflect its real value and real cost of production, financial assets are not priced according to any real returns nor even according to some expected return, but rather according to expectations of what others will pay in the future, or, even worse, expectations of future expectations that others will have of assets' future returns."[24]

Speculation can take off and snowball quickly because much of bourgeois economics rests on a delusional premise that markets will always expand. This was woefully evident in the recent rollercoaster ride of the oil and gas market, which we discussed in the previous chapter. In the years of the oil boom, production nearly doubled and spending by oil companies quadrupled. This massive expansion was fueled by enormous outlays of credit, and predicated on an expectation that oil prices could rise forever. As a result, the global oil and gas industry nearly tripled its debt from $1.1 trillion to $3 trillion between 2006 and 2014. Energy economist Philip Verleger described it as a "classic bubble" to the *Financial Times.* "It was irrational investment: expecting prices to rise continually. Companies that borrowed heavily when prices were high are going to have a very tough time."[25] The combination of high oil prices and cheap credit brought about by near-zero interest rates created, said the *Times,* a "potent mix."

The entry of speculators into a market itself plays a significant role in inflating prices. If, for instance, the tulip market of the seventeenth century only consisted of people who grew tulips, and shop owners that bought them for their flower stores, prices could fluctuate above or below a base value based on changes in supply or demand. Unfavorable growing conditions might diminish supply and therefore increase prices. Or a season of perfect weather might lead to a greater abundance of tulips, with roughly the same number of buyers, and therefore to a lower price. But these vacillations would be confined to a somewhat narrow range.

If, however, financial investors, noticing a trend in higher costs for tulips, started buying up more flowers in anticipation of continued price increases, they would be engaged in speculation. Their participation in the market would drive prices further by vastly increasing demand far past the tulip supply. This effect can easily snowball and create considerable price bubbles. As professor and blogger Lawrence Mitchell described it: "Think of the shape of a tornado. The productive asset—the asset that generated the revenue to pay the claims—was a point at the bottom. As claims proliferated from that point up, they expanded higher and higher, wider and wider, far beyond the capacity of the energy at the bottom—the earnings—to sustain it."[26]

To take a more current example, a real estate market that simply consisted of sellers of homes (who either built new houses or were selling their own houses) and buyers (who intended on moving into a new house) would also experience limited fluctuations in market prices. But the housing market has many more complicated players. Some investors buy up homes in order to rent them, and others "flip houses," i.e. they buy the property only for the sake of quickly reselling it at an even higher price. During the recent housing bubble, speculation played a significant role in creating a massive bubble.

According to the New York Federal Reserve's blog, *Liberty Street Economics*:

At the peak of the boom in 2006, over a third of all US home purchase lending was made to people who already owned at least one house. In the four states with the most pronounced housing cycles, the investor share was nearly half—45 percent. Investor shares roughly doubled between 2000 and 2006. While some of these loans went to borrowers with "just" two homes, the increase in percentage terms is largest among those owning three or more properties. In 2006, Arizona, California, Florida, and Nevada investors owning three or more properties were responsible for nearly 20 percent of originations, almost triple their share in 2000.[27]

Speculators play reckless and destructive roles in the economy. As Rosa Luxemburg explained, "[Credit] stimulates. . . the bold and unscrupulous utilization of the property of others. That is, it leads to speculation. Credit not only aggravates the crisis in its capacity as a dissembled means of exchange, it also helps to bring and extend the crisis by transforming all exchange into an extremely complex and artificial mechanism that, having a minimum of metallic money as a real base, is easily disarranged at the slightest occasion."[28]

Credit therefore allows for a great deal of speculation and gambling that has little relationship to production and the "real" economy. With it, the pace and growth of bubbles can be spectacular. The unrealizable expectation of an ever-expanding market, that someone will always be found to pay more, eventually hits the market's saturation point and the bottom falls out. Once it does, credit dries up just as quickly as it had appeared. Only at this point does the relationship between speculation and more systemic economic developments of overproduction in the economy become clear.

CREDIT FLEES IN CRISES

Credit's role of facilitating the expansion in times of boom also lays the basis for more dramatic crashes. Capitalists, we said, see any limitations of demand in the market as simple barriers to be overcome and "laughed off," leading to crises of overproduction. Credit further exacerbates this problem as it easily (at least temporarily) removes barriers to both production and consumption. And it hides any growing gaps between supply and demand for long periods of time. As Marx wrote, "The credit system appears as the main lever of over-production and over-speculation in commerce solely because the reproduction process, which is elastic by nature, is here forced to its extreme limits."[29]

On the other end of the boom and bust cycle, credit dries up when earnings start to shrink. A crisis of profitability will trigger a credit squeeze and further impede production. Following on the heels of the Great Recession, banks sat on reserve piles of over $1 trillion in 2010. The previous record had been set at $19 billion dollars in 2001.[30] No matter how cheap the US government made credit available to banks to loan through its central bank, the Federal Reserve, they simply wouldn't extend loans. Luxemburg wrote:

> After having (as a factor of the process of production) provoked overpro-
> duction, credit (as a factor of exchange) destroys, during the crisis, the very
> productive forces it itself created. . . . At the first symptom of the crisis,
> credit melts away. It abandons exchange where it would still be found in-

dispensable, and appearing instead, ineffective and useless, there where some exchange still continues, it reduces to a minimum the consumption capacity of the market.[31]

But we don't have to leave it to Marx and Luxemburg to make the case. Even the mouthpiece of the ruling class, the *Financial Times*, explained the role of credit and finance capital this way in an editorial:

> Modern capitalism needs well-functioning banks. Businesses and individuals need liquidity and an effective means of turning their savings into productive investments. But banks perform this function by making bets on the future. This is the purpose for which they exist—but it makes them inherently unstable. They tend to over-extend themselves in the good times and are over-cautious in the bad, exacerbating booms and busts.[32]

To return to the example of oil, companies that accrued titanic piles of debt during the boom in production were no longer able to pay the interest on their loans or take out new loans once their profit margins diminished. The industry, explains the *Financial Times*, "had a cost structure and debt burden that were manageable if crude stayed at about that [price] level" of over $100 a barrel. "Now the boom has gone, but the debt remains."[33] Just at the moment when credit would be most necessary to keep companies afloat, banks and investors sense the ship is sinking, and refuse to lend, for fear of getting stuck with more bad loans.

This process played out quite clearly, and explosively, during the years of the Great Recession. To set the context for how that crisis unfolded, we will first take a step back to see how the perfect storm of overproduction, economic polarization, and the monstrous growth of finance gave rise to the deepest recession since the Great Depression.

THE CAPITALIST FUNHOUSE

We can see that finance capital has always been a critical—if highly volatile and destructive—mainstay of capitalism. Yet in recent decades, the size, complexity, and influence of finance in the economy have intensified wildly. Economists have used the term FINANCIALIZATION to describe its ascendancy. In the words of economist Gerald Epstein, we are witnessing "the increasing importance of financial markets, financial motives, financial institutions, and financial elites in the operation of the economy and its governing institutions."[34] Indeed the scale of its evolution has been so immense that mainstream economic discussion often paints the financial sphere as floating off on its own, independent from capitalism's productive sphere and the process of accumulation, and as responsible for self-generating massive amounts of wealth.

Since the 1970s, changes in the US and international economies have led to a set of unique changes to the financial systems, which hit a fever pitch by the 1990s. As *Monthly Review* editor John Bellamy Foster explained: "The average daily volume of foreign exchange transactions rose from $570 billion in 1989 to $2.7 trillion dollars in 2006. Since 2001 the global credit derivatives market (the global market in credit risk transfer instruments) has grown at a rate of over 100 percent per year. Of relatively little significance at the beginning of the new millennium, the notional value of credit derivatives traded globally ballooned to $26 trillion by the first half of 2006."[35]

Deregulation and the increasing autonomy of the financial sector have created a series of smoke and funhouse mirrors, and intensified the tendencies toward speculative bubbles and financial meltdowns. As Greek economist Demophanes Papadatos explained: "The rise of finance was combined with a broad set of other practices: deregulation, direct confrontation with the workers' movement and unions, a policy favorable to larger mergers, and new methods of corporate governance favorable to the interests of shareholders."[36]

In the 1970s, what became known as the "neoliberal revolution" overthrew much of the regulatory structures that were imposed on finance in the wake of the Great Depression. We'll discuss neoliberalism further later. This decade saw the breakdown of the Bretton Woods agreement[37] and floating exchange rates, increased capital mobility, deregulation, and privatization of social benefits, such as pensions. All this provided fertile ground for risk hedging and speculation. Deregulation opened the door to an explosion of currency markets and a drive to "securitize" everything: i.e. transform debt into financial instruments, which can be publicly traded. This trend followed, but also exacerbated, a surge of consumer, financial, and corporate debt.

THE COMMODIFICATION OF DEBT: PHANTOMS OF THE MIND

Profiteering off of debts and credits has since become tremendously lucrative. While in 1973, David McNally explained, "financial returns made up just 16 percent of total profits in the American economy—a level that remained steady until the mid-1980s," by 2007, "financial gains had soared to fully 41 percent of all US profits: And because these profits derive overwhelmingly from loans, their stupendous rise could only mean one thing: mounting levels of indebtedness throughout the economy. . . from slightly more than $10 trillion [in 1987] to $43 trillion [in 2005]."[38] US household debt exploded to

130 percent of disposable income (income minus taxes) in 2007.[39] But while consumer debt doubled between 1980 and 2007, the amount of debt held by financial institutions quintupled as a proportion of GDP.[40]

The US elite was looking for a means to profitably invest their growing capital. This process accelerated in the early 2000s, as oil prices doubled, and individuals rich off the oil industry as well as governments of oil-producing nations found themselves holding even greater piles of cash, searching for an outlet. Increasingly, financial institutions handling these investments looked outside of traditional venues such as treasury bonds, where low interest rates produced too-low returns. In the 1970s, 10-year government bonds yielded 9 percent returns per year, by 2002, they yielded only about 4 percent returns.[41] "Everyone was looking for a yield," explained T.J. Lim, one of the early members of J.P. Morgan's swaps team. "You could do almost anything you could dream of, and people would buy it. Every week, somebody would think of a new product." [42] And so, capital investment found an effective channel in the form of packaging up and selling consumer debt, ushering in an "age of securitization."

New types of SECURITIES—financial assets that are tradeable—have been created that repackage any manner of existing debt. Basic securities include bonds: tradeable debt; and stocks: tradeable equity in a company. More complex packages allow a bank to mix-and-match. They can break up your mortgage, your neighbor's student loan, and thousands of other loans into tiny pieces. Then they create a basket with bits of each of these debts and repackage them into a new DERIVATIVE—a type of security or financial contract that *derives* its value from another asset. Derivatives include a variety of instruments, including futures, forwards, swaps, and options, some of which we'll discuss later.

Securitization of debt took off in the 1990s, and reached explosive proportions in the 2000s. In 2000, "the amount of debt Wall Street bought, packaged, and sold equaled $1 trillion . . . . Five years later, the number was $2.7 trillion, a 270 percent increase in half a decade."[43] The exponential growth of derivative markets was aided by the deregulatory drive of broader neoliberal policies. As David Harvey described in his *History of Neoliberalism*, "Increasingly freed from the regulatory constraints and barriers that had hitherto confined its field of action, financial activity could flourish as never before, eventually everywhere. A wave of innovations occurred in financial services to produce not only far more sophisticated global interconnections but also new kinds of financial-market-based securitization, derivatives, and all manner of futures trading. Neoliberalism has meant, in short, the financialization of everything."[44]

The rush to securitize debt thus took the concept of fictitious capital to new and absurd proportions. Claims on future value, not only stocks and loans, but much more complex financial derivatives, became commodities in their own right. Lacking any tangible qualities, and increasingly removed from any physical entity they may have originated from, these new securities can be bought, sold, traded, and borrowed against. As Marx laid out: "Profits and losses that result from fluctuations in the prices of these ownership titles [securities]. . . are by the nature of the case more and more the result of gambling, which now *appears* in place of labor as the original source of capital ownership."[45] [Emphasis added. Marx often used the word "appear" to signal that something different is happening below the surface.]

A first layer of debt-based securities is organized into COLLATERAL-IZED DEBT OBLIGATIONS (CDOs). These are bits and pieces of thousands of loans, packaged up and sold off to investors, who buy the rights to collect on streams of interest payments due on each of these loans. The resulting pools are then divided into "tranches," representing different levels of risk, and organized into different rates of return.

In the lead up to the Great Recession, at the heart of many CDOs lived SUBPRIME MORTGAGES—loans that require little money down and skirt credit requirements for borrowers looking to purchase a new home. But these loans incur steeply rising, high interest rates down the road. The high interest rates are a boon to investors. And slicing up the debts and bundling them into new baskets spreads the risk out to many investors. The expectation was that although it is likely that one or a handful of mortgages will go into default, if they are pooled with thousands of others, and then widely dispersed, the overall level of risk declines. (Of course, this only works if there isn't a wave of defaults, generalized across the business. Oops.)

Further, investors paying for the riskier tranches take the "first loss" position. That is, in exchange for the higher rate of return, they agree to assume the first level of defaults that occur, protecting investors in the less-risky tranches. Essentially, the chancier the loan, the higher the rates of return. Thus first debt is commodified, then risk, too, is commodified. The commodification of risk, and the tremendous rates of profit that could be achieved through trading it, provided added incentive for banks to push subprime and other unsound loans as widely as possible.

If this model wasn't problematic enough, financial institutions also came up with a product called CREDIT DEFAULT SWAPS (CDSs), which further magnified the damaging impact of these wild gambling schemes when mortgages started to sour at unprecedented rates. CDSs are supposed to function as a form of insurance; i.e., an investor that has purchased securities could acquire a CDS from another entity that promises to pay the investor its expected returns in the event that the security failed.

Say you owned a security that promised a $100 payout per month based on the monthly payments generated by the mortgages that were pooled together. You could then approach a third party and for the cost of, say, $1 per month, enter a credit-default swap whereby the third party would agree to pay you $100 per month in the event that the pool failed. In functioning market conditions, this seems like a great arrangement for all involved. The investor gets their $100 payout per month, but for just $1 acquires some insurance. The entity on the other side is essentially getting a $1 payout for doing nothing.

But the doomsday scenario of the pool failing suddenly means the entity that had been collecting $1 per month is now suddenly on the hook for the $100 payout it promised to insure through the CDS. This is exactly what happened in 2008 at great speeds, and the entities that issued the swaps did not have the liquidity on hand to make good on the CDSs that they had issued.

To make matters many orders of magnitude worse, because the CDS market is not bound by the typical rules of insurance, it became a playing field for mass speculation.[46] Traditionally, the way insurance works is that you have to actually own an asset to purchase insurance for it. So, for example, you are not allowed to buy a fire insurance policy on your neighbor's house and then collect on it if your neighbor's house is destroyed. (Such an arrangement would not only incentivize arson, it would also be disastrous for insurance companies who could then be on the hook for many insurance payouts from the destruction of just one house.)

But none of this was true for the CDS market. Instead, it was perfectly legal to buy credit default swaps on assets you didn't own. And, in fact, the value of the CDS market came to dwarf the value of the actual securities that were supposedly being insured. By 2007, the CDS market was approximately $60 trillion strong, despite the fact that it was insuring about $6 trillion worth of CDOs![47] The value of CDSs was also, incidentally, five times the size of the entire US economy. In a sense, every new layer of securitized debt seemed to duplicate the original credit in multiple hands. As Marx put it, "everything in this credit system appears in duplicate and triplicate, and is transformed into a mere phantom of the mind."[48] So when the market crashed, the amount owed by CDS issuers was astronomical and, in fact, so were the claims that could not be paid out. The worst in the field was the insurance giant that went bust: AIG. AIG alone had insured more than $440 billion worth of CDOs—about 3 percent of the total Gross Domestic Product for the entire United States that year—far surpassing the amount they had on hand to cover them. [49]

THE EVOLUTION OF MODERN BANKING

What has become of the role traditionally ascribed by Hilferding and others to banks—that of organizing, concentrating, and distributing capital? In their fundamentals, these functions have stayed the same, because banks' commitment to profit above all else has *always* guided the way in which they carry out their "social" role. The treacherous practice of pushing subprime loans onto working class and poor people in no way represents a departure for banks. They have found it profoundly profitable to thrust all manner of financial products onto sections of the population that were previously cut off from the system. And they have gotten away with imposing the highest interest rates on workers, the poor, and people of color.

Thus subprime mortgages have joined overdraft fees, high-interest rate credit cards complete with astronomical fees and penalties, and payday loans in a long list of predatory products, which are designed to sap income from the poor. Banks, credit cards, and other financial institutions prey on poor people with these measures, knowing that they don't have other means to access cash. As anti-apartheid activist Steve Biko once remarked, "It is very expensive to be poor."[50]

Yet, in the era of intensifying financialization, banks have increasingly turned toward further flung methods of "financial expropriation"[51] by slicing and dicing risk, and collecting huge sums from transaction fees along the way. Historically, commercial banks have operated as entities that "borrow short" and "lend long." That is, they borrow in the *short-term* from deposits of individuals (every time we deposit paychecks in our bank accounts) and from other banks, including Central Banks. And they originate *long-term* debt in the form of mortgages and loans. Because they "lend long," they have certain liquidity requirements in order to deal with day-to-day deposit withdrawals and their own daily activities.

Securitization, however, provides a way to circumvent this model by enabling banks to get their "long" assets off the books quickly. Rather than having a mortgage on its books for thirty years, the loan can be pooled, repackaged, and sold off. This process has the potential to be very profitable. A bank can make a lot of loans with little regard to how likely it is that they'll ever be repaid. Rather than holding on to the loans (and therefore the risks associated with them), debts can be sliced up and sold to institutions that specialize in the creation of financial instruments. Banks thus move loans off their books in short order, shifting their income stream to the quick fees associated with selling securities, rather than long-term interest payments from loans. Other financial institutions charge fees as well: a whole host of intermediary institutions and corporations make money off transaction fees every time these baskets of debt exchange hands.

At the same time, the process of deregulation, which let banks siphon off debts and decrease the amount of cash reserves they had on hand, also allowed for a proliferation of other institutions and companies accessing financial markets. Corporations thus increasingly rely on direct access to markets either by creating their own financial wings, or through SHADOW BANKS—financial intermediaries that perform bank-like activity, but are not regulated as banks. With assets totaling tens of trillions of dollars, so-called shadow banks account for a hefty share of the global financial system—half if you include insurance and pension funds, which similarly deal in financial instruments without banking regulation.[52]

As explained in the *Economist*, shadow banks include everything from "mobile payment systems, pawnshops, peer-to-peer lending websites," to "hedge funds and bond-trading platforms set up by technology firms. Among the biggest are asset management companies. In 2013 investment funds that make such loans raised a whopping $97 billion worldwide."[53] But among the most influential of the shadow banks are the ones set up by banks themselves, like STRUCTURED INVESTMENT VEHICLES (SIVs) created in order to repackage bank loans into bonds. SIVs were just another way for banks to off-load their riskier loans from the balance sheets, and increase the amount of debt that the bank could therefore take on. But because sponsoring banks were ultimately on the line to back up any liquidity gaps, when the debt went south they dragged the banks down with them rather than containing risk.

"These vehicles," argued one *Economist* writer,

> were meant to expand credit, and thus bolster the economy, while spreading the risks involved; at least that was the justification for excluding them from the banks' liabilities and allowing them to hold relatively little capital to protect against potential losses. Yet when they got into trouble, the banks had to bail them out on such a scale that many of the banks them-

selves then needed bailing out. The vehicles turned out to be an accounting gimmick dressed up as a service to society.[54]

While SIVs have faced some tightening regulations following the financial crisis, by and large the tendency toward shadow banking has only increased in recent years, as banks have worked to reduce their liability, and greater lending is left to the purview of their shadowy cousins. Today, the *Economist* continued, "the world's biggest asset manager, BlackRock, with about $4 trillion under management, is now considerably larger than the biggest bank, the Industrial and Commercial Bank of China, with assets of roughly $3 trillion. Before the crisis the reverse was true."[55]

Corporations, too, set up financing wings to get in directly on the financialization schemes. So, for instance, as a *Business Week* article noted: "While General Motors Corporation (GM) is having trouble selling cars, its ditech.com mortgage business is going great guns. GM's financing operations earned $2.9 billion last year, while GM lost money on cars."[56] Similarly, "when US Steel changed its name to USX (purchasing strong stakes in insurance) the chairman of the board, James Roderick replied to the question 'What is X?' with the simple answer 'X stands for money.'"[57]

The control of finance in private hands, in arenas subject to even less government regulation, aided in the proliferation of financial mechanisms and in reaching new heights of speculation.

THE ROOTS OF THE GREAT RECESSION

Given the staggering level of financial speculation let loose over the past few decades, it should come as no surprise that the house of cards eventually collapsed. Yet the roots of the Great Recession of 2007 into 2009 run deeper than the world of banking and finance. In fact, the recession was the outcome of two crises of overproduction. The first developed in the late 1990s in Asia. Unresolved issues of this crisis culminated in a second, even greater crisis a decade later. We'll see that finance played a magnifying and integral role in the way that these played out, but one that is intrinsically tied to the so-called "real" productive economy.

Marx argued that crises do not originate in the field of credit, but nevertheless first *appear* there. He wrote: "In a system of production where . . . the reproduction process rests on credit, a crisis must inevitably break out if credit is suddenly withdrawn . . . in the form of a violent scramble for means of payment. At first glance, therefore, the entire crisis presents itself as simply a credit and monetary crisis."[58] In other words, because the system depends on credit, and because the extension of credit both prolongs the expansion of production and then dries up when boom turns bust, it gives the impression that this is where the crisis begins. Marx continued:

> [The crisis] does involve. . . the convertibility of bills of exchange [extension of credit] into money. The majority of these bills represent actual purchases and sales, the ultimate basis of the entire crisis being the expansion of these far beyond the social need. On top of this, however, a tremendous number of these bills represent purely fraudulent deals, which now come to light and explode; as well as unsuccessful speculations conducted with borrowed capital, and finally commodity capitals that are either devalued or unsaleable, or returns that are never going to come in.[59]

In other words when banks come collecting on debts some of these cannot be repaid because corporate investments overshot "effective demand." Others are exposed as speculations gone bust or fraudulent Ponzi schemes.

Marx's analysis did not, of course, encompass today's particular alphabet soup of complex derivatives, which did not exist during his day. But the overall point stands: the 2007 to 2009 crisis appeared first at the outer layers of the economy—credit, financialization, and monetary policies. Below the surface, the roots of the Great Recession lay in an overproduction of goods and an overaccumulation of capital, itself the result of the neoliberal boom. NEOLIBERALISM ushered in a period of financial deregulation; but it also played a corresponding role in rehabilitating the system's profitability and heating up production levels.

Neoliberalism was the ruling elite's answer to the system's last deep recession—in the 1970s—of declining profitability, rising inflation, and slow growth. In one short decade, from 1973 to 1982, the United States went through three recessions. In response, a concerted restructuring of the economy along free-market principles ushered in a twenty-five-year-long boom that restored profitability with a vengeance. As socialist writer Lee Sustar described it:

> The capitalist solution to this crisis was to go back to market fundamentals. Economists like Milton Friedman, for decades seen as a right-wing crank, were suddenly promoted as sages for preaching deregulation of business, privatization of government services and "flexible" labor policies. Politicians like Ronald Reagan in the US and Margaret Thatcher in Britain turned Friedman's ideas into policies by smashing unions, slashing government spending and turning finance capital loose. The Clinton administration shaved off some of the rough edges of these policies, but basically consolidated what is now known as "neoliberalism."[60]

The ideology of neoliberalism thus served as a blueprint to attack the working class. Speedups, increased productivity, and declining wages transferred wealth from the bottom rungs of society to the top. Social costs were meanwhile passed on to working families through cuts to public services and welfare. The desired outcome of this restructuring was growing profitability for the ruling class alongside staggering inequality. Over the course of three decades, the wealthiest 1 percent nearly doubled its share of national earnings; while over a quarter of the population came to live on poverty wages, producing a society as unequal as the one which preceded the Great Depression.[61]

A heightened rate of exploitation laid the basis for business to boom again. And the deregulation that let loose the capitalist funhouse of financialization poured fuel on the fire. By the 1990s, happy commentators declared a "miracle economy," which would put an end to the business cycle. From 1991 to 2001, the US economy witnessed its longest-ever continual expansion. Gross Domestic Product grew, profits doubled, unemployment fell, and even wages began to rise—a miracle indeed. But the twin features of neoliberalism—economic polarization and deregulation—gave rise to contradictions that would implode down the line: overaccumulation, mountains of debt, and soaring speculative bubbles.

Rapid accumulation gave way to overproduction. This came to a head in the late 1990s, in what became known as the Asian financial crisis. A global glut of goods first appeared in Southeast Asia. For years the poster child of the free market, billions of dollars' worth of international loans and investments fueled high, export-driven growth rates. Overly-optimistic investors inundated the region with loans, vastly increasing the productive capacity of local economies but with little regard to the market's capacity to absorb the amount of goods being produced.[62]

Beginning in the 1990s, investment levels had risen throughout the region.[63] China's particularly rapid industrial growth in the middle of the decade tipped the scales towards overproduction. When markets proved incapable of absorbing the increased output, production started to slow—factories operated at capacities between 60 and 75 percent. Even so, the river of international investments kept rushing forward. But falling exports eventually led to defaults in loan repayments. When they did, the river of capital reversed course. Just as quickly as it had rushed in, and investors attempted to withdraw capital as financial panic spread.[64]

The crisis was global in nature. Much of the world was mired in conditions of recession or depression, as currencies and banking systems collapsed, world trade declined, rates of profit tumbled, and industry limped along. But the impact of the crisis was largely checked—or at least postponed—in the United States. Here the spigot of credit kept flowing through low interest rates set by the Federal Reserve Bank, trade deficits, and tax cuts to corporations. Essentially the market for commodities—both the means of production and consumptive goods—was extended as corporations and consumers borrowed more to spend more.

Piling up consumer, corporate, and state debts allowed the US to become the "buyer of last resort" of goods from other countries as well. Thus American (over)spending came to play a large role in pulling the world out of recession, propping up global production by generating demand. From 1997 to 2000, the yearly value of goods and services imported to the US jumped from just over a trillion dollars (at 2017 value) to almost $1.5 trillion.[65] During this time China's economy experienced an Industrial Revolution and double-digit annual growth rates. This in turn allowed a growing market in China to absorb output from the rest of the globe.

In short, US debt undergirded a global expansion of production and the realization of extraordinary profits, despite never resolving the worldwide glut of goods. The United States federal budget surplus was at its high of $236 billion in 2000 and flipped to a deficit of over $300 billion by 2005.[66] During those same years, a trade deficit also ballooned from $373 billion to $714 billion.[67] Along with huge budgetary and trade deficits, asset bubbles grew throughout the 1990s and 2000s.[68]

Throughout the 2000s, notwithstanding a mild recession in 2001, the engine of growth kept going, powered by debt. Businesses took in trillions of dollars of loans from banks and tapped into the vast "shadow banking" system. Working class debt allowed production to barrel ahead at great speeds, despite declining incomes that would otherwise have limited the market for consumer goods. Household debt during the peak of the boom was 120 percent of personal income. (By way of comparison, it was 31 percent during the post-World War II boom, and had climbed to 81 percent by 2000.)[69]

FIGURE 10. U.S. DEBT-TO-INCOME RATIO

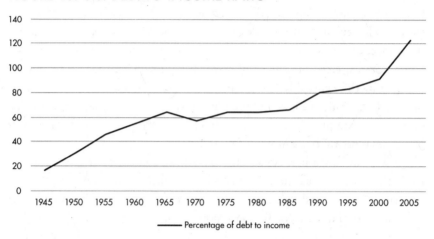

Source: Federal Reserve Board and Bureau of Economic Analysis

Yet even as the economy expanded through the 2000s, capital invest-ment in new plants and means of production was slow, as industries were still grappling with unresolved issues of overproduction from the 1990s. There was no incentive to build new factories while existing factories were still functioning at partial capacity. Even at the height of the boom in 2005, capacity utilization barely hovered at 80 percent, significantly lower than previous booms.[70] "Capitalists invested internationally or in high-profit US industries like finance and real estate, but did not pour money into develop-ing new production technologies domestically."[71]

HOUSING BUBBLES OVER

It was in this context that investment flowed heavily to a profitable housing industry, and with it swelled a bubble of extraordinary proportions. Low in-terest rates for mortgages put home ownership in reach to a wider-than-ever layer of people despite rising real estate prices. The low teaser rates of sub-prime loans helped drive demand. Working people were led to believe that property values would continue to rise indefinitely and that they would be able to refinance their loans before the higher rates built into subprime mort-gages set in.

Meanwhile, investor demand for mortgage-backed securities incentiv-ized banks to extend evermore mortgages, slice them up, repackage and re-sell them, collecting fees hand over fist in the process. Banks pushed these predatory loans hard: subprime mortgages rose from 8 percent in 2003 to at least 20 percent of mortgages by 2005.[72] At the height of the housing boom, between 2004 and 2006, banks, thrifts, credit unions, and mortgage compa-nies issued over 10 million high-interest mortgage loans, generating a com-bined total of $1.5 trillion of toxic debt.[73]

Along with the frenzied flurry of mortgage lending, the activity of spec-ulators also drove up demand for houses, and therefore their prices. Specu-lators used subprime mortgages to buy up as much property as they could. Because these loans didn't necessitate putting down much money upfront, they were able to continue to buy housing even while prices rose. Ironically, while poor and working-class people were being blamed for causing the hous-ing crisis through nonpayment of loans, investors were among the first to de-fault on their loans when housing prices began to fall. (See sidebar: "Who's to Blame for the Subprime Mortgage Crisis?") Because they didn't live in those homes, they had very little interest in holding on to bad debt. Investors were responsible for more than a quarter of seriously delinquent mortgage balanc-es, according to the New York Fed blog, *Liberty Street Economics*.[74]

While the bubble grew and grew, so too did the delusions of those that benefited from it. In 2005, at the peak of the bubble, the appraised value of homes made up 145 percent of gross domestic product. Just at this moment, Frank Nothaft, chief economist at mortgage company Freddie Mac told *Busi-ness Week*, "I don't foresee any national decline in home price values. Freddie Mac's analysis of single-family houses over the last half century hasn't shown a single year when the national average housing price has gone down."[75] Mean-while, David Lereah of the National Association of Realtors (NAR) distribut-ed "Anti-Bubble Reports" to "respond to the irresponsible bubble accusations made by your local media and local academics." Readers were assured: "There is virtually no risk of a national housing price bubble based on the fundamen-tal demand for housing and predictable economic factors."[76]

But a bubble it was. As it grew, it also encouraged heavier debt loads, as working-class people squeezed for cash used their homes as collateral for more credit, and banks went on a lending spree to take advantage of the superprofits being made. The *Economist* described this process in 2008. It is worth quoting at length:

An important reason why the American economy has been so resilient and recessions so mild since 1982 is the energy of consumers. Their spending has been remarkably stable, not only because drops in employment and income have been less severe than of old, but also because they have been willing and able to borrow. The long rise in asset prices—first of stocks, then of houses —raised consumers' net worth and made saving seem less necessary. And borrowing became easier, thanks to financial innovation and lenders' relaxed underwriting, which was itself based on the supposedly reliable collateral of ever-more-valuable houses. On average, consumers from 1950 to 1985 saved 9% of their disposable income. That saving rate then steadily declined, to around zero earlier this year. At the same time, consumer and mortgage debts rose to 127% of disposable income, from 77% in 1990.[77]

But this was an unsustainable state of affairs. Surging real estate prices and interest rates eventually put home ownership out of reach from the working class and undercut effective demand for new homes. As sales started to plummet, falling demand dragged down housing prices, and along with it home equity. Banks had dangled the prospects of home ownership to America's poor, and now came knocking down their doors for debt repayment. A tipping point arrived to turn bubble to bust.

You don't have to be a Marxist to see that skyrocketing real estate prices and stagnating incomes wouldn't add up to anything good. Analysts at Harvard University's Joint Center for Housing Studies described the state of housing in a 2008 paper. The paper is worth quoting at length, as it describes a classic case of overproduction, straight from the establishment's elite corridors:

> [E]ven lax lending standards and innovative mortgage products could not keep housing markets going indefinitely. With interest rates on the rise starting in 2004, price appreciation showed signs of weakening in late 2005. Investors quickly exited markets and homebuyers lost their sense of urgency. But builders had ramped up to meet the higher level of demand from investors as well as buyers of first and second homes, pushing single-family starts [construction of housing units] from 1.3 million in 2001 to 1.7 million in 2005. Just as housing demand started to abate, record numbers of new single-family homes were coming on the market or were in the pipeline.
>
>   With excess supplies beginning to mount and the temporary lift from mortgage product innovations coming to an end, nominal house prices finally turned down on a year-over-year basis in the third quarter of 2006. Meanwhile, interest rates on some adjustable loans began to reset and mortgage performance deteriorated as poor risk management practices took their toll. Lenders responded by tightening credit in the second half

of 2007, dragging the market down even more sharply and exacerbating the threat of a prolonged housing downturn.[78]

Thus an overheated housing market gave way to mortgage defaults and vacant homes, which then (as supply overtook demand) put a downward pressure on housing prices. Cancellations of construction projects skyrocketed. In 2007 alone, over 200,000 construction jobs were lost.[79] But as noted in the previous chapter, a significant time lag existed between the time in which the market was saturated and levels of production adjusted. This lag was exacerbated by layers of financial cocktails, several steps removed from the production of homes. By the end of 2007, the *Wall Street Journal* could report:

> Housing peaked in 2005. By early 2006 it was widely recognized the boom was likely over, and by mid-2006 it was beyond question. In June 2006, sales of existing single-family homes were 9% below their year-earlier level, sales of new homes were down 15% and framing lumber prices were down 19%. The Dow Jones Wilshire index of home-building shares had fallen 41% from its July 2005 peak. Yet throughout 2006, the folks who financed the housing bubble turned up the volume on their party. Issuance of collateralized debt obligations—investments that held heaps of risky mortgage securities and other asset-backed securities—hit $187 billion in 2006, according to Dealogic. That was up 72% from 2005.[80]

Inevitably the reality of overproduction would catch up with the delusions of finance. Mass delinquencies left mortgage fees, which had been at the heart of complex Wall Street cocktails, unpaid. The "fictitious capital," in Marx's words, behind mortgage-backed securities was exposed as completely toxic. Defaults on mortgages turned financial cocktails sour. As foreclosures nearly doubled to a million by the end of 2007, the "dominoes of debt began to fall," as Lee Sustar put it.[81] Or in the words of Marx, "The chain of payment obligations," suddenly broke "in a hundred places."

Demand for mortgage backed securities dropped off so quickly that investors were forced to sell them at a loss. The declining prices of homes in turn decreased home equity against which workers could borrow money and put a tighter squeeze on consumer spending. Writing at the end of 2008, the *Economist* described: "House values have fallen 18% since their peak in 2006. Banks and other lenders have tightened lending standards on all types of consumer loans. As a consequence, consumer spending fell at a 3.1% annual rate in the third quarter.... The golden age of spending for the American consumer has ended and a new age of thrift likely has begun."[82]

The hyperextension of debt and the inflation of the value of homes and other assets was a phenomenon that occurred throughout the financial system. It was merely at its weakest point—the subprime market—where the contradictions first came to a head. But the depth of the crisis quickly became clear. What began in the US subprime mortgage market became a global financial credit crunch, as capitalists were forced to reckon with the fact that assets of all types were overvalued. Stock prices crashed. Commercial real estate cratered. Over-indebted companies were unable to access sufficient cash. Many firms found that even funding day-to-day operations became impossible without the functioning of capital markets. The system itself was pushed to the brink of collapse, and only a herculean, internationally coordinated series of bailouts was able to keep the financial system from imploding entirely.

The multi-trillion-dollar bailouts came at a great price, through austerity measures forced on working class and poor people around the world. Meanwhile massive rounds of layoffs, cutbacks, and deactivation of facilities resulted in skyrocketing unemployment and a sizable drop in production around the world. The crisis created by Wall Street and financial institutions led to a devastating recession for working people.

THE STATE AND FINANCE

In the wake of the financial meltdown, states made vast sums of public funds available to the financial system in the form of bailouts, loans and, in some cases, nationalizations. In the United States, a $700-billion-dollar bailout of the banks known as Troubled Asset Relief Program (TARP) sparked mass outrage when it first passed. But TARP was just the tip of the iceberg. More than 30 programs overseen by the Treasury Department and Federal Reserve paid, loaned, insured, or reserved money to bail out Wall Street.[83]

The actual size of the bailout is unknown, since it is still ongoing, but estimates range from $14 trillion to twice that amount.[84] As Matt Taibbi wrote for *Rolling Stone*: "What we actually ended up doing was. . . committing American taxpayers to permanent, blind support of an ungovernable, unregulatable, hyperconcentrated new financial system that exacerbates the greed and inequality that caused the crash, and forces Wall Street banks like Goldman Sachs and Citigroup to increase risk rather than reduce it."[85]

The Treasury Department and Federal Reserve took large volumes of bad debts onto their books directly, relieving pressure on banks and other institutions. Shaken by the disastrous shock to the economy delivered by Lehman Brothers' (previously the fourth largest investment bank in the US) bankruptcy, governments made it clear that large institutions deemed "too big to fail" would be saved by the state. As a consequence, this also incentivized further consolidation since size has meant safety—encouraging strong banks to take over weaker ones.

Around the world, states mounted stimulus spending packages to help prop economies, but only by buying bad debt and shoring up banks. Public intervention to promote production and reduce unemployment was not mounted, nor were homeowners assisted with their debts.[86] In the US, the amount of money spent bailing out Wall Street could have paid off every mortgage in the country. Instead, bailouts, guarantees, assumption of bad debts, and pressures on state revenues resulted in a rapid turn to austerity measures as government debts quickly mounted. The cost of the bailout and recession was in this way passed on to workers in the form of cutbacks in state spending and payrolls, and reductions in pensions. Perversely, the same banks that benefited from the state's largesse began demanding higher interest rates in bond markets to fund new state borrowing.

In keeping with neoliberal principles, the US government rescued the financial system without violating the concept of private ownership of the system. In the wake of the crisis, when financial reform entered political discussion, banks and their lobbyists succeeded in dictating the terms of the debate, resulting in largely preserving the status quo. Capitalists that had railed against state regulation were perfectly happy for state intervention to prop up their businesses' bottom lines. Privatize the gains and socialize the losses, was the name of the game. As socialist Eric Ruder argued:

> Now that those investments have become toxic, however, the push for deregulation has been replaced—for all but the most ideologically blinkered—by the gospel of state intervention. "The goal is to get the engine of capitalism going as productively as possible," Nancy Koehn, a historian at the Harvard Business School, told the *New York Times*. "Ideology is a luxury good in times of crisis." The bailout of various financial firms and nationalization of the banks, however, is nothing more than a way to use the taxes paid by the working class to "socialize" the losses incurred by Wall Street's gamblers—ironically, the very same bankers and speculators whose multimillion-dollar paychecks are defended by free-market apologists as deserved compensation for their unique ability to make wise decisions.[87]

The trillions of dollars mobilized by federal officials to bail out banks following the financial implosion in 2007 to 2008 highlights an important point: the state is not a neutral body overlooking the social health of its population. Rather, as Marx and Engels wrote: "The executive of the modern state is but a committee for managing the common affairs of the whole bourgeoisie."[88] At times, this means letting the free market rip, at other times it means stepping in to prop up banks and industries. There may be tactical debates within the ruling class about which approach to take, and at times of deep economic crisis they may experience deadlock or uncertainty when the status quo become discredited. But thus far the ruling class has never found a crisis it wasn't able to get out of—by making the working class pay for it.

Governments use fiscal policy (government spending and taxation) along with monetary policy (the cost and availability of credit, in the case of the US set by its central bank, the Federal Reserve) to intervene in the economy. Central banks determine interest-rate policy and guarantee a portion of bank deposits. By dictating the cost of capital, central banks can influence financial activity. And by ensuring that depositors do not lose their money in the event of a bank bankruptcy, they prevent runs on bank deposits the likes of which occurred during the Great Depression.

In this sense, there has never been a truly "free market" that acts with no state mediation. But fiscal and monetary policies can only impact the economy in a limited way because the underlying principle of production and capital accumulation is unplanned. This was proven all too true by Ben Bernanke who in 2005 declared, "history proves . . . that a smart central bank can protect the economy and the financial sector from the nastier side effects of a stock market collapse."[89] Two years later, as chair of the Federal Reserve, he failed to do just that.

A TOOL FOR IMPERIALISM

Among the most important roles that the state plays in "managing the affairs" of the ruling class is to act on behalf of the capitalist class abroad. Finance is a central weapon toward that end. In "good times" the extension of credit is used as a tool for imperialist countries to control the economies of developing nations. Institutions like the IMF and World Bank are wielded to impose policies that undermine autonomous economic development and favor hyper-exploitative conditions to the benefit of first-world based multinationals. In the lead up to the Great Recession, many nations were in effect required to carry dollar reserves in order to protect their currencies. The result is a net tax on developing nations benefiting the United States as issuer of fiat world money.

In "bad times" states with stronger economies are able to impose devastating austerity measures on weaker states, as Eurogroup ministers have done in subjecting the moribund Greek economy to the priorities of Europe's bankers and bosses. Greece's problems originated in EU "rescue" plans following the Great Recession, which resulted in unemployment rates of more than 25 percent, a 30 percent drop in real wages, and a shrinking of the country's overall economic output by 25 percent between 2009 and 2015. Successive EU "bailouts" of the Greek economy have allowed European banks to get repaid, forced unforgiving austerity measures on Greece's already suffering working class, and delivered a clear message to other struggling European countries of what awaits them if they don't keep their economies in line.

Historically, just as finance played a critical role in the development of capitalism, so too it has always been a necessary tool for imperialism. Rosa Luxemburg powerfully captured the process by which the "Great Powers" used loans to subjugate colonies during the nineteenth century and destroy local economies. In *The Accumulation of Capital*, Luxemburg recounts the way Egypt was opened up to the ravages of European industrialists first through loans from Britain and France to finance the construction of the Suez Canal and to develop cotton production. "These operations of capital," wrote Luxemburg, "at first sight, seem to reach the height of madness. One loan followed hard on the other, the interest on old loans was defrayed by new loans, and capital borrowed from the British and French paid for the large orders placed with British and French industrial capital."[90]

The high cost of the interest on these loans was paid for through the land, labor, and tax payments of the Egyptian peasants (or fellahs). Luxemburg wrote:

> The greater the debt to European capital became, the more had to be extorted from the peasants . . . All over Upper Egypt people were leaving the villages, demolished their dwellings and no longer tilled their land—only to avoid payment of taxes . . . North of Siut, 10,000 fellaheen are said to have starved in 1879 because they could no longer raise the irrigation tax for their fields and had killed their cattle to avoid paying tax on it.
>
> Now the fellah had been drained of his last drop of blood. Used as a leech by European capital, the Egyptian state had accomplished its function and was no longer needed . . . Now British commissions to 'regulate'

the finances of Egypt went into action. Strangely enough, European capital was not at all deterred by the desperate state of the insolvent country and offered again and again to grant immense loans for the salvation of Egypt . . . With the financial position growing hopelessly desperate, the time drew near when the country and all her productive forces was to become the prey of European capital. October 1878 saw the representatives of the European creditors landing in Alexandria. British and French capital established dual control of finances and devised new taxes; the peasants were beaten and oppressed, so that payment of interest, temporarily suspended in 1876, could be resumed in 1877.[91]

Having seized control of the country's finances, military control was quickly to follow. By decade's end, hundreds of thousands of acres were taken by Britain as collateral for public debt. A mutiny in the Egyptian army provided a pretext for invasion. "The British military occupied Egypt in 1882, as a result of twenty years' operations of Big Business, never to leave again." Luxemburg continued: "This was the ultimate and final step in the process of liquidating peasant economy in Egypt by and for European capital. . . Stripped of all obscuring connecting links, these relations consist in the simple fact that European capital has largely swallowed up the Egyptian peasant economy. Enormous tracts of land, labor, and labor products without number, accruing to the state as taxes, have ultimately been converted into European capital and have been accumulated."[92]

United States' imperial ambitions followed closely on the heels of European colonialism. Throughout the nineteenth century, US banks floated unfavorable loans to Caribbean countries and sent in the Marines when payments were delinquent. In the early twentieth century American forces entered Haiti first through the National City Bank. Then when the Haitian government refused to cede power of its customs houses to the bank, the Marines invaded.[93]

By the time anti-colonial movements in the Global South won formal independence in the years following World War II, policies which had purposefully underdeveloped their economies and pillaged their resources ensured that new states would remain subordinate to the former colonial powers. The "Great Powers" had turned entire regions into suppliers of single commodity exports while systematically stunting or destroying the infrastructure for internal growth. When ex-colonies set to developing their own economies, they by and large had to request credit from the same countries that had looted their resources and subjugated their markets.

In the 1970s, Third World debt had reached nearly half a trillion dollars. And when spikes in interest rates made it impossible to repay the debts, the IMF and World Bank—institutions set up to serve the interests of the US and other global powers—stepped in to manage the debts. They did so by enforcing "structural adjustment programs"—loan conditions which typically impose brutal austerity measures and privatization schemes, and pry open developing nations to multinationals through "special economic zones" that exploit cheap labor. Along with these policies, "debt for equity" swaps have allowed creditors to claim assets or resources in exchange for delinquent debts. It seemed that colonialism had only found a new form.

Today the Global South is drowning in debt. Despite astronomical sums spent on debt repayments, their financial obligations keep growing. Large parts of their budgets are allocated to just servicing the interest on their debts. As David McNally described: "Between 1980 and 2002, the developing countries made $4.6 trillion in debt payments. This represents about eight times what they owed at the beginning of the period (580 billion in 1980). Yet, after making these payments, thanks to the magic of interest, they now owed $2.4 trillion."[94] The social cost of servicing these debts is in of itself a crime, leading to sky-high infant mortality rates and death rates due to curable diseases such as malaria and tuberculosis. Approximately 800,000 Africans died of AIDS in 2015. Meanwhile, payments to service the billions of dollars' worth of interest on debts continue.

Mozambique, one of the poorest nations in the world, holds public debt equal to 70 percent of its GDP. Over 60 percent of it is owed to foreign institutions.[95] The so-called "emerging markets" became a popular investment destination for speculators searching for high-yield returns. They readily lapped up a record of $1.4 trillion worth of debt from emerging markets' governments and companies. But when prices of commodities produced in the Global South fell, booming growth slowed, and speculators responded by pulling back investments and calling in debts. Economies were left in a tailspin, or sunk in a deep depression.

Of course, full on, old-fashioned colonialism still operates in the US colony of Puerto Rico. To this day Puerto Rico is under the economic and political control of Washington DC, without even a pretext of democratic representation.[96] Systematic economic underdevelopment has ensured that Puerto Rico has to import 85 percent of its food (mostly from the US). And thanks to a draconian law called the Jones Act, all of the island's imports are subject to a mafia-like shakedown before they enter the country, courtesy of the United States.

Following the Great Recession, Puerto Rico became known as the "Greece of the Caribbean." The extent to which its economy went into a free fall was prescribed by two decades of neoliberal austerity and privatization measures, and the racking up of billions of dollars' worth of international debt. Puerto Rico is unable to access loans from the IMF and World Bank, and instead relies heavily on infamously parasitic hedge funds, which according to the watchdog site Hedgeclippers.org, have swooped in like vultures "during a fast-moving economic crisis to prey on the vulnerable island." The watchdog site explained:

> Several groups of hedge funds and billionaire hedge fund managers have bought up large chunks of Puerto Rican debt at discounts, pushed the island to borrow more, and are driving towards devastating austerity measures. At the same time, they are also using the island as a tax haven . . . They are fueling inequality by demanding low taxes on wealthy investors, higher taxes on working people, lower wages, harsh service cuts and privatization of public schools . . . The spoils they ultimately seek are not just bond payments, but structural reforms and privatization schemes that give them extraordinary wealth and power—at the expense of everyone else.[97]

CONCLUSION

The neoliberal restructuring of the economy has led to seismic shifts in the world of finance. So much so that at times it has appeared that finance capital possessed magical powers to escape the limitations of the productive economy. If financial capital has become detached from productive capitalism, this raises fundamental questions about Marx's law of value. Can surplus value be created outside of production and the exploitation of labor? In the words of French sociologist Jean Baudrillard, money has become "utterly detached from production and its conditions," and we are experiencing: "The end of labor. The end of production. The end of political economy."[98]

Yet to pose these questions assumes a divide between the "real" economy of industrial capital, which engages in the production and selling of goods, but has little capital of its own from which to seed this activity, and of finance capital, which plays a purely facilitating role in circulation. In reality there is no hard line between financial and non-financial firms. Quite the contrary: the last few decades have witnessed an increasing overlap and merging of productive and financial capital. Non-financial firms have had greater access and connectivity to financial markets. "In practice," argued Demophanes Papadatos,

> borrowing capitalists typically possess some of their own capital plus some that they borrow. Second, revenue in the form of interest tends also to accrue to industrial and commercial capitalists, and it is not the exclusive foundation of a separate social group, such as financial capitalists. The separate and often opposing interests of lending and borrowing capitalists cannot be fully analyzed in terms of the functioning-industrial section of the capitalist class confronting the financial-moneyed section.[99]

Financial and industrial capital are completely interdependent. The experience of the Great Recession proved, rather than refuted, this point when the very real and concrete market for homes hit its limit and brought wild financial dreams back down to earth in a devastating crash. Still, the relative strength of finance vis-à-vis industrial capital has given increased momentum to arguments that we are in a "post-industrial" phase of capitalism, such as has been popularized by post-Marxist philosophers Antonio Negri and Michael Hardt; or that we are in a stagnant stage of the system, propped up only by ongoing investment in finance, as is the editorial line held by the *Monthly Review* since the 1970s.

Current *Monthly Review* editor John Bellamy Foster has dubbed this phase of capitalism as "monopoly-finance." He has argued: "financialization has become a permanent structural necessity of the stagnation-prone economy. . . . Stagnation and enormous financial speculation emerged as symbiotic aspects of the same deep-seated, irreversible economic impasse."[100] The argument goes that capitalists are no longer able to find a sufficient rate of return in industrial production and are therefore increasingly dependent on finance capital as a means to increase capital. But since finance capital cannot, in the end, expand indefinitely without a base in the productive economy, we are prone to both speculative bubbles and spectacular busts.

In fact, the massive investment in financial cocktails was the product of an *opposite* trend. So much profitability had been restored through neoliberal restructuring that capital needed additional outlets for investment. Since the 1970s tremendous material growth in production and output has taken place, most dramatically in China, but throughout other regions of the world as well. Rather than a permanent state of stagnation intermittently propped up with new financial innovations, we see continual dynamism and growth—at the expense of the world's poor and working class.

Despite the outrageous and grotesque growth of finance capital in the economy today, capitalism, as McNally has argued, "still depends on exploiting labor in workplaces—be it cleaners in office towers, farm workers in fields, data processors in packed cubicles, sewing machine operators in back street sweatshops, or autoworkers on giant assembly lines."[101] Profits cannot be created without the exploitation of labor at the point of production, even if large sums are traded and lost.

Financialization quickly generated spectacular sums of *fictitious* capital—promises of future profits—along with plentiful fees for the many hands involved in the transactions. The fictitious nature of this new capital only became clear when the value promised melted away, causing the bizarre appearance and disappearance of trillions of dollars seemingly overnight. "This fictitious money capital," explained Marx, "is enormously reduced during crisis, and with it the power of its owners to borrow money in the market. The reduction of the money value of these securities. . . has nothing to do with the real capital they represent. As against this, it has a lot to do with the solvency of their owners."[102]

Despite specific developments that Marx could not have foreseen, the evolution and explosion of the financial sector is consistent with classical Marxist economic analysis. Finance capital has surely reached a new phase in its size and strength. But its presence—and its seemingly mystical qualities—has existed for as long as modern industry. Many years before the days of the toxic alphabet soup of CDOs, CDSs, and SIVs—Marx could write about a "new financial aristocracy, a new variety of parasites in the shape of promoters, speculators and simply nominal directors; a whole system of swindling and cheating by means of corporation promotion, stock issuance and stock speculation."[103]

WHO'S TO BLAME FOR THE SUBPRIME MORTGAGE CRISIS?

When the subprime market went bust, the common trope from mainstream commentators was that poor and working-class people, who should not have been able to afford homeownership, irresponsibly took out mortgages that they could not pay back. Somehow we were expected to believe that poor people cheated or pressured banks to make these loans to them. A somewhat more oblique version of the same argument placed the blame on the Community Reinvestment Act (CRA), which was passed in 1977 to address discriminatory loan practices known as "redlining" (whereby banks would not lend within African American and Latinx neighborhoods).

Washington Post columnist Charles Krauthammer, for instance, wrote:

> Much of this crisis was brought upon us by the good intentions of good people. For decades, starting with Jimmy Carter's Community Reinvestment Act of 1977, there has been bipartisan agreement to use government power to expand homeownership to people who had been shut out for economic reasons or, sometimes, because of racial and ethnic discrimination. What could be a more worthy cause? But it led to tremendous pressure on Fannie Mae and Freddie Mac—which in turn pressured banks and other lenders—to extend mortgages to people who were borrowing over their heads. That's called subprime lending. It lies at the root of our current calamity.[104]

This line turns reality on its head. First, the CRA never mandated loose lending requirements or extortionary, rising interest rates. The problem was not that the goal of expanding homeownership put too much pressure on banks and the state, but rather that without a strong commitment to enforcing anti-discrimination in housing, the legislative efforts of the CRA could not go far enough.[105] Nor was it the case that subprime borrowers were necessarily too poor to afford to buy homes. Well over half of subprime mortgages went to people who had credit scores high enough to obtain conventional loans.[106] But more importantly even if they *couldn't* afford the loans, and dared to dream of homeownership anyway, that was certainly not their fault. Blame lies with a system that is based on low-wage and precarious labor, where people work hard all their lives, and still find that basic needs like decent shelter are luxuries for the rich.

Instead banks preyed upon the dreams of working-class people, and took advantage of their vulnerable and weak bargaining positions to drive millions of prospective homeowners toward subprime loans. This was not because poor people demanded risky, high-interest loans, but because Wall Street did. A ferocious appetite for high-yielding, mortgage-backed securities put pressure on banks and other mortgage lenders to turn over more and more high-risk loans. As Ira Rheingold of the National Association of Consumer Advocates put it: "Wall Street wanted the mortgage brokers to keep making loans even though they were riskier and riskier. They didn't care that . . . people were getting loans they couldn't afford because there was so much money to be made."[107]

Frances Darden, a disabled mother of three from Boston "long dreamt of owning her own home," reported the *Financial Times:*

> Several banks turned her down for a mortgage because she did not earn enough. She was starting to give up hope. But in September 2004, an advertisement in the local newspaper for a home buyers' seminar caught her eye. "It was so appealing," she recalls. "It said: 'You can afford your dream home. Let's make history.'" . . . She says the agent encouraged her to buy a multi-family property, where she could become not only homeowner but landlady as well. At that time, her monthly income was made up of not much more than $1,800 in disability payments, a small amount of child support and a modest rent subsidy. Much to her surprise, Ms. Darden was "pre-approved" for a loan worth $894,000. "When they told me, I couldn't believe it. But they said: 'We're different from everyone else, we can help you.'" Ms. Darden put no money down. She says she was assured that her monthly repayments would be $5,000 and that rental income would fully cover those costs—and put money in her pocket to boot. As it turned out, the repayments were more than $7,500 a month. The annual interest rate was 11.7 percent, nearly double the level a creditworthy borrower would be charged. By November the following year she had fallen hopelessly behind on her mortgage. One flat in the two-unit house she had bought was foreclosed on and sold. The other is soon to go to auction.[108]

Rather than being the culprits of the housing market, poor and working-class families were its victims, roped into predatory loan agreements with growing interest rates that could not be maintained on stagnating wages. And this was particularly true of Blacks and Latinxs, who had been kept out of home ownership through racist redlining policies for decades. When money was to be made off of this same population, racial exclusion gave way to "predatory inclusion," as African American Studies Professor and writer Keeanga-Yamahtta Taylor put it, granting access to financing but at unequal terms. "Racism and the economic exploitation of African Americans was the glue that held the American housing market together and would necessarily need to be overcome to fully include Black buyers in the real estate market. But inclusion did not bring an end to predacious practices; it intensified them."[109]

Of course it can't be said that African Americans and Latinxs were "formerly" excluded from homeownership. A 2018 study by Reveal News showed that modern-day redlining is alive and well across the country. An analysis of 31 million Home Mortgage Disclosure Act records found that Blacks and Latinxs are denied mortgage loans of *any kind* at rates far higher than whites in 61 metropolitan areas "even when controlling for applicants' income, loan amount and neighborhood."[110] The report explained: "The disproportionate denials and limited antidiscrimination enforcement help explain why the homeownership gap between whites and African Americans, which had been shrinking since the 1970s, has exploded since the housing bust. It is now wider than it was during the Jim Crow era."[111] In Washington DC, JP Morgan Chase granted 23 out of 1,119 home purchase loans to African Americans in 2015 to 2016. In Philadelphia, banks placed "nearly three-quarters of their branches in white-majority neighborhoods," keeping any type of financial service literally out of reach.

Yet where people of color have been able to secure loans, it has been at great and extortionary—subprime—costs. A study conducted by a group of fair housing agencies found that in every major city, Blacks and Latinxs were many times more likely to land subprime mortgages than their white counterparts with similar incomes. In greater Boston, for instance, "71 percent of blacks earning above $153,000 in 2005 took out mortgages with high interest rates, compared to just 9.4 percent of whites, while about 70 percent of black and Hispanic borrowers with incomes between $92,000 and $152,000 received high-interest rate home loans, compared to 17 percent for whites."[112] Cassandra Hedges, a Black mother of two explained: "One of the first things my broker asked me was 'How do you know you are ready to buy a house. Have you done any research?' We said 'No'. At that point I think he realized 'Okay I got some people that don't know what the heck they are doing'."[113]

When the higher interest rates that were built into the loans set in, homeowners were not able to refinance their loans, as many had been led to believe that they could. This was because at just that moment banks tightened their lending standards. Falling house prices also removed the option of selling their homes to pay off their mortgages. And when the rising interest rates of subprime loans hit, again, people of color, who were also bearing the brunt of high unemployment and declining incomes, were disproportionately affected by the foreclosures that followed. Black households lost between $71 and $93 billion of wealth through subprime mortgage payments and defaults between 1998 and 2006.[114] It was no wonder that those suffering from every end of economic disenfranchisement were the first to lose their homes.

Lastly, countless others could not afford to buy homes at all, subprime mortgages or not. An overheated housing market and speculation drove prices up beyond the reach of many. Think of the impact that New York City's "billionaire's row" has on the fantastically overblown real estate market there. While 59th street in Manhattan houses some of the world's richest people overlooking Central Park, two blocks down at 57th street, sleek glass skyscrapers are largely vacant for most of the year. They are investment properties for foreign capital. "If you put money in the bank in Germany, you're getting negative interest. You can buy an apartment in Manhattan and get exponentially higher returns. It has caused all this money to flow into New York," Stephen Shapiro of JLL's New York capital markets group told the *Financial Times*.[115]

In New York City, journalist Derek Thompson reported that "rampant luxury-home building" and the simultaneous "cratering of middle-class-home construction" has driven up the average price of a newly listed condo from $1.15 million to $3.77 million in the past decade.[116] By putting homeownership out of reach, most working-class residents are forced to rent, rather than own. This then has the effect of also overheating the *rental* market, driving up rents in the process.

CAPITALISM'S GRAVEDIGGERS

On March 22, 2016, the *Financial Times* ran an article titled, "'Peak Death' Might Not Be Enough to Save the Japanese Funeral Industry." Apparently, the last two decades have seen a "boom of activity for the sector" in Japan, as the population ages and graveyards fill. Sadly. . . *for the funeral industry*. . . increasing numbers of deaths aren't translating into higher profits, because the number of mourners have in any case halved. Apparently, the prohibitive cost of putting on funerals has decreased their numbers. As has the fact that fewer Japanese workers have full-time jobs, so the cultural convention of "duty appearance" at funerals by employees has also diminished. The *Financial Times* soberly reported: "Securing sustainable profit growth even amid rising mortality could become harder, say industry heads."[1] Capitalism is an absurd and irrational beast that can't muster caring about lives over profit. But at least the *Financial Times* has the decency to be honest about it.

As Marx and Engels wrote in the *Communist Manifesto*: "All that is solid melts into air, all that is holy is profaned, and man is at last compelled to face with sober senses his real conditions of life, and his relations with his kind."[2] Capitalism, we are compelled to face, is driven only by what is profitable, and this dictates every facet of our lives—and deaths. The profit motive dishes out material deprivation and ecological destruction. Our relationships with each other face deep alienation. A few make fantastic profits at the expense of the many, who in turn spend most of our waking hours in conditions we have little say over. We live in a society where every decision made by those with power is driven by how much money can be made. In a nutshell, "exchange-value" rules over "use-value." Profits, over human beings.

This state of affairs has been so normalized that we've come to take it for granted—if not as the way things *should* be—at least the way they *must* be. We go to work, we pay the bills, we go on with our day. Yet the insanity and brutality of it all can't but rear its ugly head all over our planet, our communities, our lives, every time a cut corner leads to breached levies that could have stopped a hurricane from destroying a city, or a mining disaster buries workers alive. Its ugly head rears through the billions of dollars directed toward speculation in meaningless financial cocktails, or Bitcoins, or other Wall Street gambles, while our public-school systems and hospitals languish in poverty. Its ugly head rears again, climate summit after climate summit, when no agreement with actual teeth is reached because it simply is not profitable to rein in an entire manufacturing edifice built around cheap and dirty energy. It rears again and again and again, when millions of poor people are sacrificed to curable diseases by both the pharmaceutical industry and the global industrial debt complex, which cripples state funding of public health programs. The list goes on, literally ad infinitum.

If there are just three points that I hope you'll take away from this book they're these:

One: These are not accidents. They are not isolated incidents of greed. They are simply products of the way the system works. Competition is the mainstay of capitalism. It can't be made friendlier or softer because it *requires* an accumulation of capital at any cost, in order to get ahead, or get left behind.

Two: These same processes of accumulation necessarily lead to contradictions that threaten the very profits that capitalists seek. Every contradiction for capitalism is both a great hazard to our lives—since we are made to pay the price—and also an important crack in the system. Every periodic crisis is a potential point around which to organize. If the system seems impenetrable, all the more reason to find its weakest links.

Three: "The point, however, is to change it," argued Marx.[3] And this too is the point of this book. Better understanding the system, as Marx wrote: "to reveal the economic law of motion of modern society"[4] is a critical first step. These laws of motion help us to assess the balance of forces, the relative strength or weakness of the ruling class, and their strategies for increasing their profits and our immiseration. But Marx had more to say about how the very development of capitalist industry not only concentrates capital in few hands, but also concentrates workers together into a force that can challenge the system. Capitalism, wrote Marx and Engels, creates its own gravediggers.[5]

For the first time in human history, there exists a class with both the interest and the ability to abolish classes and liberate humanity. This is not because workers are inherently heroic, nor because capitalists are inherently evil. Though our respective positions in society do set us against each other in ways that bring out truly heroic working-class struggles, and truly evil repression. But capitalists cannot turn a profit without our labor. Because the system depends on exploitation, the exploited are in a unique position to bring that system down. Workers (sometimes literally, sometimes metaphorically) have our hands on the gears of production. If we collectively withdraw our labor-power, along with it, we withdraw the means to turn a profit. Without profits, the system cannot survive.

This is why New York City transit workers were able to shut down the entire city when they struck for a very powerful few days in 2005. The threat to profits was so great that the entire political and media establishment went on the attack, jailed their union leader, and broke the strike.[6] In 2014, just seventy workers at Chrysler's Piston Automotive factory in Toledo forced their bosses to capitulate in a single day by going out on strike. Chrysler's just-in-time production meant that a strike by Piston's parts suppliers could have too quickly shut down production at plants across the country. So after unsuccessfully threatening the workers, the company quickly gave into their demands instead.[7]

Train conductors, Starbucks baristas, teachers, and IT workers—despite differing levels of income, education, and internet savvy—share a common experience of exploitation, and a common enemy in the capitalist class. Whether this shared interest and experience is obscured by cultural propaganda and manipulation or not, does not change the *potential* for unity.

Finally, working-class struggle cannot be wielded individually. I can't simply throw down my shovel (or my laptop) and go on strike, but need the participation of all my coworkers to effectively stop production. Nor can the goal be to win only individual gains. Taking home a shovel, a coffee machine, or a printer will do me little good, but the entire workplace, owned collectively by my coworkers and me could be put to use.

Of course, the *potential* to stop production, let alone to unite the working class to bring down the profit system, is not the same as having the actual strength, consciousness, and organization to do so. Quite a few significant obstacles stand in our way. Foremost among them, workers have been effectively divided through the manipulation of racist, sexist, and nationalist ideas. In the United States, racism has been the most important tool in protecting the status quo from a united working class, with its most recent, grotesque chapter manifesting itself in the Trump era. Racism has been weaponized not only to destroy the lives and families of immigrants, Muslims, and people of color, it has also been used to devastate the living standards of all workers by undermining the solidarity that we need to effectively fight and win.[8]

Working-class organization has also been physically broken throughout the last couple of centuries, whether by the police, the National Guard, private strikebreakers assaulting picket lines, or through the concerted effort of McCarthyite witch-hunts to root out socialist and radical organizers from the union movement. The challenges of building the fighting capacity of our side are great enough to warrant many other books and discussions, and are easier to see than the episodic glimpses of strength we've witnessed in the recent past. Nevertheless, the basic organization of capitalism pushes workers together to fight back, even as these struggles ebb and flow.

Working-class power is not an abstract concept of historical significance. Capitalism, with its immense productive capacity, has created, for the first time, the ability to wipe out hunger, want, and poverty. The fact that it won't—and in fact *can't*—is its crime. Only the working class has the interest and collective power to bring about a system based on wants instead of profits, by organizing the massive productive powers unleashed by capitalism in collective and sustainable ways. Though a thorough discussion of workers' power and the prospects for socialism is beyond the purview of this book, it seems appropriate to give Marx the final word:

> As soon as this metamorphosis has sufficiently decomposed the old society throughout its depth and breadth, as soon as the workers have been turned into proletarians, their means of labor into capital, as soon as the capitalist mode of production stands on its own feet, the further socialization of labor and the further transformation of the soil and other means of production into socially exploited and therefore communal means of production takes on a new form. What is now to be expropriated is not the self-employed worker, but the capitalist who exploits a large number of workers.
>
> . . . [T]he mass of misery, oppression, slavery, degradation, and exploitation grows; but with this there also grows the revolt of the working class, a class constantly increasing in numbers, and trained, united, and organized by the very mechanism of the capitalist process of production. The monopoly of capital becomes a fetter upon the mode of production which has flourished alongside and under it. The centralization of the means of production and socialization of labor reach a point at which they become incompatible with their capitalist integument. This integument is burst asunder. The knell of capitalist private property sounds. The expropriators are expropriated.[9]

THE CORONAVIRUS CRISIS

We managed to stop this book on its way to the printer so that I could add some remarks about the unfolding economic collapse. At the moment that this book was going to print, we were in the early stages of a devastating public health catastrophe, which in its first few months had already claimed a hundred thousand lives, and the economic consequences of which seemed to be pushing us off a financial cliff.

Rereading the conclusion to this book, I wondered how long it would be before the *Financial Times* would follow up on their morbid assessment of the Japanese funeral industry, which is still unable to revive despite truly "peak death." The extent to which capitalism utilizes profit metrics, but understands nothing of life metrics, has become unambiguously transparent to billions of people around the world. Barely a month after most states in the US issued stay-at-home orders politicians of all stripes started clamoring for dates to return to work. The system can't comprehend a scenario in which we prioritize public health for so long that it might interfere too greatly with economic output. Ultimately, every political decision is measured as a cost-benefit analysis.[1]

How many will have gone through the experience of losing friends and family members to a pandemic that could have been avoided, or at minimum mitigated until a vaccine was developed? How many will have bitterly digested the fact that authorities stepped in to save the stock market before looking out for the well-being of their loved ones? 2020 will go down as the year that the system showed itself to be utterly disinterested in saving hundreds of thousands, possibly millions, of lives. Capitalism in general, its US brand in particular, failed spectacularly at handling a predicted viral threat.

It's impossible at this moment to make predictions about the economic consequences of the pandemic beyond stating the obvious: they are already extreme and unprecedented. The exact trajectory of the crisis will be greatly impacted by the still-unknown biological timeline of the novel coronavirus. And while I write this afterword, we appear to be entering the beginning stages of a recessionary spiral. But a few points seem worth sketching out.

First, the coronavirus pandemic is a capitalist pandemic: From the role of factory farming in exposing humans to zoonotic diseases (originating in animals), to health care systems stripped bare by decades of budget cuts, to states and hospitals buckling under the pressures of bidding wars for masks and ventilators, to a for-profit pharmaceutical industry that has until now refused to undertake developing a general cure for the flu and its deadly variants, because while it may be *possible* it is not *profitable*. The state, too, has confirmed its decidedly partisan role as the "a committee for managing the common affairs of the whole bourgeoisie."[2]

The United States government took the most criminal of approaches. Despite repeated briefings in which analysts concluded, as early as November of 2019, that a viral infection could cause a "cataclysmic event," Trump and his administration dragged their feet for months. "It's one person coming in from China, and we have it under control. It's going to be just fine," Trump said in January.[3] With no nationwide response to the virus in place, COVID-19 spread to literally every county in the country. The administration finally stepped in to save Wall Street, and only secondarily committed a fraction of the bailout resources to Main Street.

The government may well get pushed into taking a few positive steps, simply for the sake of forestalling a complete social and economic meltdown, but so far their actions have been wildly inadequate. Less than 10 percent of stimulus spending is going to the health care sector. And the much-touted direct payments to individuals of $1200 will barely cover a week's worth of expenses for most.

Second, the working class will once again be made to pay—with our lives, our livelihoods, and our well-being. While the rich and famous were reporting their Coronavirus test results on social media at the outset, millions of people could not access testing, including health care workers on the frontlines of fighting the pandemic. State and local officials waited far too long to issue stay-at-home orders and close down schools and other institutions, leaving workers (particularly low-wage and frontline workers) vulnerable, and allowing the virus rip through many communities.

People of color, who already bear the brunt of economic inequalities and discrimination, are therefore inordinately vulnerable to the spread and deathly impact of the virus. Conditions of poverty, which disproportionately impact people of color, exacerbated the COVID-19 disaster: cramped living conditions that make social distancing impossible, pre-existing chronic diseases like high blood pressure, heart disease and diabetes, and jobs that don't allow for telecommuting and/or are deemed essential (as grocery workers, delivery people, nurse aides and nurses, and sanitation). In New York City, the *New York Times* reported death rates for Black and Latinx people were twice as high as those of white people. In Chicago, Black people account for 72 percent of deaths, despite the fact that they make up less than a third of the city's population.[4] The neighborhoods that are majority Black or Latinx are those that suffer most from lack of testing sites and available hospital beds, while those that make it to a hospital are then less likely than their white counterparts to be treated properly once they arrive.[5]

Though middle-income tourists and travelers may have set in motion the initial global spread of the virus, the virus is rooting itself in the world's poorest neighborhoods and slums, where it wreaks havoc. In densely populated cities with weak health care infrastructure, few resources, and no economic wiggle-room, entire communities may be destroyed. For years down the line, economies that already carried extreme debt burdens will be unable to access new lines of credit. They will suffer the simultaneous impacts of the disease and the dried-up funding to deal with its consequences.

Finally, while I promised to stay away from making predictions, there is one forecast I will make: the talking heads of the mainstream media and the Federal Reserve will get *their* predictions wrong. At the first sign of financial turmoil, the Fed swooped in with trillions of dollars into unchartered territory, buying up every kind of security—from US treasuries, to mortgage-backed securities, to junk bonds. The purpose was to inject cash into the financial system and prop up every major credit market. In response to the Fed's early actions, and despite the steepest ever drop in employment numbers, the stock markets rebounded and investors were giddy: "It is both shocking and almost amazing," said one investment banker to the *Financial Times*.[6]

But there was more to the stock market's wild swings than just elation at the Fed's giveaways. The early bounces were an indication of confidence among investors who thought that the economy could be turned off with stay-at-home shutdowns, and then simply turned back on again once the pandemic passes. Federal Reserve Chairman Jerome Powell gave a reassuring spin on April 9: "When the spread of the virus is under control, businesses will reopen, and people will come back to work. There is every reason to believe that the economic rebound, when it comes, can be robust. . . . We would expect there to be a fairly quick rebound."[7]

It's hard to know whether this is a lie or a delusion or some combination of the two. Even in an unlikely best-case scenario, in which we only have to contend with one wave of coronavirus infections, and can wake up one morning to safely return to work, the economy will not suddenly rebound. The dramatic scale of the layoffs in the first weeks of the crisis cannot be overcome easily and many businesses will have gone bankrupt in the process. Even those large corporations that survive the crisis, will come back online with much reduced capacity.

Supply chains have also been severely broken, unevenly and in many places. Some companies will find themselves lacking raw materials and inputs when they attempt to restart production. Demand too, has utterly cratered. The ripple effects will engulf much of the world economy. For instance, as auto factories idle across the US and Europe, demand for steel, electronics, and other components will collapse. And millions of unemployed people won't start spending until they find full and stable employment again.

In short, the scale of disruption to economy is hard to exaggerate, and even harder to imagine a seamless recovery from. Instead, we will likely see mountains of bad debt and defaults from both bankrupt corporations and among the millions of unemployed. As this happens, banks will call in their debts, causing credit to dry up. Just as in 2008, actions by the Federal Reserve to lower interest and pump money into the economy will not necessarily translate to banks making loans when they see no profitable rates of return.

In fact, the global economy was already on shaky foundations before the pandemic hit. The World Trade Organization is currently forecasting shrinkage of 13 to 32 percentages in global trade volume. But global trade growth in 2019 had already slowed to its lowest level since the Great Recession. Throughout the Great Recession's recovery, GDP growth rates as well bordered on stagnation in most advanced economies.[8] Business earnings slumped, corporate debt hit record highs, while corporate investments were historically low. Wage growth has been practically nonexistent, and millions of working families are saddled with more debt than ever. The country's pre-coronavirus low unemployment rate was based on the addition of poorly paid, low-skilled, temporary, and part-time work.

The contradictions that had set off the crisis of 2007 to 2008—economic polarization, corporate and consumer debt, and financial deregulation—were never resolved. Rather than a classic capitalist crisis in which bankruptcies and a destruction of capital give way to a recovery, and the most efficient capitals advance at the expense of the least efficient, the federal government bailed the system out. Central banks provided a multi-trillion-dollar lifeline to the financial system and to thousands of unprofitable companies.

Among the consequences of these policies was the growth of corporate debt to a record $13.5 trillion worldwide.[9] The stock market surged, in the form of corporate stock buybacks, but business investment and advances in productivity lagged. The "age of austerity" of the past decade meant that we saw too little fiscal stimulus (government spending), but instead witnessed a constant injection of monetary stimulus (tinkering with interest rates and money supplies). The heavily indebted corporations, the frayed global trade system, and millions of struggling families will not easily weather the severe shocks to supply, demand, production, and employment.

The federal government will continue to try more of the same policies, albeit with greater force and speed. The problem is that to the extent to which they have financial strategies (limited and contradictory though they might be), they have no health care strategies. The system is simply not set up to prioritize our health. Rather than fortifying a threadbare health care system or a nonexistent social safety net, the government is committed to bailing out climate-change inducing industries and financial markets. Capitalism is a system that revolves around exchange-values, and cares little for use-values.

Like other crises, the current crisis also exposes important cracks in the system. Because of its scale, and because of its life-or-death consequences, these cracks are likely to be more indicting than at any other time since the Great Depression. The next few years will likely be brutal, and will most certainly require struggles on every front for defensive demands: funding of basic medical supplies, tests, and hospital beds; and for offensive demands, too: Medicare for All, the expansion of social security and unemployment benefits, the demand to nationalize banks and make issuance of credit a social function, and investment in a Green New Deal, for the rebuilding of the economy on ecologically sustainable lines.

More than ever, we need determined organizing efforts alongside of a vision for a different kind of society—one that is organized around principles of planetary survival, human health, and justice. There is nothing easy or automatic about waging these struggles, but we know that the alternative is a system that fails us every time.

ACKNOWLEDGMENTS

Thanks first to David Bodamer. Dave and I initially conceived of this book together, and he poured countless hours of work into getting it off the ground. Circumstances led us to decide that it was best approached as a solo venture, but Dave's vision and clarity persist in the completed project.

Thanks as well to the dream team at Haymarket Books: Anthony Arnove's encouragement and support made this book possible; Nisha Bolsey's care, thoroughness, and incredible patience was heroic; Maya Marshall's edits made the manuscript considerably more readable and precise. And I am so grateful for the behind-the-scenes heavy lifts from Charlotte Heltai, Rachel Cohen, and Eric Kerl in shepherding this book through to publication with skill and finesse.

Daphna Thier and Amy Muldoon slogged through early drafts of the book when it was barely coherent, and their comments helped me move the manuscript onto a more lucid and accessible path. Paul D'Amato's thoughtful attention and engagement challenged me to grapple more rigorously with many of the book's themes, and offered innumerable suggestions that improved its substance and arc. Key pieces of the book are better for my discussions with and feedback from Paul Heideman, Michael Zweig, Meghan Behrent, Ashley Smith, Ela Thier, and Charlotte Heltai. Finally, Tania Guerra helped bring my vision for the book to life with her creativity, dedication, and humor.

When I first started to write this book, I was unemployed and childless. Writing a book seemed like a great idea at the time. Years and many drafts later I am neither childless nor unemployed and the idea seemed much more dubious. In short, I wrote this book about capitalism but under the confines of capitalism, and it was, I'll be honest, really hard.

I couldn't be more grateful for the tremendous support I received from my family. Daphna, Ela, Tzvia, and Uri Thier each provided countless hours of free childcare in order that this book could be written. My roommates, Daphna, Chris Dols, and Matt Swagler showed perhaps excessive patience with my messiness, grumpiness, and overall ill-mannered behavior throughout the process. And Naim, it seems, tolerated my behavior as well when we should have been out feeding the ducks or roaring like dinosaurs. John Jordan, Holly LaDue, and Maisha Inniss helped me keep my head above water when the discouragement set in. And finally, to every person who told me that they wanted or needed to read this book—thank you, it was those many conversations along the way that kept me on course.

Thanks most of all to my best friend, comrade, and partner Matt Swagler. Parenting and writing are both wonderfully exhaustive projects, and I found them nearly impossible to pull off simultaneously. Without his indefatigable support, and his insistence that we collectively make this book our priority, it would not have been written.

GLOSSARY

Absolute surplus value (Chapter 4): Surplus value created through an extension of the workday.

Accumulation (Chapter 5): The part of surplus value that is reinvested as capital (as opposed to consumed by capitalists themselves).

Bonds (Chapter 7): Publicly traded debt. A company or state can borrow from public markets by issuing certificates, which will be repaid at a set time, with interest.

Bourgeoisie (Chapter 1): The bourgeoisie, or capitalists, are the class of people who privately own the social means of production. Industrial capitalists employed workers to manufacture goods. Other capitalists employ workers to provide services, and finance capitalists, in the form of bankers and other investors, also play a central role in the capitalist economy.

C-M-C (Chapter 4): The circuit of simple commodity exchange, in which goods exchange for their equivalents, using money as an intermediary.

Capital (Chapter 4): Money that is used to accumulate more money. Capital's power of self-expansion derives from a *social relation* in which workers are compelled to labor and produce value for the capitalists.

Capital markets (Chapters 5 & 7): Financial markets in which long-term debt (bonds), shares of the company (stocks), or other financial assets are issued and traded.

Capitalist class (Chapters 1 & 4): A class of people made up of those who control the means of production, have political power, dictate the terms of other's working conditions, or own capital that can be invested in production.

Centralization (Chapter 5): The process through which industries come to be dominated by fewer and larger companies through the consolidation (mergers, acquisitions, etc.) of already existing capitals.

Collateralized debt obligations (Chapter 7): CDOs are debt-based securities that package up bits and pieces of loans that are then divided into "tranches," representing different levels of risk and organized into different rates of return, and then sold off to investors.

Commodity (Chapter 2): A good, which has had human labor performed upon it, satisfies a demand within society, and is produced for the purpose of sale.

Commodity fetishism (Chapter 2): Real social relations of production and exchange in capitalist society are hidden behind a veil of what appears to be a relationship between money and commodities.

Concentration (Chapter 5): The process of a company growing through time, by way of accumulation.

Constant capital (Chapter 4): Capital invested in the means of production. Its value reappears in the commodities produced. This value is transmitted as is through the production process.

Credit default swaps (Chapter 7): CDSs function as a form of insurance on securities. They are purchased from a third entity that promises to pay the investor its expected returns in the event that the security fails.

Dead labor (Chapter 2): Previous generations of labor, which carry past value into the process of production.

Derivatives (Chapter 7): Types of securities or financial contracts (e.g. futures, forwards, swaps, and options) that derive their value from another asset or set of assets (e.g. stocks, bonds, currencies, or commodities).

Economies of scale (Chapter 5): Cost advantages gained by businesses through operational efficiencies and economic leverages associated with an increased scale of production.

Equivalent value (Chapter 3): An equivalent value provides a measurement for some other good's value.

Exchange-value (Chapter 2): The quantitative aspect of value: the ratio with which one commodity exchanges for other commodities.

Fictitious capital (Chapter 7): Claims on future capital, which are "fictitious" in that their current values are based on expectations of future values.

Financialization (Chapter 7): A process in which financial markets and in·stitutions have grown in size, complexity, and influence.

Gold standard (Chapter 3): A system in which major currencies around the world were fixed against, and could ultimately be redeemed for, their worth in gold. It resulted in fixed exchange rates between currencies, since they were all measured against gold.

Great Recession (Introduction & Chapter 7): The economic crisis of 2007 into 2009 was the longest and deepest crisis in the United States since the Great Depression. It began with a collapse of a giant housing bubble followed by a stock market crash, the failure of the largest US investment banks, plummeting commodity prices, freezing of credit, and slowing international trade.

Human labor in the abstract (Chapter 2): Quantities of generalized labor; i.e. not *what kind* of labor went into making something, rather *how much* of it was required.

Inflation (Chapter 3): Inflation describes a situation in which prices of commodities rise. It can have many causes, but always reflects a fall in the value of money (against which commodities' prices are measured). Each monetary unit can thus buy fewer goods than it used to.

Labor-power (Chapter 4): The ability to work, sold to the capitalist for an agreed upon amount of time.

Labor theory of value (Chapter 2): A commodity's value is measured by the amount of generalized (or "abstract") labor socially necessary to its production.

Living labor (Chapter 2): Human labor engaged in the production of a commodity.

M-C-M' (Chapter 4): The circuit of capital: money is invested in the production of commodities, which are sold on the market and result in a greater sum of money. Rather than money serving an *intermediary* role, the expansion of money is the *driver* of the process.

Manufacture (Chapter 1): A system of production where groups of workers are assembled under one roof with machinery and raw materials, supervised, and paid a wage to construct commodities.

Means of production (Chapters 1 & 4): Tools and materials necessary for production (e.g. factories, office buildings, land, machinery, IT infrastructure, and so on).

Middle class (Chapters 1 & 4): A layer of society that stands between the working class and the capitalist class. It includes small business owners, as well as middle managers, supervisors, and professional occupations that have a fair amount of autonomy at their jobs.

Monopoly (Chapter 5): A lone company that dominates its market. Pure monopolies are rare, but monopolistic tendencies and practices, whereby large companies take advantage of their preeminent positions, are common.

Moral depreciation (Chapter 4): A machine loses value when newer machines are produced more cheaply. Its value is measured by the socially necessary labor-time that would now be needed to produce it, not the original labor-time objectified within it.

Necessary labor (Chapter 4): The part of the workday required to reproduce the cost of labor-power.

Neoliberalism (Chapter 7): The ideology and policies associated with free market liberalization: privatization, speedups, increased productivity, and deregulation.

Oligopoly (Chapter 5): A market dominated by a handful of companies.

Organic composition of capital (Chapter 6): The ratio of the value invested in constant capital to the value invested in variable capital: c/v.

Overaccumulation (Chapter 6): When capitalists cannot find a profitable outlet to invest their surplus. This leads to unused capacity in the form of idle factories, machinery, etc.

Overproduction (Chapter 6): When supply outpaces demand. If this occurs in key industries and is generalized across the economy, it results in a "crisis of overproduction."

Price (Chapter 3): The ratio between a given quantity of a commodity and its equivalent in money.

Proletarians (Chapters 1 & 4): Proletarians, or workers, are the class of people who must sell their labor-power for a wage.

Rate of exploitation (Chapter 4): See "rate of surplus value."

Rate of profit (Chapter 4): The ratio of surplus value to the total amount of capital invested: $s/(c+v)$.

Rate of surplus value (Chapter 4): The ratio of surplus value to variable capital (s/v). That is the amount of extra value pocketed by capitalists relative to capital investment in labor-power. It expresses the degree of exploitation of labor-power by capital (and is therefore synonymous with a "rate of exploitation").

Relative surplus value (Chapter 4): Surplus value created by shortening the amount of time necessary to produce the equivalent of the workers' wages.

Relative value (Chapter 3): A value that is being determined relative to another value.

Reserve army of laborers (or surplus population) (Chapter 4): Unemployed people. Unemployment is a necessity for capital, which uses it as a tool to discipline the paid workforce through the threat of being easily replaced.

Securities (Chapter 7): Tradable financial assets.

Shadow banks (Chapter 7): Financial intermediaries that perform bank-like activity, but are not regulated as banks.

Social reproduction (Chapter 4): The daily and generational reproduction of class relations via the maintenance of the capitalist class and the working class.

Socially necessary labor-time (Chapter 2): The average amount of time that it takes to produce a commodity, using the common tools and technology available in a given society.

Stocks (Chapter 7): Claims to the total value of a company (its assets minus its debts, or "equity"). Each *share* is a claim to a fraction of the company's worth.

Structured investment vehicles (Chapter 7): SIVs are non-bank financial institutions often created by banks offshore in order to avoid taxes and regulation. They give sponsoring banks the ability to invest in securities, without having to keep the riskier loans on their balance sheets. Money for investments are raised through borrowing funds from investors, but their sponsoring banks are on the line to back up any liquidity gaps if the SIVs are not able to raise enough through loans.

Subprime mortgages (Chapter 7): Mortgage loans that require little money down and skirt credit requirements for borrowers looking to purchase a home.

These loans incur steeply rising high interest rates when the loans "reset" down the road.

Surplus labor (Chapter 4): The part of the workday that produces additional value once the value of workers' labor-power has been reproduced.

Surplus value (Chapter 4): Accumulated product of the unpaid labor-time of workers (see "surplus labor").

Tendency for the rate of profit to fall (Chapter 6): A historic tendency for the rate of profit to fall as a result of the growing productivity of labor (reflected in a rising organic composition of capital). As capitalists employ less labor and invest more in machinery, the part of the investment that generates *new, added* value drops. That is, the surplus value per unit of capital falls.

Turnover rate of capital (Chapter 6): The time that elapses between the investment of capital towards the production process, and when the produced goods are sold. The faster the speed in which invested capital becomes sold, the more rounds of production can happen within a given span of time.

Universal equivalent (Chapter 3): A universal equivalent is a commodity against which all other commodities are measured.

Use-value (Chapter 2): The qualitative aspect of value: how it is used. The item itself could also be called a "use-value" to refer to it as an item of want. E.g. the use-value of bread is that it provides nourishment. But you could also call bread a "use-value" because people want or need bread.

Variable capital (Chapter 4): Capital invested in labor-power, which reproduces the equivalent of labor-power itself, and also produces an excess surplus value.

Working class (Chapters 1 & 4): A class of people made up of anyone that must sell their labor in order to work and has no access to the means of production themselves.

FURTHER READING

ECONOMICS

Karl Marx, *Capital*, Volumes 1–3

David Harvey, *A Companion to Marx's Capital*, Volumes 1–2

Ben Fine and Alfredo Saad-Filho, *Marx's Capital*

Ernest Mandel, *Marxist Economic Theory*, Volumes 1–2

Simon Clarke, *Marx's Theory of Crisis*

David Smith and Phil Evans, *Marx's Capital Illustrated: An Illustrated Introduction*

David McNally, *Global Slump: The Economics and Politics of Crisis and Resistance*

INTRODUCTION TO SOCIALISM AND MARXISM

Karl Marx and Frederick Engels, *The Communist Manifesto*

Friedrich Engels, *Socialism: Utopian and Scientific*

Rosa Luxemburg, *Reform or Revolution?*

Danny Katch, *Socialism. . . Seriously: A Brief Guide to Human Liberation*

Bhaskar Sunkara, *The Socialist Manifesto: The Case for Radical Politics in an Era of Extreme Inequality*

Bhaskar Sunkara (ed.), *The ABCs of Socialism*

Vivek Chibber, *The ABCs of Capitalism*

Paul D'Amato, *The Meaning of Marxism*

MARXISM AND OPPRESSION

Keeanga-Yamahtta Taylor, *From #BlackLivesMatter to Black Liberation*

Sherry Wolf, *Sexuality and Socialism: History, Politics, and Theory of LGBT Liberation*

Deepa Kumar, *Islamophobia and the Politics of Empire*

Cinzia Arruzza, Tithi Bhattacharya, and Nancy Fraser, *Feminism for the 99%: A Manifesto*

Justin Akers Chacón and Mike Davis, *No One is Illegal: Fighting Racism and State Violence on the US-Mexico Border*

MARXISM AND ECOLOGY

Chris Williams, *Ecology and Socialism: Solutions to Capitalist Ecological Crisis*

John Bellamy Foster, *Marx's Ecology: Materialism and Nature*

Paul Burkett, *Marx and Nature: A Red and Green Perspective*

Michael Löwy, *Ecosocialism: A Radical Alternative to Capitalist Catastrophe*

THE US WORKING CLASS

Howard Zinn, *A People's History of the United States*

Kim Moody, *An Injury to All:* The Decline of American Unionism

Kim Moody, *On New Terrain: How Capital Is Reshaping the Battleground of Class War*

Michael Zweig, *The Working-Class Majority: America's Best Kept Secret*

Sidney Lens, *The Labor Wars: From the Molly Maguires to the Sit Downs*

Jeremy Brecher, *Strike!*

Art Preis, *Labor's Giant Step: The First Twenty Years of the CIO: 1936–55*

Alice and Staughton Lynd, *Rank and File: Personal Histories by Working-Class Organizers*

NOTES

INTRODUCTION

1. Lorena Mongelli, Julia Marsh, and Carl Campanile, "Former Top Nurse at Jacobi, Worried about Lack of Testing, Dies of Coronavirus," *New York Post,* March 30, 2020, https://nypost.com/2020/03/30/former -head-nurse-of-jacobi-medical-center-psychiatric-unit-dies-of-coronavirus/.
2. Arundhati Roy, "The Pandemic Is a Portal," *Financial Times,* April 3, 2020, https://www.ft.com/content/10d8f5e8-74eb-11ea-95fe-fcd274e920ca.
3. See Rob Wallace, *Big Farms Make Big Flu: Dispatches on Infectious Disease, Agribusiness, and the Nature of Science* (New York: Monthly Review Press, 2016).
4. Roy, "The Pandemic is a Portal."
5. Board of Governors of the Federal Reserve System, "Distribution of Household Wealth in the US."
6. Christopher Ingraham, "The Richest 1 Percent Now Owns More of the Country's Wealth than at Any Time in the Past 50 years," *Washington Post,* December 6, 2017. Danielle Kurtzleben, "Middle Class Households' Wealth Fell 35 Percent from 2005 to 2011," *Vox,* August 23, 2014.
7. Samuel Brannen, Christian Stirling Haig, Katherine Schmidt, "The Age of Mass Protests: Understanding an Escalating Global Trend," Center for Strategic & International Studies, March 2, 2020, https://www.csis.org/analysis /age-mass-protests-understanding-escalating-global-trend.
8. Frank Newport, "Democrats More Positive About Socialism Than Capitalism," Gallup, August 13, 2018.
9. David Cecere, "New Study finds 45,000 Deaths Annually Linked to Lack of Health Coverage," *Harvard Gazette,* September 17, 2009.
10. Eric Holt-Gimenez, "Malnutrition in Children" UNICEF Data, April 2019; and "We Already Grow Enough Food For 10 Billion People—and Still Can't End Hunger," December 18, 2014.
11. Bhaskar Sunkara, *The Socialist Manifesto: The Case for Radical Politics in an Era of Extreme Inequality,* (New York, NY: Basic Books, 2019), 49.
12. Karl Marx, *Capital: A Critique of Political Economy,* vol. 1 (New York: Penguin, 1990), 17.
13. Marx, *Capital,* vol. 1, 90.

14. We'll see throughout the book that when Marx talks about how something *appears*, he is usually making a point about underlying reality being different than appearance.
15. Marx, *Capital*, vol. 1, 876.
16. Marx, *Capital*, vol. 1, 104.

CHAPTER ONE: THE BIRTH OF CAPITAL

1. Marx, *Capital*, vol. 1, 925–926.
2. Will Wilkinson, "Capitalism and Human Nature," *Cato Policy Report* 27, no. 1 (January/February 2005), 13.
3. We'll discuss classes in future chapters, but broadly defined, they are social groups with different relationships to the production and distribution of society's wealth.
4. See Eleanor Burke Leacock, *Myths of Male Dominance* (New York: Monthly Review Press, 1981). Chris Harman also provides a broad overview of the origins of class society in: "Engels and the Origins of Human Society," *International Socialism* 2, no. 65 (winter 1994). It is based on (and seeks to update) Engels's seminal work, *The Origin of the Family, Private Property, and the State* (London: Penguin Classics, 2010).
5. Leacock, *Myths*, 139.
6. Quoted in Leacock, *Myths*, 49.
7. The British Marxist Chris Harman summarized this point: "Such groups could not keep the surplus in their own hands at times when the whole of society was suffering great hardship unless they found ways of imposing their will on the rest of society, unless they established coercive structures, states, and legal codes and ideologies to back them up. But once such structures and such ideologies were in existence, they would perpetuate the control of the surplus by a certain group even when it no longer served the purpose of advancing production. A class which emerged as a spur to production would persist even when it was no longer such a spur." Harman, "Engels and the Origins of Human Society," *International Socialism* 2, no. 65, (winter 1994).
8. This long and complex history is outside the purview of what can be explained in a few short sentences here. A good summary can be found in Harman, "Engels and the Origins of Human Society," *International Socialism* 2, no. 65, (winter 1994). See also James Scott, *Against the Grain* (New Haven: Yale University Press, 2017) for a fuller account.
9. Much of the debate revolves around what newly defined capitalism as against feudalism and which elements of the transition—the development of productive forces within feudalism, agrarian class struggle, the emergence of an international market—drove the process forward. A short introduction can be found within a brief debate: Paul Heideman and Jonah Birch, "In Defense of Political Marxism," *International Socialist Review*, July 2013, https://isreview. org/issue/90/defense-political-marxism and Neil Davidson, "Is There Any-

thing to Defend in Political Marxism?" *International Socialist Review*, winter 2013–14, https://isreview.org/issue/91/there-anything-defend-political-marxism. Deeper overviews can be found in Robert Brenner, "Property and Progress: Where Adam Smith Went Wrong," in *Marxist History-Writing for the Twenty-First Century*, ed. Chris Wickham (London: British Academy, 2007) and Chris Harman, "From Feudalism to Capitalism," *International Socialism 2*, 45 (Winter 1989), 35–87, https://www.marxists.org/archive/harman/1989/xx/transition.html. A series of essays which debate the argument more fully can be found in T. H. Aston and C. H. E. Philpin, eds., *The Brenner Debate: Agrarian Class Structure and Economic Development in Pre-Industrial Europe* (New York: Cambridge University Press, 1987).

10. Trade and markets, which expanded during this period, allowed lords to purchase luxuries and weaponry. To a lesser extent, peasants also used markets to sell excess crops to get cash for salt or other basic items. But so long as they were able to till their own land and produce the necessities of survival, they were not dependent on the market to sell their produce or buy goods from others. Despite the increasing production of non-agricultural goods and their exchange over the course of many centuries, economies remained primarily agricultural. Commodity production of goods sold on a market still existed only in pockets of society. The majority of the population—still as much as 80 or 90 percent worldwide between 1400 and 1800—lived in the country, subsisted on the meager foods and goods of their own production, and couldn't afford to buy the products of the town's craftsmen. See Robert Marks, *The Origins of the Modern World: A Global and Environmental Narrative from the Fifteenth to the Twenty-First Century* (Lanham: Rowman & Littlefield, 2015), 21.

11. Marx, *Capital*, vol. 1, 273.

12. Marx, *Capital*, vol. 1, 873.

13. Marx wrote: "The history of this expropriation assumes different aspects in different countries, and runs through its various phases in different orders of succession, and at different historical epochs. Only in England, which we therefore take as our example, has it the classic form." Marx, *Capital*, vol 1, 876.

14. William Cobbett, *Rural Rides, Project Gutenberg e-book, 17*. Karl Marx wrote about Cobbett: "The great changes attending the decomposition of the old English Society since the eighteenth century struck his eyes and made his heart bleed." Karl Marx, "Layard's Inquiry. Fight over the Ten-Hour Working Day," *New York Daily Tribune*, July 22, 1853, https://www.marxists.org/archive/marx/works/1853/07/22a.htm. Marx wrote glowingly about Cobbett's writings, but he also critiqued the limitations of his political understanding. "But if he saw the effects, he did not understand the causes, the new social agencies at work. He did not see the modern bourgeoisie, but only that fraction of the aristocracy which held the hereditary monopoly of office, and which sanctioned by law all the changes necessitated by the new wants and pretensions of the middle-class. He saw the machine, but not the hidden motive power."

15. Cobbett, *Rural Rides*, 17–19.

16. These processes, which have often been attributed solely to European advances, were in fact taking place in China, India, and Egypt among others. The technical and manufacturing prowess in China was particularly advanced, and developed much earlier than comparable European accomplishments. Chinese engineering, transportation, and mechanization feats, many of which took hold centuries before they were known in Europe—from printing to the magnetic compass to the ploughshare to windmills—propelled the Chinese economy forward.

17. J. M. Blaut, *The Colonizer's Model of the World: Geographical Diffusionism and Eurocentric History* (New York: Guildford Press, 1993), 166.

18. Marx, *Capital*, vol. 1, 272–273.

19. Marx, *Capital*, vol. 1, 719.

20. Marx, *Capital*, vol. 1, 875.

21. Oliver Goldsmith, *The Deserted Village* (London: Longmans, Green and Co, 1876).

22. Paul Mantoux, *La révolution industrielle au XVIIIe siècle : essai sur les commencements de la grande industrie moderne en Angleterre*, cited in: Michel Beaud, *A History of Capitalism: 1500–2000* (New York: Monthly Review Press, 1983), 71.

23. Quoted in Beaud, *A History of Capitalism*, 53.

24. Marx, *Capital*, vol. 1, 899.

25. Marx, *Capital*, vol. 1, 896–897.

26. Marx, *Capital*, vol. 1, 896–897.

27. Marx, *Capital*, vol. 1, 899–900.

28. Consider the role of border police and immigration officers in threatening violence and deportation on migrant workers, the role of mass incarceration on African-American and Latinx communities, or the role of police and National Guard at picket lines. The threat—and use—of violence keeps communities disempowered and economically desperate and backs up the otherwise day-to-day, "smooth" operations of capitalist relations.

29. Marx, *Capital*, vol. 1, 875.

30. Economic progress for the new order meant, of course, progress in productivity and therefore profits. It did not translate into *human* progress and the equitable distribution of goods to meet needs!

31. For a fuller discussion, see Neil Davidson, "How Revolutionary Were the Bourgeois Revolutions?" *Historical Materialism*, 13, no. 3 (2005), 3–33, DOI: 10.1163/1569206054927563. This too is a point of controversy among Marxists. See for instance: Ellen Meiksins Woods, "Capitalism's Gravediggers," *Jacobin*, December 15, 2014.

32. Chris Harman, "The Rise of Capitalism," *International Socialism* 2, 102, (Spring 2004), Marxist Internet Archive.

33. The account in this chapter generally follows the argument laid out by Harman above. But see also Ellen Meiksins Wood, "Eurocentric Anti-Eurocentrism," *Against the Current*, no. 92 (May–June 2001).

34. W. E. B. Du Bois recounts advertisements in Southern papers such as these: "Fifty Dollars reward. Ran away from the subscriber, a Negro girl, named Maria. She is of a copper color, between 13 and 14 years of age—bareheaded and barefooted. She is small for her age—very sprightly and very likely. She stated that she was going to see her mother at Maysville." Or "Fifty Dollars reward. Ran away from the subscriber, his Negro man Pauladore, commonly called Paul. I understand Gen R. Y. Hayne has purchased his wife and children from H. L. Pinckney, Esq., and has them on his plantation at Goosecreek, where, no doubt, the fellow is frequently lurking." W. E. B. Du Bois, *Black Reconstruction in America:1860–1880* (New York: Free Press, 1998), 12.

35. Du Bois, *Black Reconstruction, 9.*

36. Howard Zinn, *A People's History of the United States* (New York: Harper Collins, 1995), 28–29.

37. Du Bois, *Black Reconstruction, 4.*

38. Du Bois, *Black Reconstruction, S.*

39. Eric Williams, *Capitalism and Slavery* (Chapel Hill: University of North Carolina Press, 1994 [1944]), 103.

40. Walter Rodney described in his groundbreaking book, *How Europe Underdeveloped Africa*: "In the seventeenth and eighteenth centuries, the Portuguese carried most of the East African ivory which was marketed in India; while Indian cloth and beads were sold in East and West Africa by the Portuguese, Dutch, English, and French. The same applied to cowry shells from the East Indies. Therefore, by control of the seas, Europe took the first steps towards transforming several parts of Africa and Asia into economic satellites."

41. Marx, *Capital*, vol. 1, 925.

42. Here again a critical topic hits the limits of what this book can cover. I encourage readers to pick up *An Indigenous Peoples' History of the United States (ReVisioning American History)* by Roxanne Dunbar-Ortiz.

43. Marx wrote: "These methods depend in part on brute force, for instance the colonial system. But they all employ the power of the state, the concentrated and organized force of society, to hasten, as in a hothouse, the process of transformation of the feudal mode of production into the capitalist mode, and to shorten the transition" (vol. 1) 915–916.

44. Marx, *Capital*, vol. 1, 895.

45. Marx, *Capital*, vol. 1, 283.

46. Karl Marx, *Grundrisse* (London: Penguin, 1977), 410.

47. Marx, *Capital*, vol. 1, 638.

CHAPTER TWO: THE LABOR THEORY OF VALUE

1. Marx, *Capital*, vol. 1, 164.

2. Marx, *Capital*, vol. 1, 125.

3. Mandel, *Marxist Economic Theory*, vol. 1, 58.

4. Marx, *Capital*, vol. 1, 89–90.

5. See Sheena McKenzie, "The Smell of Success? $115 Bottles of British Air Sold to Chinese Buyers," CNN, February 8, 2016, http://www.cnn.com/2016/02/08/world/fresh-air-britain-china-bottles/ and "Whiff of Fresh Swiss Mountain Air on Sale for Just $167," RT, February 28, 2017, https://www.rt.com/viral/378831-swiss-air-for-sale/. And, of course, water has not fared as well as air in staying out of the clutches of the market.

6. Marx, *Capital*, vol. 1, 125.

7. The question of prices will only be taken up in upcoming chapters. But it has to be said that only in a twisted society would people be willing to pay $1,400 for a talking Teddy Ruxpin: see Brian Galindo, "25 Toys of the 80s That Are Worth an Absolute Fortune Now," BuzzFeed, August 8, 2014, https://www.buzzfeed.com/briangalindo/25-toys-of-the-80s-that-are-worth-an-absolute-fortune-now?utm_term=.bkPVVkwZjo#.prd99zP6OX

8. Vladimir Ilyich Lenin, *Karl Marx: A Brief Biographical Sketch With an Exposition of Marxism*, Lenin's collected works, (Moscow, 1974), Volume 21, 43–91.

9. Marx, *Capital*, vol. 1, 182.

10. The use-value of grain only matters to capitalists in the sense that if grain were *not* edible, or if people didn't want or need to eat, then it would not be able to be exchanged. As we'll discuss, a thing needs to have a use-value in order to have an exchange-value.

11. Marx, *Capital*, vol. 1, 177.

12. Karl Marx, *A Contribution to the Critique of Political Economy*, in *Marx and Engels Collected Works*, vol. 29 (New York: International Publishers, 1976), 270.

13. David Harvey, *A Companion to Marx's Capital* (New York: Verso, 2010), 23.

14. William Stanley Jevons, *The Theory of Political Economy*, 3rd ed. (London: MacMillan and Co., 1888), 7, Library of Economics and Liberty, http://www.econlib.org/library/YPDBooks/Jevons/jvnPE1.html

15. Jevons, *Theory of Political Economy*.

16. Brendan Cooney, "Law of Value 8: Subject/Object," *Kapitalism101*, November 15, 2011, https://kapitalism101.wordpress.com/2011/11/15/law-of-value-8-subjectobject/

17. John Cazenove, quoted in Ronald Meek, *Studies in Labor Theory of Value* (New York, NY: Monthly Review Press, 1977), 124.

18. We'll discuss supply and demand further in chapters 3 and 6.

19. Friedrich Engels's letter to Nikolai Danielson, *Marx and Engels Collected Works*, vol. 48 (Electric Book: Lawrence & Wishart, 2010), 136–7.

20. Marx, *Capital*, vol. 1, 133.

21. Karl Marx, *Critique of the Gotha Programme*, in *Marx and Engels Collected Works*, vol. 24 (Electric Book: Lawrence & Wishart, 2010), 81.

22. Paul D'Amato, *The Meaning of Marxism* (Chicago: Haymarket Books, 2006), 50.

23. David McNally, *Global Slump* (Oakland: PM Press, 2011), 71.

24. Marx, *Capital*, vol. 1, 142.

25. Marx, *Capital*, vol. 1, 135–136.

26. Adam Smith, *An Inquiry into the Nature and Causes of the Wealth of Nations* (Indianapolis: Liberty Classics, 1981), 10.

27. Smith, *Wealth of Nations*, 47–48.

28. David Ricardo's *Principles of Political Economy and Taxation*, published some forty years after *The Wealth of Nations*, also argued: "The value of a commodity, or the quantity of any other commodity for which it will exchange, depends on the relative quantity of labor which is necessary for its production, and not on the greater or less compensation which is paid for that labor." David Ricardo, *Principles of Political Economy and Taxation* (Harmondsworth: Penguin, 1971), 55. Ricardo investigated the law of value more systematically than did Smith, though Marx sees both as limited and contradictory. See Marx, *Theories of Surplus Value*, chapters 3 and 10. Benjamin Franklin, too, wrote: "Trade in general being nothing else but the exchange of labour for labour, the value of all things is justly measured by labour."

29. Marx, *Capital*, vol. 1, 129.

30. Marx, *Capital*, vol. 1, 168.

31. Alex Callinicos, *The Revolutionary Ideas of Karl Marx* (London: Bookmarks, 2004), 109.

32. Marx, *Capital*, vol. 1, 289–290.

33. Marx, *Capital*, vol. 1, 181.

34. Harvey, *Companion to Marx's Capital*, 39–40.

35. Marx, *Capital*, vol. 1, 165.

36. Marx wrote of feudalism: "Labor and its products... take the shape in the transactions of society, of services in kind and payments in kind... Whatever we may think, then, of the different roles in which men confront each other in such a society, the social relationships between individuals appear in any event as their own personal relations, are not disguised as social relations between things, between the products of labor," Marx, *Capital*, vol. 1, 165.

37. Marx, *Capital*, vol. 1, 175.

38. See chapter seven.

39. Size estimates vary, but a 2016 aerial survey by the Dutch foundation Ocean Cleanup found that the heart of the garbage patch is about 386,000 sq. miles, with the periphery spanning a further 1,351,000 sq. miles. Texas, by way of comparison, is about 269,000 sq. miles. See: "'Great Pacific garbage patch' far bigger than imagined, aerial survey shows," *Guardian*, October 4, 2016, https://www.theguardian.com/environment/2016/oct/04/great-pacific-garbage-patch-ocean-plastic-trash.

40. Save On Energy, "Land of Waste: American Landfills and Waste Production," https://www.saveonenergy.com/land-of-waste/. And Marcia Anderson, "Confronting Plastic Pollution One Bag at a Time," EPA Blog, November 1, 2016, https://blog.epa.gov/blog/tag/plastic-bags/.

41. Heather Rogers, *Gone Tomorrow: The Hidden Life of Garbage* (New York: New Press, 2005), 2.

42. "Advancing Sustainable Materials Management: 2017 Fact Sheet," United States Environmental Protection Agency, November 2019, accessed at https://www.epa.gov/sites/production/files/2019-11/documents/2017_facts_and_figures_fact_sheet_final.pdf.

43. For a discussion of these estimates see Max Liboiron, "Municipal versus Industrial Waste: Questioning the 3–97 ratio," *Discard Studies* (blog), March 2, 2016. https://discardstudies.com/2016/03/02/municipal-versus-industrial-waste-a-3-97-ratio-or-something-else-entirely/.

44. US Department of Transportation, Bureau of Transportation Statistics, "Number of US Aircraft, Vehicles, Vessels, and Other Conveyances," https://www.bts.gov/content/number-us-aircraft-vehicles-vessels-and-other-conveyances.

45. US Department of Transportation, Bureau of Transportation Statistics, "World Motor Vehicle Production, Selected Countries," https://www.bts.gov/content/world-motor-vehicle-production-selected-countries

46. Hannah Ritchie and Max Roser (2020), "Plastic Pollution". Published online at University of Oxford, OurWorldInData.org, https://ourworldindata.org/plastic-pollution.

47. Eriksen M, Lebreton LCM, Carson HS, Thiel M, Moore CJ, Borerro JC, et al., Plastic Pollution in the World's Oceans: More than 5 Trillion Plastic Pieces Weighing over 250,000 Tons Afloat at Sea. PLoS ONE 9(12): e111913 (2014). https://doi.org/10.1371/journal.pone.0111913

48. David Harvey, *A Brief History of Neoliberalism*, (New York: Oxford University Press, 2005), 165.

CHAPTER THREE: MONEY

1. Marx, *Capital*, vol. 1, 202.
2. Marx, *Capital*, vol. 1, 188.
3. Marx, *Capital*, vol. 1, 140.
4. Marx, *Capital*, vol. 1, 155.
5. Marx, *Capital*, vol. 1, 143.
6. Mandel, *Marxist Economic Theory*, vol. 1, 72.
7. Marx, *Capital*, vol. 1, 159.
8. Marx, *Capital*, vol. 1, 169.
9. According to Mandel: "Those people who are engaged in both agriculture and cattle-raising usually choose as their universal equivalent either cattle, wheat, or rice. Thus Greeks and Romans adopted the ox as the first universal equivalent down to the sixth and fifth centuries BCE. The Indians' word for the national currency, *rupee,* is derived from *rupa*, meaning a herd. The Iranians of the *Avesta* and the Germans of the *Lex Saxonum* also chose the ox as the universal equivalent, which indicates the predominance of cattle-raising in the epoch when this happened. In North, East, and South Africa, cattle, in the shape of camels, sheep, goats or cows, likewise constituted the universal

equivalent among people who were essentially cattle-breeders," Mandel, *Marxist Economic Theory*, vol. 1, 74.

10. Doug Orr, "What is Money?" in *Real World Macro: A Macroeconomics Reader from Dollars & Sense*, 28th edition, ed. Amy Gluckman, et al. (Boston: Economic Affairs Bureau, 2011), 147.

11. Mandel, *Marxist Economic Theory*, vol. 1, 77.

12. Decorative edges on coins were used to keep people from clipping off small amounts of metal from around the edges of coins and sell off the shavings! The current ridges on quarters are remnants from the time when quarters were made of real silver. Another practice from the time when real precious metals were used was to cut coins in half for change! See Matt Soniak, "How Many Ridges Are on a Quarter? (And Why Are They There in the First Place?)" *Mentalfloss*, June 22, 2011, http://mentalfloss.com/article/28044/how-many-ridges-are-quarter-and-why-are-they-there-first-place.

13. Marx, *Capital*, vol. 1, 208.

14. Jay Greene, "Third-party Merchants Selling on Amazon Hit Record Numbers," *Seattle Times*, January 9, 2014. See also Jeffrey Pfeffer, "Here's Why Amazon Is More Ruthless Than Walmart," *Time*, June 11, 2014.

15. Marx, *Capital*, vol. 1, 207.

16. This point, as we'll see in chapter seven, was made all too well in the recession following the financial meltdown of 2007 to 2008. No matter how low interest rates were set by the Federal Reserve (the central bank of the United States government) to encourage investment, capitalists simply did not see profitable enough returns to advance their capital.

17. Michel Foucault, *The Order of Things: An Archaeology of the Human Sciences* (London: Tavistock Publications, 1970), 173.

18. Accessed at http://onlygold.com/Info/History-Of-Gold.asp.

19. The British pound itself was first a measurement of silver. But by the thirteenth century, both gold and silver currencies were circulating in Britain, and by the eighteenth century, while silver was increasingly in short supply throughout much of Western Europe, gold became the basis of the pound.

20. Pierre Vilar, *A History of Gold and Money, 1450 to 1920* (New York: Verso, 1991), 211.

21. The transformation in the nature of agriculture was producing surplus far beyond what was possible through small-scale subsistence farming. At the same time, large landowners increasingly collected rent in money form, rather than rent-in-kind (i.e. in the form of goods). Money thus grew out of the confines of pockets of the elite. "Agricultural rents had to be paid in money, not in kind; more and more people were earning a daily wage and not living on subsistence production, and this meant a growing domestic market. People increasingly went over to commercial or industrial production of such things as wine, brandy, and dye-stuffs," Pierre Vilar, *A History of Gold and Money, 1450 to 1920* (New York: Verso, 1991), 259.

22. Vilar, *A History of Gold and Money*, 281.

23. See Joel Geier, "International Monetary Fund: Debt Cop," *International Socialist Review* 11 (2000).

24. Marx, *Capital*, vol. 1, 230.

25. Stanford, *Economics for Everyone, A Short Guide to the Economics of Capitalism* (London: Pluto Press, 2008), 214.

26. "The magic of mining," *Economist*, January 8, 2015.

27. "Bitcoin Mining Consumes More Electricity a Year Than Ireland," *Guardian*, November 27, 2017.

28. "The magic of mining," *Economist*, January 8, 2015, https://www.theguardian.com/technology/2017/nov/27/bitcoin-mining-consumes-electricity-ireland

29. Frank Chaparro, "Morgan Stanley: 'Bitcoin acceptance is virtually zero and shrinking,'" *Business Insider*, July 12, 2017.

30. "The Magic of Mining," *Economist*, January 8, 2015.

31. Asia Simone Burns, "Cryptocurrency Investors Worry, Wait After Bitcoin Price Drop," *NPR*, January 18, 2018.

32. "The Magic of Mining," *Economist*, January 8, 2015.

33. Harvey, *A Companion to Marx's Capital*, vol. 1, 59.

34. See chapter six, "System Failure."

35. Karl Marx, *Wage-Labour and Capital & Value, Price, and Profit* (New York: International Publishers, 2006), 51–52.

36. Harvey, *A Companion to Marx's Capital*, vol. 1, 82.

37. Quoted in Vilar, *A History of Gold and Money*, 14.

38. Marx, *Capital*, vol. 1, 196. The Marx/Engels Internet Archive (marxists.org) version also includes the line: "As soon as magnitude of value is converted into price, the above necessary relation takes the shape of a more or less accidental exchange ratio between a single commodity and another, the money commodity."

CHAPTER FOUR: WHERE DO PROFITS COME FROM?

1. Marx, *Capital*, vol. 1, 292.

2. Mandel, *Marxist Economic Theory*, vol. 1, 53.

3. While this sort of transaction (people making things and selling them for cash to buy other things) has existed for as long as money has existed, it is not clear whether there was ever a *historical period* of "simple commodity production," because from very early on the development of systematic trade involved merchants whose goal was never C–M–C, but always "buying cheap and selling dear."

4. Mandel, *Marxist Economic Theory*, vol. 1, 84.

5. Marx, *Capital*, vol. 1, 253.

6. Marx, *Capital*, vol. 1, 279–280.

7. The capitalist must also invest in raw materials, but Marx simplifies the formula to include labor-power (L) and the means of production (MP).

8. Marx, Capital, vol. 1, 270.

9. Marx, *Capital*, vol. 1, 300–301.

10. Marx, *Capital*, vol. 1, 300–301.
11. Marx, *Capital*, vol. 1, 655.
12. Of course, workers are regularly paid below the value of their labor-power, as we'll discuss further below.
13. Tithi Bhattacharya, "What Is Social Reproduction Theory?" *Socialist Worker*, September 10, 2013.
14. Marx, *Capital*, vol. 1, 325.
15. As Engels wrote: "The transaction, then, may be thus described—the workman gives to the Capitalist his full-day's working power; that is, so much of it as he can give without rendering impossible the continuous repetition of the transaction. In exchange he receives just as much, and no more, of the necessaries of life as is required to keep up the repetition of the same bargain every day. The workman gives as much, the Capitalist gives as little, as the nature of the bargain will admit. This is a very peculiar sort of fairness." Engels, "A Fair Day's Wages for a Fair Day's Work," *Labour Standard* no. 1, May 7, 1881.
16. It is also the basis on which companies can take advantage of monopoly positions, as we'll discuss in the next chapter.
17. Marx, *Capital*, vol. 1, 229.
18. Marx, *Capital*, vol. 1, 321.
19. Marx, *Capital*, vol. 1, 509.
20. Marx, *Capital*, vol. 1, 528.
21. The rate of surplus value is the same as the ratio of surplus labor to necessary labor. Marx explained: "In other words, the rate of surplus value, $s/v =$ surplus labor/necessary labor. Both ratios, s/v and surplus labor/necessary labor, express the same thing in different ways; in the one case in the form of objectified labor, in the other in the form of living, fluid labor. The rate of surplus value is therefore an exact expression for the degree of exploitation of labor-power by capital, or the worker by the capitalist." See Marx, *Capital*, vol. 1, 326. However, in the simplified version of this same example, I said the ratio of surplus labor/necessary labor was 7/1. This is because here we didn't account for the capitalists' expenditure of constant capital. Once we take this into account, we see that the ratio of necessary to surplus labor is 4:1, or 6.4 hours of surplus labor to 1.6 hours of necessary labor.
22. Oxfam, "Reward Work, Not Wealth," January 2018.
23. Unfortunately for Starbucks execs, their rate of profit is not 100 percent in real life. But for the sake of numerical simplicity, we'll stick to these hypothetical numbers.
24. Marx, *Capital*, vol. 1, 255.
25. Marx, *Capital*, vol. 1, 932.
26. Marx, *Capital*, vol. 3, (London: Penguin Classics, 1991), 132.
27. Marx, *Capital*, vol. 1, 275.
28. I say "mostly" because private day cares and schools also contribute to social reproduction but are cites of surplus value as well.
29. Marx, *Capital*, vol. 1, 717.

30. Marx, *Capital*, vol. 1, 717.

31. Lise Vogel, "Domestic Labor Revisited," *Science & Society*, vol. 64, no. 2 (summer, 2000), 161.

32. "Right-to-work" laws unfortunately don't mean that you are guaranteed the right to work. They are union-busting laws which bar unions from collecting dues from every worker in a shop that has voted to be represented by the union. It's no longer the case that "right-to-work" states are primarily in the American South, where the labor movement has been historically most divided by racism. Now an emboldened Right has passed union-busting legislation in other states including Wisconsin and Missouri, as well as organized campaigns for national legislation.

33. "The State of the Gender Pay Gap 2019," Payscale online resource, https://www.payscale.com/data/gender-pay-gap.

34. Lizzy Goodman, "The Best Women's Soccer Team in the World Fights for Equal Pay," *New York Times*, June 10, 2019.

35. Elise Gould, Janelle Jones, and Zane Mokhiber, "Black workers have made no progress in closing earnings gaps with white men since 2000," Economic Policy Institute, September 12, 2018.

36. Elise Gould, "Latina workers have to work nearly 11 months into 2019 to be paid the same as white non-Hispanic men in 2018," Economic Policy Institute, November 19, 2019.

37. Patricia Cohen, "Racial Wealth Gap Persists Despite Degree, Study Says," *New York Times*, August 17, 2015. "The Simple Truth About the Gender Pay Gap," fall 2015, American Association of University Women, http://www.aauw.org/files/2015/09/The-Simple-Truth-Fall-2015.pdf.

38. Catherine Hill, et al., "The Simple Truth About the Gender Pay Gap," fall 2017, American Association of University Women; Eileen Patten, "Racial, Gender Wage Gaps Persist in US Despite Some Progress," Pew Research Center, July 1, 2016.

39. Justin Akers Chacón, "The Case Against 'The Case Against Open Borders,'" *Socialist Worker*, November 27, 2018.

40. The cost of materials and equipment is also reflected in the prices of Boeing products. But the overall point is that higher wages do not always translate to lower rates of exploitation. Furthermore these "comfortable" jobs are not guaranteed, as higher-paid workers are pushed to work faster for stagnating wages, see their benefits cut, and lose jobs when factories close in order to pay substantially lower wages elsewhere. Boeing, for instance, announced in 2014 the relocation of its engineering center from Washington State (where engineer salaries averaged $125,000 a year) to Alabama (where the going rate is $89,000). See Leada Gore, "Boeing will save $60,000 per job by moving engineering center to Alabama; average salary will be $89,000," *AL.com*, April 27, 2014, http://www.al.com/business/index.ssf/2014/04/boeing_will_save_60000_per_job.html.

41. This chapter section relies on much of the analysis and methodology in Michael Zweig's book *The Working Class Majority: America's Best Kept Secret*, 2nd ed. (Ithaca, NY: Cornell University Press, 2011).

42. Gwen Ifill, "Clinton's Standard Campaign Speech: A Call for Responsibility," *New York Times*, April 26, 1992.

43. Michael Zweig, *The Working Class Majority*, 2.

44. Whether or not teachers or nurses are considered part of the working class has been debated by Marxists and other radical labor historians. See endnote 195. A related point of debate is whether those that work for the government (as opposed to private, for-profit schools, or other companies, as Marx's quote about the teacher in the "teaching factory" refers to) are producing surplus value, and if not, how this impacts their classification as workers (or as "proletarians," a term which Marx often used interchangeably with the term workers, but sometimes distinguished as only those "productive workers" who produce surplus value). See endnote 189. However you address these questions, it seems evident that public-sector workers face working-class conditions, have higher representation by unions, are often at the forefront of strikes and class struggle, and hold significant social power.

45. Marx, *Capital,* vol. 1, 644. Marx here is referring to the concept of a "productive" worker, versus an unproductive one, in order to specifically delineate workers who generate surplus value. "Unproductive" workers are also workers; they just have a different relationship to the creation of capital. American socialist Hal Draper had a very useful description of the working class as existing in concentric circles. An industrial "core" sits strategically at the center of capitalist production, while outer rings of workers are less likely to be direct producers, but nonetheless contribute to the collective process of the extraction of surplus value. See Hal Draper, *Karl Marx's Theory of Revolution: The Politics of Social Classes,* vol. 2, (New York: Monthly Review Press, 1978), 35–38.

46. Geoffrey de Ste. Croix, "Class in Marx's Conception of History, Ancient and Modern," *New Left Review* I/146 (July-August 1984) 100.

47. Board of Governors of the Federal Reserve System, "Report on the Economic Well-Being of US Households in 2016," May 2017, https://www.federalreserve.gov/publications/files/2016-report-economic-well-being-us-households-201705.pdf.

48. Organization for Economic Cooperation and Development Employment Outlook 2016, Statistical Annex, 238, accessed at http://www.oecd.org/els/oecd-employment-outlook-19991266.htm.

49. Adjuncts now make up the majority of university instructors. See Tyler Kingkade, "9 Reasons Why Being an Adjunct Faculty Member Is Terrible," *Huffington Post,* November, 11 2013, updated December 6, 2017.

50. Marx and Engels, *The Communist Manifesto*, 43.

51. Zweig, *The Working Class Majority*, 13–36; Kim Moody, *On New Terrain* (Chicago: Haymarket Books, 2017), 37–40. These estimates include some teachers, social workers, and other professions, which Zweig and Moody both classify as a

mixed bag of some middle-class and some working-class jobs. These professions, Moody and Zweig argue, are proletarianizing professions. And this is particularly significant because, as Moody points out, many of these proletarianizing professionals are today leading some of the most militant class struggles in the US. My take is that teachers and nurses have not had enough autonomy or independence to be considered part of the middle class for a long time, and certainly not today in the days of "teaching to the test." Even if a degree of flexibility within the classroom affords some creativity on the job, teachers have no control over any of the basic parameters of the job—size of the class and therefore workload, schedule, benefits, etc. I also think that greater sections of many other professions from accountants to web developers should be accounted for within the ranks of the working class. Many of these jobs entail routinized and tedious tasks, require long hours, and offer meager compensation. Lastly, though supervisors can generally be considered part of the middle class, there are many instances in which this is not the case. Many, if not most, of BLS-classified "first line supervisors" in retail and food prep/service jobs, for instance, are probably working class. These supervisors often have such "privileges" as coming up with shift schedules or opening or closing the store, but have no jurisdiction to hire and fire, or hold any other meaningful authority. Taking into consideration these variables, my own very rough analysis of data from the Bureau of Labor Statistics led me to estimate that these numbers could be as high as 75 percent.

52. Moody, *On New Terrain*, 41.

53. Marx and Engels, *The Communist Manifesto*, 40.

54. Ste. Croix, "Class in Marx's Conception of History," 100.

55. Mr. Burns's laugh, https://www.youtube.com/watch?v=YuoToHKCas4.

56. We'll discuss this point further in the following chapter. In the meantime, take the example of a company like Etsy, founded as a quirky e-commerce shop for handmade items by three Brooklyn hipsters in 2005. By 2011, the company's board had pushed out its founders, and in 2013 they changed their terms of service to allow the sale of manufactured goods. By 2015, Etsy generated over $2 billion dollars in sales, but, still not generating a profit to satisfy shareholders, pushed out another CEO in 2017, laid off 8 percent of its staff, and brought in former American Express executive Josh Silverman as CEO. Company balconies were locked to keep employees from jumping, as layoffs were announced.

57. In addition to increasing the amount of surplus value extracted from the workforce through an extension of the workday, capitalists also have an interest in making sure their machines are always running. They are in a race against time to get the most use out of their investments before moral depreciation devalues their equipment, and therefore the value that these machines or technologies pass on to their products.

58. Marx, *Capital*, vol. 1, 527.

59. Marx, *Capital*, vol. 1, 645.

60. Marx, *Capital*, vol. 1, 534.

61. Marx, *Capital,* vol. 1, 534.

62. Tony Smith, *Technology and Capital in the Age of Lean Production* (Albany: State University of New York Press, 2000), 60.

63. Kim Moody, "US Workers in the Late Neoliberal Era," *New Politics,* vol. 16 (summer 2017) 3.

64. Marx, *Capital,* vol. 1, 433.

65. Quoted in Braverman, *Labor and Monopoly Capital,* 56–57.

66. Marx, *Capital,* vol. 1, 530.

67. Marx, *Capital,* vol. 1, 433.

68. Marx, *Capital,* vol. 1, 723–724.

69. Frederick Winslow Taylor, "The Principles of Scientific Management," in *Scientific Management* (New York: Harper & Row, 1947 [1911]), 39.

70. Taylor, "Principles of Scientific Management," 43–44.

71. Taylor, "Principles of Scientific Management," 45–46.

72. Taylor, "Principles of Scientific Management," 59.

73. Leon Trotsky, "Terrorism and Communism," chapter 8, https://www.marxists.org/archive/trotsky/1920/terrcomm/ch08.htm.

CHAPTER FIVE: THE ACCUMULATION OF CAPITAL

1. Marx, *Capital,* vol. 1, 739.

2. Upton Sinclair, *The Flivver King: A Novel of Ford-America* (London: T. Werner Laurie LTD, 1908), 50.

3. Friedrich Engels, *Anti-Dühring,* (Chicago: Charles H. Kerr & Co., 1935), 282–284.

4. Charles Duhigg, "How Companies Learn Your Secrets," *New York Times,* February 16, 2012.

5. For instance, according to Duke University's biannual report on marketing trends, social media spending has more than tripled since 2009 as a share of marketing budgets, despite the fact that nearly half of firms say they haven't been able to show the impact of marketing on social media. See "The CMO Survey, Highlights and Insights Report," Duke Fuqua School of Business, American Marketing Association, Deloitte, August 2017, https://cmosurvey.org/results/august-2017/.

6. Kana Inagaki, "Toyota: Emission Control," *Financial Times,* March 17, 2016.

7. Paul La Monica, "Apple Reaches $1,000,000,000,000 Value," *CNN Money,* August 2, 2018.

8. Vlad Savov, "The Entire History of iPhone vs. Android Summed up in Two Charts," *Verge,* June 1, 2016.

9. Marx, *Capital,* vol. 1, 777.

10. Cision PR Newswire, "Global Remote Patient Monitoring Market Report 2018–2023," April 27, 2018.

11. Alison Diana, "8 Technologies Changing Home Healthcare," *Information-Week: Connecting the Business Technology Community,* December 18, 2014.

12. Marx and Engels, *The Communist Manifesto*, 44.

13. Engels, *Anti-Dühring*, 286.

14. See, for instance, Louis Woodhill, "General Motors Is Headed for Bankruptcy—Again," Forbes, August 15, 2012. https://www.forbes.com/sites/louiswoodhill/2012/08/15/general-motors-is-headed-for-bankrupcy-again/#8bbb9476bb98.

15. Marx, *Capital*, vol. 1, 726.

16. Jeff Spry, "Upgrade Your Geek Lifestyle with This Lavish $25 Million Star Trek-Themed Mansion," Syfy Wire, May 17, 2019. And while the expensive drinking habits of the ultrarich are nothing new, a blogger who went on a Tinder date with pharmaceutical executive Martin Shkreli (the man responsible for jacking up the price of antiparasitical drug Daraprim by 5000% percent overnight) discovered that he shelled out $120 for a cup of "Gold Medal Sencha" tea, despite admitting that he's "not really a big tea drinker." Jacklyn Collier, "My Tinder date with 'Pharma Bro' Martin Shkreli," *Washington Post Blog*, January 5, 2016.

17. Chuck Collins, Omar Ocampo, and Sophia Paslaski, "Billionaire Bonanza 2020: Wealth Windfalls, Tumbling Tazes, and Pandemic Profiteers," Institute for Policy Studies, https://ips-dc.org/billionaire-bonanza-2020/.

18. Marx, *Capital*, vol. 1, 739.

19. See Todd Leopold, "Your Late Fees Are Waived: Blockbuster Closes," CNN, November 7, 2013., https://www.cnn.com/2013/11/06/tech/gaming-gadgets/blockbuster-video-stores-impact/index.html.

20. Marx, *Capital*, vol. 1, 742.

21. Of course, this is a big "if." In the next chapter, we'll discuss the myriad ways in which the economy goes awry.

22. Marx, *Capital*, vol. 1, 727.

23. See "Defining Capital" in the previous chapter.

24. Harvey, *A Companion*, 259.

25. Daniel Fisher, "The Best Little Factory in Texas," *Forbes,* June 10, 2002.

26. Bill Breen, "Living in Dell Time," *Fast Company*, November 1, 2004.

27. Breen, "Living in Dell Time."

28. "Global 500," *Fortune*, http://fortune.com/global500/; "Labor force, total," The World Bank Open Data, http://data.worldbank.org/indicator/SL.TLF.TOTL.IN.

29. Jeff Desjardins, "Most Valuable US Companies Over 100 Years," Visual Capitalist, November 14, 2017.

30. Marx, *Capital*, vol. 1, 776.

31. Jeffrey Pfeffer, "Here's Why Amazon Is More Ruthless than Walmart," *Time,* June 11, 2014.

32. McDonald's restaurants grew from 31,046 in 2006 to 36,899 in 2016 according to Statistica.com.

33. These numbers fluctuate and encompass everything from stock and bond markets to real estate and derivative markets, which will be discussed in

chapter seven. See Jack Malvey, "The History and Future of Global Capital Markets," Center for Global Investment & Market Intelligence, June 2016.

34. Marx, *Capital*, vol. 1, 777.

35. General Motors was founded by Durant in 1908 as a holding company for Buick. That same year, it acquired Oldsmobile. In 1909, General Motors acquired Cadillac, Cartercar, Elmore, Ewing, Oakland (which later became the Pontiac brand), Reliance Motor Truck, and Rapid Motor Vehicle Co. In 1911, Durant left the firm and cofounded Chevrolet Motor Co. Five years later, Durant and Chevrolet had amassed a 54.5 percent ownership stake in GM and the two companies were merged. In 1925, GM bought English car company Vauxhall and an 80 percent stake in German automaker Opel. In 1931 it acquired the Australian firm Holden. By the 1950s, GM had become the largest corporation in the United States in terms of its revenues as a percent of GDP where it remained until 2008.

36. Marx, *Capital*, vol. 1, 779.

37. Marx, *Capital*, vol. 1 (Moscow: Progress Publishers, 1887). In the Penguin edition, the translation reads: "one capitalist always strikes down many others?" (929), but I prefer the Progress Publishers translation in this case for its succinctness.

38. "List of mergers and acquisitions by Microsoft," *Wikipedia*.org, http://en.wikipedia.org/wiki/List_of_mergers_and_acquisitions_by_Microsoft; "List of mergers and acquisitions by Apple," *Wikipedia*.org, https://en.wikipedia.org/wiki/List_of_mergers_and_acquisitions_by_Apple.

39. In the summer of 2016, as music start-up Omnifone filed for bankruptcy, for instance, Apple bought up select streaming technologies and hired sixteen engineers and other employees in a "talent grab."

40. Under the auspices of its parent company, Alphabet Inc., "List of mergers and acquisitions by Alphabet," *Wikipedia*.org, https://en.wikipedia.org/wiki/List_of_mergers_and_acquisitions_by_Alphabet.

41. "M&A Statistics," Institute for Mergers, Acquisitions and Alliances, https://imaa-institute.org/mergers-and-acquisitions-statistics/.

42. Stephen Grocer, "A Record $2.5 Trillion in Mergers Were Announced in the First Half of 2018," *New York Times*, July 3, 2018..

43. Quoted in Steven Rosenfeld, "US Economy Increasingly Dominated by Monopolies as 2015 Corporate Mergers Continue," *AlterNet*, November 17, 2015.

44. James Kynge, Gabriel Wildau, and Don Weinland, "China Inc: The Quest for Cash Flow," *Financial Times*, March 18, 2016.

45. Marx, *Capital*, vol. 1, 777–8.

46. Marx, *Capital*, vol. 1, 779–80.

47. Marx, *Capital*, vol. 1, 777.

48. Marx, *Capital*, vol. 1, 445.

49. . . . or over the course of years if, like Johnny Cash, you get the component parts "one piece at a time."

50. Byron Olsen and Joseph Cabadas, *The American Auto Factory* (St. Paul, MN: MBI Publishers, 2002), 20–42.
51. McNally, *Global Slump*, 66.
52. Cited in Braverman, *Labor and Monopoly Capital*, 45.
53. "Economies of Scale and Scope," *Economist* online extra, October 20, 2008, adapted from the *Economist Guide to Management Ideas and Gurus* by Tim Hindle.
54. Again, it will not require one hundred times the number of printers to produce a hundred times the pages. Rather the printers will likely run without interruption, producing less waste and less set-up costs. Once these costs are covered, the difference between printing 100 or 1000 copies will be marginal.
55. Jennifer Smith and Sarah Nassauer, "Walmart Toughens Delivery Demands for Suppliers," *The Wall Street Journal*, March 6, 2019. And Emily Schmitt, "The Profits and Perils of Supplying to Walmart," *Bloomberg*, July 14, 2009.
56. Ayşegül Şahin, Sagiri Kitao, Anna Cororaton, and Sergiu Laiu, "Why Small Businesses Were Hit Harder by the Recent Recession," *Current Issues in Economics and Finance,* Federal Reserve of New York, vol. 17, no. 4, http://www.newyorkfed.org/research/current_issues/ci17-4.pdf.
57. Ed Crooks, "US Oil and Gas Sector Reboots to Survive," *Financial Times,* April 4, 2016.
58. Karl Marx, "The Accumulation of Capitals and the Competition among the Capitalists," *Economic and Philosophical Manuscripts of 1844,* https://www.marxists.org/archive/marx/works/1844/manuscripts/capital.htm#4.
59. As *the Wall Street Journal* noted: "At McDonald's, international revenue rose 24 percent since 2009, three times as fast as in the US At Starbucks, international revenue jumped 35 percent the past two years, more than double the 14 percent increase in the US." See Scott Thurm, "For Big Companies, Life Is Good Large Corporations Emerge from Recession Leaner, Stronger—and Hiring Overseas," *Wall Street Journal*, April 9, 2012.
60. As of 2017, Amazon held 46 percent of the online retail market share. It spent 15 billion dollars on acquiring other companies from 2014 to 2017 alone. See Matt Stoller, "The Return of Monopoly," *New Republic*, July 13, 2017.
61. Mary Anne Henderson, "Warehouse Woes: Amazon and the New 'Middle Class,'" *San Antonio Current,* September 10, 2013.
62. According to "Demographia World Urban Areas, 14th Annual Edition," April 2018, 55 percent of the world's population live in urban areas and 13 percent of the world's population live in cities of over 5 million inhabitants. See also United Nations, Department of Economic and Social Affairs, Population Division (2019) World Urbanization Prospects 2018: Highlights (ST/ESA/SER.A/421).
63. Donald Armbrecht, "The World's Fastest Growing Cities," World Economic Forum, November 25, 2015, http://www.weforum.org/agenda/2015/11/the-worlds-fastest-growing-cities

64. United Nations, Department of Economic and Social Affairs, Population Division (2019), World Urbanization Prospects 2018: Highlights (ST/ESA/ SER.A/421).

65. "Demographia World Urban Areas, 14th Annual Edition," Demographia.

66. Winsome Tan, "The History of a 'City Without History,'" Asia Society, May 4, 2010, http://asiasociety.org/history-city-without-history

67. Andrew Malone and Richard Jones, "Revealed: Inside the Chinese Suicide Sweatshop Where Workers Toil in 34-hour Shifts to Make Your iPod," Daily Mail (UK), June 11, 2010.

68. Malone and Jones, "Inside the Chinese Suicide Sweatshop."

69. Malone and Jones, "Inside the Chinese Suicide Sweatshop."

70. Alissa Walker, "A Day in the Life of the Fastest Growing Megacity in the World," Gizmodo, March 31, 2015, http://gizmodo.com/a-day-in-the-life-of-the-fastest-growing-megacity-in-th-1694822923. See also Tim Franco's Metamorpolis photo series for some stunning visualizations of this explosion, http://www.timfranco.com/photographer/photojournalism/documentary/ chongqing/china/vertical-communism/

71. Charles Clover, "Delivering the Jack Ma Economy," Financial Times, September 15, 2015. Despite the truth behind this statement, it should be noted that the era of seeming unending rural migration is coming to a close. Labor shortages in China are increasingly a reality.

72. Clover, "Delivering the Jack Ma Economy."

73. Haya El Nasser, "LA Garment Industry Rife with Sweatshop Conditions," Aljazeera America, September 9, 2015.

74. Marx, Capital, vol. 1, 799.

75. Matt Stoller, "The Return of Monopoly," New Republic, July 13, 2017.

76. Howard Means, Money and Power: The History of Business (New York: Wiley, 2001), 156.

77. Taken for a Ride, dir. Martha Olson and Jim Klein, 1996.

78. Vandana Shiva, "The Seeds of Suicide: How Monsanto Destroys Farming," Asian Age, April 5, 2013, https://web.archive.org/web/20130329155150/ http://www.asianage.com/columnists/seeds-suicide-650.

79. Quoted in Steven Rosenfeld, "US Economy Increasingly Dominated by Monopolies as 2015 Corporate Mergers Continue," AlterNet, November 17, 2015.

80. Robert Boroujerdi, et al., "Does Consolidation Create Value?" Goldman Investment Research, February 12, 2014.

81. Daniel Victor and Matt Stevens, "United Airlines Passenger Is Dragged from an Overbooked Flight," New York Times, April 10, 2017.

82. For more on the calculated misery wrought by the airline industry, see Tim Wu, "Why Airlines Want to Make You Suffer," New Yorker, December 26, 2014.

83. "Pharmaceutical Industry," World Health Organization, http://www.who.int /trade/glossary/story073/en/.

84. See Daniel J. McGraw, "How Big Pharma Gave America Its Heroin Problem," Pacific Standard, November 30, 2015, for a discussion of Big Pharma's

relationship to heroin addictions. The World Health Organization itself has argued: "As a result of this pressure to maintain sales, there is now 'an inherent conflict of interest between the legitimate business goals of manufacturers and the social, medical, and economic needs of providers and the public to select and use drugs in the most rational way.' This is particularly true where drugs companies are the main source of information as to which products are most effective. Even in the United Kingdom, where the medical profession receives more independent, publicly-funded information than in many other countries, promotional spending by pharmaceuticals companies is fifty times greater than spending on public information on health." See "Pharmaceutical Industry," World Health Organization website, http://www.who.int/trade/glossary/story073/en/.

85. Lydia Ramsey, "Drug Companies are Reeling after the Martin Shkreli Incident—and It Could Shake Up the Entire Industry," *Business Insider*, September 30, 2015.

86. David Crow, "Valeant Under Pressure over Price Rises," *Financial Times*, October 9, 2015.

87. Nadia Kounang, "Why Pharmaceuticals Are Cheaper Abroad," CNN, September 28, 2015. https://www.cnn.com/2015/09/25/health/us-buys-more-for-drugs/index.html.

88. Kounang, "Why Pharmaceuticals are cheaper abroad."

89. Petrino DiLeo, "The $16 Trillion Dollar Bailout," *Socialist Worker* (US), September 7, 2011.

90. Otmar Issing, "Too Big to Fail Undermines the Free Market Faith," *Financial Times*, January 19, 2012.

91. Richard Waters, "Tesla Chief in Driving Seat as Pre-Orders Reflect Strong Interest in New Model," *Financial Times*, April 2, 2016.

92. V.I. Lenin, *Imperialism: The Highest Stage of Capitalism,* (New York: International Publishers, 1990), 88.

93. For a good introduction, read Phil Gasper, "Lenin and Bukharin on Imperialism," *ISR*, Spring 2016, 69–87.

94. Robert Holly, "Agribusiness Companies Capitalize on Tax Breaks, Grants, Subsidies and Loans," Midwest Center for Investigative Reporting, May 12, 2015.

95. Thomas Friedman, "A Manifesto for the Fast World," *New York Times Magazine*, March 28, 1999.

96. Marx and Engels, *The Communist Manifesto*, 44.

97. Marx and Engels, *The Communist Manifesto*, 46–7.

98. Engels, "The Part Played by Labor," 460.

99. Marx, *Capital*, vol. 3, 368.

100. Marx, *Capital*, vol. 3, 911.

101. Andy Sharman, "VW Scandal Fuels Fears over 'Death of Diesel,'" *Financial Times*, September 30, 2015.

102. Geoff Dyer and Ed Crooks, "US and Canada to Cut Methane Emissions by 40–45%," *Financial Times,* March 10, 2016.

103. Karl Marx, *Grundrisse* (London: Penguin, 1977), 410.

104. Chris Williams, "Why U.N. Climate Talks Continue to Fail," *Indypendent,* September 12, 2014.

105. Lester Brown, "Our Global Ponzi Economy," Earth Policy Institute webpage, October 7, 2009, adapted excerpt from Lester R. Brown, *Plan B 4.0: Mobilizing to Save Civilization* (New York: W.W. Norton & Company, 2009).

106. Chris Williams and Marcella Olivera, "Can Bolivia Chart a Sustainable Path Away from Capitalism?" *Truthout,* January 28, 2015, https://truthout.org/articles/can-bolivia-shatter-the-vise-of-capitalism.

107. Andres Schipani, "Bolivia's Water People Are Left High and Dry," *Financial Times,* March 14, 2016.

108. Schipani, "Bolivia's Water People."

109. Marx and Engels, *The Communist Manifesto,* 47.

CHAPTER SIX: CAPITALIST CRISIS

1. Marx and Engels, *The Communist Manifesto,* 48.

2. Marx, *Capital,* vol. 3, 363.

3. Marx, *Capital,* vol. 3, 363.

4. Laura Kusisto, "Many Who Lost Homes to Foreclosure in Last Decade Won't Return," *Wall Street Journal,* April 20, 2015.

5. Official unemployment figures don't include "discouraged" workers who have stopped looking for work, or those who are involuntary part-time or *underemployed.*

6. "US Household Debt Passes Its Pre-Recession Peak," *CBS MoneyWatch,* May 17, 2017. The article also explains: "Nearly 11 percent of that debt is 90 days overdue or more. The Fed estimates that the true figure could be double that amount, because many borrowers are able to defer loan payments if they are unemployed or continuing their studies."

7. "Tell 'The Nation': Recession Stories," *Nation,* November 23, 2009.

8. "Tell 'The Nation.'"

9. As Greek socialist, Antonis Davanellos pointed out, "servicing the public debt" is just a way of saying, "rob the people, depriving them of badly needed resources in order to serve the interests of the banks and all the other loan sharks of the international market," Antonis Davanellos, "European Capitalism's Weak Link?" *Socialist Worker,* February 10, 2010.

10. Aaron Smith, "Greenspan: It's a 'Credit Tsunami.'" *CNNMoney,* October 23, 2008, https://money.cnn.com/2008/10/23/news/economy/committee_regulatory/index.htm.

11. John Cassidy, "Interview with Eugene Fama," *New Yorker,* January 13, 2010. Fama also argued that there actually wasn't a housing or a credit bubble. (We'll discuss "bubbles" later on, but suffice to say, it was widely acknowl-

edged that they played a pivotal role in the Great Recession.) Consumers, as the theory goes, had all the information they needed to buy, so the price at every moment was right.

12. Marx, *Capital*, vol. 3, 357.

13. Simon Clarke, *Marx's Theory of Crisis* (New York: Saint Martin's Press, 1994), 16.

14. Clarke, *Marx's Theory of Crisis*, 1.

15. Clarke, *Marx's Theory of Crisis*, 3.

16. John Maynard Keynes coined the term in his *The General Theory of Employment, Interest and Money* (London: Macmillan, 1936). See also: George Akerlof and Robert Shiller, *Animal Spirits: How Human Psychology Drives the Economy, and Why It Matters for Global Capitalism* (Princeton: Princeton University Press, 2009).

17. In a speech at the American Enterprise Institute on December 5, 1996, Greenspan asked: "How do we know when irrational exuberance has unduly escalated asset values, which then become subject to unexpected and prolonged contractions as they have in Japan over the past decade?" This phrase has since been woven into the Lexicon of "behavioral economics."

18. William Stanley Jevons, "Commercial Crises and Sun-Spots," *Nature* xix, pp. 33–37, November 14, 1878.

19. David Hirshleifer and Tyler Shumway, "Good Day Sunshine: Stock Returns and the Weather," *The Journal of Finance*, vol. 58, no. 3 (June 2003), 1009–1032.

20. Jean-Baptiste Say, *A Treatise on Political Economy*, www.econlib.org/library /Say/sayT15.html

21. During a crisis of overproduction, the value of money can rise if prices of goods have dropped due to oversupply. If the prices drop, each dollar essentially has more buying power, and therefore is worth more. Investors aren't then interested in purchasing goods to sell, or in buying materials for further production, since they know that those products will be worth less on the market. They'd rather have extra dollars, which at this point are rising in value.

22. Engels, "Outlines of a Critique of Political Economy."

23. The logic of capitalism is of course at complete odds with the logic of humanity! The point of housing, its use-value, is to provide shelter. But this use is refracted through the need to make profits, and so houses are viewed as assets to buy, collect, resell. Further, as we'll discuss in future chapters, investment in mortgage-related financial products helped to inflate prices even higher. When the bubble popped, millions couldn't pay their mortgages and faced foreclosures, and families lost their homes. Capitalism's solution is not to find ways to keep people in their houses (much less to house the homeless!) but to try and find ways to restore profitability to the banks and to the real estate industry. Rather than reining in banks and financial institutions, nothing was done to provide homeowner relief, or to make houses more affordable.

24. US Bureau of Economic Analysis, "Corporate Profits After Tax" (without IVA and CCAdj) [CP], retrieved from FRED, Federal Reserve Bank of St. Louis, https://fred.stlouisfed.org/series/CP.

25. Doug Henwood, "The Profit Hoarders," *Jacobin*, September 8, 2017.

26. Marx, *Capital*, vol. 1, 208.

27. Marx, *Capital*, vol. 1, 209.

28. For a fuller discussion of Keynesianism see Petrino DiLeo, "The Return of Keynes?" *International Socialist Review* 63, (September 2008).

29. Naomi Klein's *The Shock Doctrine: The Rise of Disaster Capitalism* (New York: Picador, 2007) chronicles how governments have used neoliberal strategies to take advantage of economic and natural crises to push through pro-capital policies.

30. Marx, *Theories of Surplus Value*, chapter 17, section 8.

31. Duncan Foley, *Understanding Capital: Marx's Economic Theory* (Cambridge: Harvard University Press, 1986), 143.

32. Marx, *Capital*, vol. 3, 351–352.

33. Marx, *Capital*, vol. 3, 352.

34. Marx, *The Poverty of Philosophy*, chapter 1, section 2.

35. Marx, *Capital*, vol. 3, 353.

36. Simon Clarke, "The Marxist Theory of Overaccumulation and Crisis," *Science & Society* 54, no. 4 (1990), 454.

37. Marx, *Theories of Surplus Value*, chapter 17, section 12.

38. Engels, *Anti-Dühring*, 286.

39. Marx, *Capital*, vol. 3, 365.

40. Simon Clarke, "The Marxist Theory," 458.

41. Marx, *Theories of Surplus Value*, chapter 17, section 12. Regarding Ricardo's argument, Marx quotes him here: "Too much of a particular commodity may be produced, of which there may be such a glut in the market, as not to repay the capital expended on it; but this cannot be the case with respect to all commodities; the demand for corn is limited by the mouths which are to eat it, for shoes and coats by the persons who are to wear them; but though a community, or a part of a community, may have as much corn, and as many hats and shoes, as it is able or may wish to consume, the same *cannot be said of every commodity produced by nature or by art.* Some would consume more wine, if they had the ability to procure it. Others having enough of wine, would wish to increase the quantity or improve the quality of their furniture. Others might wish to ornament their grounds, or to enlarge their houses. The wish to do all or some of these is implanted in every man's breast; *nothing is required but the means, and nothing can afford the means, but an increase of production.*" Marx replies, in part: "What is the purpose of all this? In periods of over-production, a large part of the nation (especially the working class) is less well provided than ever with corn, shoes etc., not to speak of wine and furniture. If over-production could only occur when all the members of a nation had satisfied even their most urgent needs, there could never, in the history of bourgeois society up to now, have been a state of general over-production or even of partial over-production. When, for instance, the market is glutted by shoes or calicoes or wines or colonial products, does this perhaps mean that four-sixths of the nation have more

than satisfied their needs in shoes, calicoes, etc.? What after all has over-production to do with absolute needs? It is only concerned with demand that is backed by ability to pay. It is not a question of absolute over-production—over-production as such in relation to the absolute need or the desire to possess commodities. In this sense there is neither partial nor general over-production; and the one is not opposed to the other."

42. Marx, *Theories of Surplus Value,* chapter 17, section 12.
43. Mandel, *Marxist Economic Theory,* vol. 1, 343.
44. Marx, *Capital,* vol. 3, 366–7.
45. Marx, *Theories of Surplus Value,* chapter 17, section 14.
46. *Socialist Voice,* no. 19, summer 1983, https://www.marxists.org/history/etol/newspape/socialistvoice/marx19.html
47. Marx, *Capital,* vol. 2, 486–7.
48. Pavel Maksakovsky, *The Capitalist Cycle* (Chicago: Haymarket Books, 2009), 81.
49. Richard Day, "Introduction" in Maksakovsky, *The Capitalist Cycle,* xlii.
50. Maksakovsky, *The Capitalist Cycle,* 69.
51. Marx, *Theories of Surplus Value,* chapter 17, section 8.
52. We'll discuss the housing bubble more fully in the following chapter.
53. Claudio Katz, "Interpretations of the Economic Crisis," *International Socialist Review* 75 (January 2011).
54. Quoted in Mandel, *Marxist Economic Theory,* vol. 1, 354–5.
55. Marx, *Capital,* vol. 3, 358.
56. Henry Foy, "VW Emissions Crisis Fuels Jobs Fear in East Europe," *Financial Times,* October 12, 2015.
57. Karl Marx, *Grundrisse,* chapter 12.
58. Ed Crooks, "Oil and Gas: Debt Fears Flare Up," *Financial Times,* March 21, 2016.
59. Ed Crooks, "The US Shale Revolution," *Financial Times,* April 24, 2015.
60. Crooks, "The US Shale Revolution."
61. Fluctuations in supply and demand of raw energy materials are particularly prone to whiplash because rising demand for energy sources during a boom can't quickly be met through a sudden expansion of extractive infrastructure and application of new technologies. Once research and extraction are expanded, the products often hit the market after demand has already peaked.
62. Crooks, "The US Shale Revolution."
63. Anjli Raval and David Sheppard, "Hedge Funds Bet on Higher Oil Prices," *Financial Times,* March 29, 2016.
64. Clifford Krauss, "Oil Prices: What's Behind the Drop? Simple Economics," *New York Times,* April 18, 2016.
65. Stanley Reed and Andrew E. Kramer, "In Doha, Major Oil Exporters Fail to Agree on Production Freeze," *Financial Times,* April 17, 2016.
66. Krauss, "Oil Prices."
67. Ed Crooks, "US Oil and Gas Sector Reboots to Survive," *Financial Times,* April 4, 2016.
68. Crooks, "Oil and Gas: Debt Fears Flare Up."

69. The industry also benefitted from the fact that after several years of crippling falls in oil prices, OPEC did eventually come to an agreement to curb production. See Ellen Wald, "For How Long Will OPEC Extend Production Cuts?" *Forbes*, November 29, 2017, for an account of the ups and downs of this process.

70. Stanley Reed, "Oil Companies at Last See Path to Profits After Painful Spell," *New York Times*, August 1, 2017

71. Ed Crooks, "The Week in Energy: The Good Times Roll for Oil Producers," *Financial Times*, March 11, 2018.

72. Marx, *Capital*, vol. 3, 364.

73. Marx, *Theories of Surplus Value*, chapter 17, section 6.

74. Lukas Brun, "Overcapacity in Steel China's Role in a Global Problem," Center on Globalization, Governance & Competitiveness, Duke University, published by the Alliance for American Manufacturing, September 2016.

75. Nick Gibbs, "Europe Plant Capacity Crisis to Extend to 2016," *Automotive News Europe*, June 21, 2013.

76. Paul Lienert, "GM's Plan Only Partly Solves Gap Between Capacity and Sedan Demand," *Automotive News*, November 28, 2018.

77. Marx, *Capital*, vol. 3, 363.

78. Cited in Harvey, *A Brief History of Neoliberalism*, p. 163.

79. Marx, *Capital*, vol. 3, 362.

80. Marx, *Capital*, vol. 3, 364.

81. Maksakovsky, *Capitalist Cycle*, 97.

82. Marx, *Capital*, vol. 1, 93.

83. It's important to note that the ratio of physical machinery to concrete labor is different than how much capital is invested. (It might cost $20 a day to utilize the loom and $10 a day to hire the weaver.) This is why Marx distinguished between the "technical composition" of capital (one laborer to one loom) and the "value composition" of capital ($20 dollars to $10 dollars). There's clearly a relationship between the technical and organic compositions of capital, but you can see how they might change at different rates. Marx wrote: "By the composition of capital we mean. . . the ratio between its active and its passive component, between variable and constant capital. Two relationships are involved here. . . The first relationship depends on technical conditions and is to be taken as given, at any particular stage of development of productivity. . . A definite number of workers corresponds to a definite quantity of means of production. . . The *organic* composition of capital is the name we give to its value composition, insofar as this is determined by its technical composition and reflects it." Marx, *Capital*, vol. 3, 244–245.

84. In chapter one we talked about Joseph Marie Jacquard, who invented the mechanical loom in 1804. His father was a master weaver, who could fabricate six inches of silk in a week. The mechanical loom could produce fourteen feet in a week. The three thousand meters now possible equals almost *ten thousand feet a week*.

85. Chris Bauer, "VistaPrint—Web Masters," *Printing Impressions*, March 1, 2006.

86. A 3-D printing company recently announced it was opening a factory in Louisville, Kentucky, with one hundred high-tech 3-D printers running twenty-four hours, seven days a week. This 24/7 operation will be staffed with just three employees. CNN Money, "Louisville Factory: 100 Printers, 3 Employees," May 4, 2015.

87. Marx and Engels, *The Communist Manifesto*, 44.

88. Who remembers car phones? They were a luxury in 1988, but now cheaper smartphones could drive the car for you.

89. Since the last set of printers were not used for the full ten years that they were anticipated to last, this is value that is lost. If they were only used for, say, five years, then $7.5 million of the $15 million spent will have to be written off, unless they can sell them off for part of that value.

90. Marx, *Capital*, vol. 3, 373–4.

91. Marx, *Capital*, vol. 3, 347.

92. Roman Rosdolsky, *The Making of Marx's Capital, vol.1*, (London: Pluto Press Limited, 1980), 409. And, in general, a useful discussion of this question more generally in the appendix, 398–412.

93. This process, as we'll discuss soon in the section on "countervailing tendencies," also cheapens the creation of the means of production, thereby reducing constant capital and easing the pressure on the profit rate's fall.

94. The equalization of profit rates is one of the key reasons why (as we discussed in chapter three) prices diverge from their values.

95. Marx, *Capital*, vol. 3, 339.

96. Marx, *Capital*, vol. 3, 346.

97. It should be noted that these savings cannot be applied retroactively by those companies which, like BigBucks, already spent $10 million on their printers. For them, the drain on profitability is even greater. Now their printers pass on 20 percent less value, while the amount that they initially invested remains the same.

98. A high turnover of capital is also the secret behind the success of fast food chains. They sell products cheaply (reflecting the shorter socially necessary labor-time needed to make McDonald's Big Macs), but they turn over capital quickly from the initial investments in raw materials, labor, and equipment, to the sale of the food items.

99. Some Marxists, like Michael Roberts, do contend that the tendency for the rate of profit to fall is the main motor for cyclical crises because booms produce an expansion of production and investments in technology, leading to falls in profit rates, while the destruction of capital characteristic of crises lead to sharp falls in the organic composition of capital thereby restoring profitability.

100. Capitalism's need for unemployment, referred to by Marx sometimes as "surplus population," sometimes as "reserve army of laborers," is also discussed in chapter 4.

101. Marx, *Capital*, vol. 3, 359.

102. Clarke, *Marx's Theory of Crisis*, 243.

103. Marx, *Capital*, vol. 3, 349–50.

104. Marx, *Capital*, vol. 3, 358.

105. In the next chapter, we'll also see how finance capital plays a necessary role in the accumulation of capital, but how it too deepens and intensifies the ways that these contradictions play themselves out.

106. Mandel, *Marxist Economic Theory*, vol. 1, 346.

107. Trotsky, *Whither France*, chapter 1 (in section "How a Revolutionary Situation Arises").

CHAPTER SEVEN: CREDIT AND FINANCIALIZATION

1. Marx, *Capital*, vol. 3, 572.

2. Marx, *Capital*, vol. 3, 569.

3. Marx, *Capital*, vol. 3, 572.

4. Terry Chan, et al., "Next Debt Crisis: Will Liquidity Hold?" S&P Global Ratings, March 12, 2019.

5. Silvia Amaro, "Global Debt Hits New Record of $253 Trillion and Is Set to Grow Even More This Year," CNBC, January 14, 2020.

6. "GDP (Current US$)," The World Bank Open Data, https://data.worldbank.org/indicator/NY.GDP.MKTP.CD.

7. Ben Chu, "Global debt."

8. Marx, *Capital*, vol. 3, chapter 21, https://www.marxists.org/archive/marx/works/1894-c3/ch21.htm. In this case I found the translation in the Penguin edition (page 460) more confusing, so I am quoting the International Publishers version from Marxists.org.

9. In the case of state bonds, interest here does not draw on profit, or even future profit, but is paid out of tax revenue.

10. Marx, *Capital*, vol. 3, 528.

11. Rudolf Hilferding, *Finance Capital* (London: Routledge & Kegan Paul, 1981), chapter 5.

12. Gillian Tett, *Fool's Gold* (New York, NY: Free Press, 2009), 25.

13. Hilferding, *Finance Capital*, chapter 5.

14. Doug Henwood, *Wall Street: How It Works and for Whom* (New York & London: Verso, 1998), 13.

15. Marx, *Capital*, vol. 3, 601.

16. There are different types of bonds that act in more complicated ways, but this basic definition will suffice for our purposes.

17. Marx, *Capital*, vol. 1, 780.

18. Rosa Luxemburg, *Reform or Revolution* (London: Bookmarks, 1989), 30-31.

19. Amy Traub and Catherine Ruetschlin, "The Plastic Safety Net Findings from the 2012 National Survey on Credit Card Debt of Low- and Middle-Income Households," May 22, 2012, http://www.demos.org/publication/plastic-safety-net.

20. Zack Friedman, "Student Loan Debt In 2017: A $1.3 Trillion Crisis," *Forbes*, February 21, 2017. Nancy Welch, "Educating for austerity Social reproduction in the corporate university," *International Socialist Review* 98, (September 2012).

21. Bianca DiJulio, Ashley Kirzinger, Bryan Wu, and Mollyann Brodie, "Data Note: Americans' Challenges with Health Care Costs," Henry J. Kaiser Family Foundation, Mar 2, 2017, accessed at https://www.kff.org/health-costs/poll-finding/data-note-americans-challenges-with-health-care-costs/.

22. Workers' already low wages are made lower by the exorbitant interest they are forced to pay on credit. Credit card interest rates are now at 18 percent or higher. And most young workers today pay a significant portion of their wages or salaries out to service interest on their student loans.

23. Marx, *Capital*, vol. 3, 572.

24. Gerald Friedman, "From Tulips to Mortgage-Backed Securities," *Dollars & Sense*, January/February 2008.

25. Crooks, "Oil and gas: Debt Fears Flare Up."

26. Lawrence Mitchell, "Financial Speculation: The Good, the Bad and the Parasitic," November 11, 2014, https://www.theconversation.com/financial-speculation-the-good-the-bad-and-the-parasitic-33613.

27. Andrew Haughwout, Donghoon Lee, Joseph Tracy, and Wilbert van der Klaauw, "'Flip This House': Investor Speculation and the Housing Bubble," *Liberty Street Economics*, December 5, 2011.

28. Luxemburg, *Reform or Revolution*, 30.

29. Marx, *Capital*, vol. 3, 572.

30. Doug Orr, "What is Money?" *Dollars & Sense*, October 2010.

31. Luxemburg, *Reform or Revolution*, 30.

32. "Nationalise to Save the Free Market," *Financial Times*, October 13, 2008.

33. Ed Crooks, "U.S. Oil and Gas Sector Reboots to Survive," *Financial Times*, April 4, 2016.

34. Cited in Ramaa Vasudevan, "Financialization: A Primer," *Dollars & Sense*, November/December 2008.

35. John Bellamy Foster, "The Financialization of Capitalism," *Monthly Review*, vol. 58, iss. 11 (2007).

36. Demophanes Papdatos, "Central Banking in Contemporary Capitalism," in *Financialization in Crisis*, ed. Costas Lapavitsas (Chicago, IL: Haymarket Books, 2012), chapter 1.

37. Bretton Woods, recall from chapter 3, was created after World War II by allied nations through the United Nations Monetary and Financial Conference. It set up the International Monetary Fund and required all currencies to be tied to the US dollar at fixed rates of exchange.

38. McNally, *Global Slump*, 86.

39. Lapavitsas, *Financialization in Crisis*, 2.

40. McNally, *Global Slump*, 86.

41. Tett, *Fool's Gold*, 93

42. Tett, *Fool's Gold*, 31.

43. McNally, *Global Slump,* 102.

44. Harvey, *A Brief History of Neoliberalism,* 33.

45. Marx, *Capital,* vol 3, 609.

46. CDSs are also completely unregulated. They're not traded on an exchange, but just on the basis of intra-bank agreements. There is no centralized repository of information, and no way to know how exposed each bank or institution is.

47. Marty Wolfson, "Derivatives and Deregulation," *Dollars & Sense,* November/December 2008.

48. Marx, *Capital,* vol. 3, 603.

49. Adam Davidson, "How AIG Fell Apart," *Reuters,* Sep 18, 2008.

50. The full quote, from his paper "Black consciousness and the quest for a true humanity" is not only poignant, but as relevant today as ever: "Thus in South Africa now it is very expensive to be poor. It is the poor people who stay [farthest] from town and therefore have to spend more money on transport to come and work for white people; it is the poor people who use uneconomic and inconvenient fuel like paraffin and coal because of the refusal of the white man to install electricity in black areas; it is the poor people who are governed by many ill-defined restrictive laws and therefore have to spend money on fines for 'technical' offences; it is the poor people who have no hospitals and are therefore exposed to exorbitant charges by private doctors; it is the poor people who use untarred roads, have to walk long distances, and therefore experience the greatest wear and tear on commodities like shoes; it is the poor people who have to pay for their children's books while whites get them free. It does not need to be said that it is the black people who are poor," http://www.sahistory .org.za/archive/black-consciousness-and-the-quest-for-a-true-humanity.

51. Lapavitsas, "Introduction," in *Financialization in Crisis.*

52. A March 2018 report from the Financial Stability Board, the decidedly pro-shadow banking international group of policymakers and regulators that makes recommendations to the G20, estimated that non-banking financial in-stitutions account for $160 trillion in assets out of $340 trillion financial assets. Within this $160 they more narrowly and conservatively define "shadow banks" as making up $45 trillion in assets. See Caroline Binham, "Shadow Banking Grows to More than $45tn Assets Globally," *Financial Times,* March 5, 2018.

53. A.A.K., "The Economist Explains How Shadow Banking Works," *Economist Blog,* Feb 1, 2016, http://www.economist.com/blogs/economist-explains/2016/02/economist-explains-0.

54. Edward McBride, "Shadow and Substance," *Economist,* May 10, 2014.

55. McBride, "Shadow and Substance."

56. Cited in John Bellamy Foster and Fred Magdoff, *The Great Financial Crisis,* (New York: Monthly Review Press, 2009), 54.

57. Harvey, *A Brief History of Neoliberalism,* 32.

58. Marx, *Capital,* vol. 3, 621.

59. Marx, *Capital,* vol. 3, 621.

60. Lee Sustar, "Who Caused the Great Crash of 2008?" *Socialist Worker*, December 5, 2008.

61. Lee Sustar, "The Panic of 2008," *Socialist Worker*, October 11, 2008.

62. Joel Geier, "Can the US Escape the Global Crisis?" *International Socialist Review* 6, (winter 1999).

63. Measured as the percentage of GDP going to "fixed capital formation" (new factories, roads, and housing) was upward of 30 percent, and in some cases above 40 percent, every year in Malaysia, Thailand, and South Korea until 1997. (Compare these figures to worldwide fixed capital formation, which hovered below 24 percent of GDP during the same decade.) See "Gross fixed capital formation (% of GDP)," World Bank Open Data, https://data .worldbank.org/indicator/NE.GDI.FTOT.ZSThe .

64. See Geier, "Can the US Escape the Global Crisis?" for fuller analysis.

65. "Imports of Goods and Services (BoP, current US$)," World Bank Open Data, https://data.worldbank.org/indicator/BM.GSR.GNFS.CD.

66. Kimberly Amadeo, "US Deficit by Year: Compared to GDP, Increase in Debt and Events," *Balance*, October 27, 2017.

67. "US Trade in Goods and Services Annual Trade in Goods and Services, 1960–present," United States Census Bureau, https://www.census.gov /foreign-trade/statistics/graphs/gands.html

68. These bubbles would implode first in the dot-com industry in 2001, and a few years later in the housing industry. The one bubble gave way to the other. After the dot-com bubble burst, the Federal Reserve responded with lowering interest rates from 6.5% to 1% between 2001 and 2003 in order to jump-start the economy. This gave banks easy credit to extend mortgages and other loans. At the same time, investors increasingly looked to mortgage-backed securities for a higher return than the 1% offered by Federal Reserve. Both of these trends fed into the creation of a housing bubble. Meanwhile, more investors took money out of the stock market after the crash and invested in real estate. As Yale economist Robert Shiller argued: "Once stocks fell, real estate became the primary outlet for the speculative frenzy that the stock market had unleashed." See Jonathan R. Laing, "The Bubble's New Home," *Barron's*, June 20, 2005.

69. Carlos Garriga, Bryan Noeth, and Don E. Schlagenhauf, "Household Debt and the Great Recession," *Federal Reserve Bank of St. Louis Review*, second quarter 2017, 99(2), 183–205.

70. Federal Reserve Economic Data, "Capacity Utilization: Total Industry, Percent of Capacity, Monthly, Seasonally Adjusted," https://fred.stlouisfed.org /series/TCU.

71. Joel Geier, "Capitalism's worst crisis since the 1930s," *International Socialist Review* 62 (November/December 2008).

72. "The State of the Nation's Housing 2008," Joint Center for Housing Studies of Harvard University, 2008, 2, www.jchs.harvard.edu/sites/jchs.harvard.edu /files/son2008.pdf; Rick Brooks and Constance Mitchell Ford, "The United

States of Subprime: Data Show Bad Loans Permeate the Nation; Pain Could Last Years," *Wall Street Journal,* October 11, 2007.

73. Rick Brooks and Constance Mitchell Ford, "The United States of Subprime: Data Show Bad Loans Permeate the Nation; Pain Could Last Years," *Wall Street Journal,* October 11, 2007.

74. Haughwout, Lee, Tracy, and Van Der Klaauw, "'Flip This House': Investor Speculation and the Housing Bubble," Liberty Street Economics, December 5, 2011, http://libertystreeteconomics.newyorkfed.org/2011/12/flip-this -house-investor-speculation-and-the-housing-bubble.html.

75. June Kim, "Housing Bubble—Or Bunk," *Bloomberg,* June 22, 2015, https:// www.bloomberg.com/news/articles/2005-06-21/housing-bubble-or-bunk.

76. National Association of Realtors, "Market-by-Market Home Price Analysis Reports," October 2005, and "Housing Bubble Prospects Q&A." Outgoing Federal Reserve chair Alan Greenspan similarly declared no national bubble in home prices, but rather a "froth" in some local markets. Incoming chair Ben Bernanke denied the existence of a bubble as well, declaring instead that "price increases largely reflect strong economic fundamentals." Ben Bernanke, "The Economic Outlook," testimony before the Joint Economic Committee, October 20, 2005, https://georgewbush-whitehouse.archives.gov/cea /econ-outlook20051020.html.

77. "The End of the Affair," *Economist,* November 20, 2008.

78. "State of the Nation's Housing," 6.

79. "State of the Nation's Housing," 7.

80. Justin Lahart, "Egg Cracks Differ in Housing, Finance Shells," *Wall Street Journal,* December 24, 2007.

81. "State of the Nation's Housing," 3.

82. "The End of the Affair," *Economist.*

83. For a full list, see "Behind the Real Size of the Bailout," *Mother Jones,* December 21, 2009.

84. John Carney, "The Size of the Bank Bailout: $29 Trillion," CNBC, December 14, 2011. European countries also spent another estimated $2 trillion on bank bailouts.

85. Matt Taibbi, "Secrets and Lies of the Bailout," *Rolling Stone,* January 4, 2013.

86. One notable exception was in China, where, which Lee Sustar explained, "was able to avoid the worst of the 2007–09 recession through a big economic stimulus program—twice as big, in proportion to its economy, as those in the US and in Europe . . . [T]he booming economy in China was pulling in imports from around the world, from sophisticated machinery from the US, Europe and Japan to oil and raw materials from Latin America, Africa and other parts of Asia." In this way, China's stimulus spending "put a floor under the world economy," at least temporarily. . . undergirded as it was by mass outlays of debt. Lee Sustar, "Can the US Escape the Slump?" *Socialist Worker,* February 11, 2016.

87. Eric Ruder, "Comrade-in-Chief?" *Socialist Worker,* October 15, 2008.

88. Marx and Engels, *The Communist Manifesto*, 43.

89. Nell Henderson, "Bernanke: There's No Housing Bubble to Go Bust," *Washington Post*, Thursday, October 27, 2005.

90. Luxemburg, *The Accumulation of Capital* (Eastford, CT: Martino Fine Books, 2015), chapter 30.

91. Luxemburg, *The Accumulation of Capital*, chapter 30.

92. Luxemburg, *The Accumulation of Capital*, chapter 30.

93. See Scott Nearing and Joseph Freeman, *Dollar Diplomacy: A Study in American Imperialism* (New York: B.W. Huebsch and the Viking Press, 1925), 134–151, for a fuller account.

94. McNally, *Global Slump*, 127.

95. Andrew England and Elaine Moore, "EM Debt—a Trawl for Yield," *Financial Times*, March 18, 2016.

96. Puerto Ricans cannot vote in federal elections. While they can vote for local officials, the White House can overrule local decisions.

97. "Hedge Fund Vultures in Puerto Rico," *Hedge Papers* 17, (July 2015), 1–3.

98. Cited in McNally, *Global Slump*, 87.

99. Demophanes Papadatos, "Central Banking in Contemporary Capitalism: Inflation-Targeting and Financial Crisis" in *Financialization in Crisis*, ed. Costas Lapavitsas, 131.

100. "The Financialization of Capitalism."

101. McNally, *Global Slump*, 88.

102. Marx, *Capital*, vol. 3, 625.

103. Marx, *Capital*, vol. 3, 569.

104. Charles Krauthammer, "Catharsis, Then Common Sense," *Washington Post*, September 26, 2008.

105. See Keeanga-Yamahtta Taylor, *Race for Profit: How Banks and the Real Estate Industry Undermined Black Homeownership* (Chapel Hill, NC: University of North Carolina Press, 2019), 257.

106. Gary Dymski, "Racial Exclusion and the Political Economy of the Subprime Crisis" in *Financialization in Crisis*, ed. Costas Lapavitsas (Chicago, IL: Haymarket Books, 2012), 76.

107. Petrino DiLeo, "Prelude to a Wider Recession? Housing Bubble Deflates," *International Socialist Review* 53, (May–June 2007).

108. Ben White, et al., "How a Fiasco of Easy Home Loans Has Tripped Up America," *Financial Times*, March 15, 2007.

109. Taylor, *Race for Profit*, 17.

110. Aaron Glantz and Emmanuel Martinez, "For people of color, banks are shutting the door to homeownership," *Reveal News*, February 15, 2018.

111. This gap also has everything to do with wealth and financial stability, which are "inextricably linked to housing opportunity and homeownership," according to the National Fair Housing Alliance. "For a typical family, the largest share of their wealth emanates from homeownership and home equity." Not coincidentally, the *Reveal* article points out, "median net worth for an African

American family is \$9,000, compared with \$132,000 for a white family. Latinx families did not fare much better at \$12,000."

112. Jason Szep, "Blacks Suffer Most in US Foreclosure Surge," *Reuters*, March 20, 2007.

113. Szep, "Blacks Suffer Most."

114. McNally, *Global Slump*, 125.

115. Anna Nicolaou, "Global Elite Buys Trophy Apartments," *Financial Times*, September 29, 2015.

116. Derek Thompson, "Why Manhattan's Skyscrapers Are Empty," *The Atlantic*, January 16, 2020.

CONCLUSION: CAPITALISM'S GRAVEDIGGERS

1. Leo Lewis, "Japan's funeral sector adapts as 'peak death' looms," *Financial Times*, March 21, 2016. Peak death refers to the phenomenon wherein the deaths outnumber births and the aging population puts occupancy in the death industry on course to peak.

2. Marx and Engels, *The Communist Manifesto*, 44.

3. Marx, *Theses on Feuerbach*, 1845.

4. Marx, *Capital*, vol. 1, 92

5. Marx and Engels, *Communist Manifesto*, 44.

6. Hadas Thier, "New York Transit Strike: A Glimpse of Union Power," *International Socialist Review* 46 (2006), 26–29.

7. Jane Slaughter, "Auto Parts Workers Strike for Recognition, Strategy Was to Shut Down Assembly Plant," *Labor Notes*, April 17, 2014.

8. The places where racism could be most effectively used to stave off workplace struggles and unionization—such as in the Southern states—are also the places where both Black and white workers earn substantially lower wages than in other parts of the country. As Phil Gasper notes in *Socialist Worker*, "The Berkeley economist Michael Reich published an extensive study of this question in the 1980s. He found that 'where racism is greater, income inequality *among whites* is also greater,' and that 'most of the inequality among whites generated by racism [is] associated with increased income for the richest 1 percent of white families.'" Phil Gasper, "Capitalism, Racism and the 1 Percent," *Socialist Worker* (US), March 31, 2015.

9. Marx, *Capital*, vol. 1, 928–929.

AFTERWORD: THE CORONAVIRUS CRISIS

1. US Federal agencies in fact attach numeric values to quantify the "value of statistical life" (or VSL) and use that as a metric to calculate life "benefits" versus "costs" of health and safety regulations. There's simply no way for capitalism to treat life as priceless.

2. Marx and Engels, *The Communist Manifesto*, 43.
3. Josh Margolin and James Meek, "Intelligence Report Warned of Coronavirus Crisis as Early as November," ABC News, April 8, 2020, https://abcnews.go.com/Politics/intelligence-report-warned-coronavirus-crisis-early-november-sources/story?id=70031273.
4. Jeffery Mays and Andy Newman, "Virus is Twice as Deadly for Black and Latino People Than Whites in N.Y.C.," *New York Times*, April 8, 2020, https://www.nytimes.com/2020/04/08/nyregion/coronavirus-race-deaths.html.
5. Desha Johnson-Hargrove, "My Husband Died Trying to Protect His Bus Passengers From Coronavirus. Please Stay Home So His Death Isn't In Vain," Time.com, April 9, 2020, https://time.com/collection/coronavirus-heroes/5816894/jason-hargrove-bus-driver-coronavirus/.
6. Joe Rennison, Robin Wigglesworth, Colby Smith, "Federal Reserve Enters New Territory with Support for Risky Debt," *Financial Times,* April 9, 2020.
7. Jeff Cox, "Powell says the economic recovery can be 'robust' after the coronavirus is contained," CNBC, April 9, 2020, https://www.cnbc.com/2020/04/09/fed-chair-powell-says-the-economic-recovery-can-be-robust-after-coronavirus.html.
8. Snehal Shingavi interview with David McNally, "What happens next?" *Section 44: A Journal of Texas Marxism*, April 6, 2020, https://section44.org/2020/04/06/what-happens-next-interview-with-david-mcnally/.
9. Peter Goodman, "Coronavirus May Light Fuse on 'Unexploded Bomb' of Corporate Debt," *New York Times,* March 11, 2020, https://www.nytimes.com/2020/03/11/business/coronavirus-corporate-debt.html.

INDEX

A

abstract labor. *See* labor, abstract labor
accumulation
    centralization and concentration of
        capital and, 116–121, 130
    contradictions and crisis and, 140,
        149–150, 154–155, 161, 175–
        176, 181, 186–189, 220, 234
    finance capital and, 194, 197, 204
    imperative for, 8, 71–72, 105, 110–
        113, 139, 143, 157–158, 234
    overaccumulation and, 172–173,
        211–212
    primitive accumulation and, 14–15,
        20–22
    social reproduction and, 83
The Accumulation of Capital (Luxem-
    burg), 221
alienation, 24, 31, 99, 123, 129, 233
Amazon, 55, 106, 125–126
Anti-Dühring (Engels), 104
Apple, 28, 44, 93, 107, 116, 119, 127,
    137
austerity, 97, 149, 218–219, 221,
    223–224, 241

B

banking systems. *See* finance capital,
    banking systems
Bhattacharya, Tithi, 75
Bitcoin. *See* digital currency
bourgeoisie. *See also* class
    accumulation and, 108–109, 112, 137,
        147

    class polarization and, 91
    definition of, 16
    middle class and, 90
    rise of, 19–20
    the state and, 23, 220, 238
Bretton Woods Agreement, 59, 204
Britain. *See* United Kingdom
Bukharin, Nikolai, 136–137

C

capital. *See also* capitalism; finance
    capital
    centralization and concentration
        of, 116–121, 125, 136, 174,
        185–186
    circuit of, 73, 198
    constant capital and, 79–81, 109, 174,
        177, 184
    definition of, 8, 17, 70, 81–82, 82
    destruction of, 172, 174, 187
    expansion of, 82, 157, 164
    fixed capital and, 166, 169, 172,
        183–184
    organic composition of, 176–178, 181
    productive and unproductive capital
        and, 110
    variable capital and, 79–81, 109, 174,
        176, 178, 180
capitalism
    accumulation and. *See* accumulation
    characteristics of, 7, 13–14, 23, 28, 31,
        72–73
    climate change and, 5, 25, 47, 140–
        146, 234, 241
    commodities and. *See* commodities

competition and, 92, 103–108, 114,
    119, 122, 124–125, 157, 234
contradictions of, 8, 175, 234
COVID-19 and, 237–241
crises and. *See* crises
exploitation under, 8, 14, 17, 19, 76, 98
growth and globalization and, 46–48,
    71–72, 184, 186
imperialism and, 22, 136–137
money and. *See* money
oppression and, 5, 84–85
profit and. *See* profit
rejection by millennials of, 4
revolution and, 187, 234–236
rise of, 7, 11–16, 18–22, 24, 58
social effects of, 5, 126–127
the state and, 19, 20, 23, 220
technology and labor process and,
    95–97, 107–109, 123, 176–178,
    181
capital markets. *See* finance capital;
    capital markets
Capital, Volume 1 (Marx)
accumulation and, 103
commodities and, 29, 32, 49
crisis and, 186–187
money and, 51
nature and, 25
rise of capitalism and, 11
scientific method of, 6–8
value and, 27, 31, 37, 64, 69
Capital, Volume 3 (Marx), 82, 182–183,
    187, 189
China
economy and, 72, 85, 120, 127,
    134–136
growth and, 212–213, 225
pre-industrial development of, 13, 16
rivalry with United States and, 137,
    173, 238
urbanization and, 126–128
working conditions and industrial
    action and, 4, 127–129
Clarke, Simon, 149–151, 157–158, 186

class. *See also* bourgeoisie
capitalist class and, 88, 181
class consciousness and, 91
class society and, 11–13
class struggle and, 91–92, 94, 149, 175,
    235, 236
definition of, 8, 87–89
exploitation and, 7, 98
inequality and, 2, 5
middle class and, 87, 90
working class and, 16, 18–19, 87–90,
    212, 235, 236
climate change, 4–5, 25, 47, 140–146
Clinton, Bill, 211
C-M-C, 70
collateralized debt obligations (CDOs).
    See finance capital, securities
colonialism, 22, 185, 222–223
commodities
capitalism and, 11, 14, 16–17, 23,
    222–223
circulation of, 55–56
competition and, 104–105, 108, 122,
    130–131
exchange-value and, 27–33, 45–48
fetishism and, 44–45
finance capital and, 204, 206, 211, 213
labor theory of value and, 36–42, 67,
    69, 73–75, 79, 85, 177, 180
mainstream analysis of, 33–37,
    152–153
Marx's analysis of, 7, 23, 27–28
money and, 43–44, 49–60
overproduction and, 160–167, 173
pre-capitalist exchange of, 70–71
price and, 64–67, 165, 199–200
surplus value and, 72–74, 81–82, 95,
    97, 110, 155, 157–159
Communist Manifesto (Marx and En-
    gels), 91, 108, 137, 147, 233
constant capital. *See* capital, constant
    capital
COVID-19, 1–2, 237–241
credit default swaps (CDSs). *See* finance

capital, securitization
crisis. *See also* Great Recession; overproduction; tendency for the rate of profit to fall
  Classical and Keynesian explanations of, 150–155, 161–163, 169
  Marxist theory of, 8, 147–150, 153–155, 157, 159–160, 162–169, 175, 185
  recovery from, 171–172, 174
Critique of the Gotha Programme (Marx), 36

D

digital currency, 61–64, 234
Douglass, Frederick, 86

E

Economist (magazine), 61–64, 123, 209, 215, 217
Engels, Frederick
  capitalism and, 108–111, 158, 233–234
  class and, 89–91, 129, 234
  crisis and, 152
  criticism of classical economics and, 36, 152
  forces of production and, 140
  globalization and, 137–138
  nature and climate and, 25, 138, 146
  social reproduction and, 83
  the state and, 220
European Union, 137, 167, 221
exchange-value. *See* value, exchange-value
exploitation. *See also* surplus value
  capitalism and, 7–8, 17, 19, 70, 76, 92, 98
  class and, 88–89, 92
  fetishism and, 44
  neoliberalism and, 212
  oppression and, 85–86
  pre-capitalist societies and, 13–14, 98
  rate of, 81–82, 87, 97, 115, 178,

183–185
  superexploitation and, 86

F

Federal Reserve, 3–4, 60, 124, 134, 149, 201–202, 213–214, 218, 220, 239–240
feudalism, 13–14, 19–20, 28, 56
finance capital
  banking system and, 1, 193–194, 208–210, 218–219
  capital markets and, 118, 195–196
  credit and debt and, 97, 118, 167–168, 172–174, 187–191, 198–203, 213, 234, 241
  crisis and, 164, 190. See also Great Recession
  fictitious capital and, 192, 195, 224–226
  imperialism and, 221–222, 224
  neoliberalism and, 203–205, 211–212
  productive economy and, 210–211, 224–225
  role of, 110, 124, 191, 194, 196–198
  securitization and, 205–209
  speculation and, 186, 199–200, 201–202, 204–205, 207–208, 215, 234
financialization. *See* finance capital
Financial Times
  China and, 128–129
  concentration and centralization of capital and, 120, 125, 133, 135
  COVID-19 and, 239
  destruction of value and, 171–172
  effective demand and, 233
  finance capital and, 167–169, 194, 200, 203, 228, 230–231
  green capitalism and, 141
  overproduction and, 168–169
Fordism, 104, 108, 156
Foster, John Bellamy, 204
Foucault, Michel, 57
Foxconn, 93, 127–129

Friedman, Milton, 211

G

gender, 84–86, 94
gold standard, 58–60
Google, 87, 119–120
Great Depression, 59–60, 149, 204
Great Recession
    bailout of financial system and,
        218–219
    causes of, 8, 189–190, 195, 203,
        206–210
    effects of, 2–3, 88, 148, 168, 173, 198,
        202, 240
    housing bubble and, 200, 214–218,
        225, 227, 229, 231
    imperialism and, 221, 224
Green New Deal, 241
Greenspan, Alan, 149, 151, 154

H

Harvey, David, 32, 44, 48, 65–66,
    113–114, 205
Henwood, Doug, 153, 194
Hilferding, Rudolf, 193–194, 208

I

imperialism, 105, 136–137, 220–224
Industrial Revolution, 14, 20–21, 25,
    129, 213
inflation, 62, 66, 165
International Monetary Fund (IMF), 59,
    220, 223–224

J

Jevons, William Stanley, 34, 36, 151

K

Keynes, John Maynard, 153–154

L

labor

abstract labor and, 37–40, 52–53
complex labor, 38
labor-power and. See also capital, vari-
    able capital
    as a commodity, 14, 17, 35, 66, 69,
        73–75, 85, 87, 97, 199
    class and, 82, 88, 92, 98, 235
    migration and, 86
    social reproduction and, 75, 83–85
    value and, 34–38, 73–76, 79–81, 82,
        92, 95–98, 109, 176–179, 184
labor theory of value and, 7–8, 28, 32,
    35, 37, 39–40, 45, 67, 224–225
labor-time and
    socially necessary labor-time and,
        40–44, 51–52, 57–58, 60, 64–67,
        80, 96, 104, 107–108, 110,
        177–179, 181
    surplus and necessary labor-time
        and, 76, 93–94, 98, 101, 158,
        181–182
    value and, 34, 38–39, 50, 70–71, 75,
        184
living and dead labor and, 42, 80
nature and, 24
reserve army of labor and, 89–90
wage labor and, 14–18, 22–23, 44
Lenin, Vladimir, 30, 135–137
Luxemburg, Rosa, 198, 202, 221–222

M

mainstream economics
    classical and neoclassical economics
        and, 35–36, 39–40
    commodities and, 33–37, 152–153
    crisis and, 150–155
    effective demand and, 160, 165
    efficient market hypothesis and, 149
    marginalism and, 30, 33–36, 77–79
Maksakovsky, Pavel, 164–165, 175
Mandel, Ernest, 6, 28, 52, 54, 71, 160,
    187
Marxism. See Marx, Karl
Marx, Karl

capitalism and capital and
  accumulation and, 111–113, 121, 155
  competition and, 107–108, 122, 125
  concentration and centralization of capital and, 116–119, 121–122, 185–186, 197
  constant and variable capital and, 79–80
  consumption and, 80, 84, 158
  forces of production and, 97, 108, 140, 176
  growth and, 72, 82, 137–138, 157–158
  method of analysis of, 5–7
  rise of capitalism and, 14–15, 18–19, 23
  class and, 17, 88–89, 91–92, 94, 129, 234
  classical economics and, 36, 40, 153
  commodities and, 23, 27–29, 55–56, 70
  crisis and, 147–149, 153–155, 159–167, 172, 174–177, 180–183, 186–187, 210–211, 217
  fetishism and, 44–45, 59
  finance capital and, 121, 189–191, 193, 195, 200, 202, 206, 207, 226
  labor and
    labor-power and, 74–75, 83, 98, 122
    labor theory of value and, 32, 36, 37–38, 40–41, 43, 67, 98
    reserve army of labor and, 90, 185
    slavery and, 22
  money and, 44, 50–51, 53
  nature and, 24–25, 27, 36, 137–138, 144, 146, 186
  socialism and, 139, 175, 236
  the state and, 220
  value and
    price and, 64–65, 156
    relative and equivalent value and, 51–52
    surplus value and, 72–73, 76, 93–96,

182, 233
    use-value and exchange-value and, 29–31
M-C-M', 71–72, 104, 113, 183, 190–192
McNally, David, 37, 204, 223, 226
means of production, 16, 23, 73, 80, 164, 174
mercantilism, 71–72
Microsoft, 107, 119, 269
money
  digital currency and, 61–64, 234
  fetishism and, 44, 49, 67
  function of, 53–57, 66
  historical development of, 54, 57–61
  hoarding of, 167
  international trade and, 59, 66–67
  Marx's analysis of, 7, 50
  precious metals and, 54–55, 57–60
  value and price and, 29, 43, 50–51, 60–61, 65–66
monopoly and oligopoly, 130–134, 136
Moody, Kim, 90–91, 95
moral depreciation, 80, 164, 184. *See also* capital, fixed capital

N

nature, 24–25, 27, 36, 137–138, 144, 186. *See also* climate change
necessary labor. *See* labor, labor-time, surplus and necessary labor
neoliberalism, 204–205, 211–212, 219, 224
New York Times, 106, 170–171, 219, 239
Nixon, Richard, 60

O

Occupy Wall Street, 4, 88
oligopoly. *See* monopoly and oligopoly
oppression, 5, 85–86, 235
organic composition of capital. *See* capital, organic composition of
overaccumulation. *See* accumulation, overaccumulation

overproduction, 159–161, 165–168,
    173–175, 186–187, 189–190,
    202–203, 210–217. *See also* crisis

P

Papadatos, Demophanes, 204, 225
pre-capitalist societies, 13, 70, 98. *See
    also* feudalism
price, 39, 64–67, 164–166
primitive accumulation. *See* accumula-
    tion, primitive accumulation
private property, 20, 89
productive forces, 137–138, 147, 156,
    161, 181, 186, 190, 202, 222
productivity. *See* value, surplus value
profit. *See also* accumulation
    competition and, 108, 121, 125,
        131–132, 140, 171–172
    crisis and, 152–153, 157–158,
        160–167, 173–187, 213, 234.
        See also tendency for the rate of
        profit to fall
    exploitation and oppression and, 82,
        86–87, 89, 129, 170, 183–184
    finance capital and, 118, 190–198, 200,
        202–206, 208–209, 211–212,
        214–215, 225–226
    imperative for, 5, 25, 110–116, 141–
        144, 154–155, 233, 237–238
    mainstream explanations of, 33–36,
        77–79
    rate and distribution of, 65, 81,
        97, 109–110, 147–148, 175,
        182–183, 193, 196–197
    source of, 7–8, 23, 72–73, 79, 92–93,
        104, 235. *See also* value, surplus
        value
    superprofits and, 107, 133, 163, 166
proletariat. *See* class, working class

R

race and racism. *See* oppression
Reagan, Ronald, 211

reserve army of labor. *See* labor, reserve
    army of labor
revolution, 15, 175, 187
Ricardo, David, 39–40, 159, 186

S

Sanders, Bernie, 4–5, 88
securities. *See* finance capital, securiti-
    zation
sexuality. *See* oppression
shadow banks. *See* finance capital; bank-
    ing system
slavery, 20–22, 184
Smith, Adam, 14, 22, 39–40
Smith, Tony, 95
socialism, 4–5, 101, 137–139, 236
socially necesaary labour-time. *See* labor,
    labor-time, socially necessary
    labor-time
social reproduction, 75, 83–85
the state, 19–20, 23, 134, 136–137,
    220–221
Ste. Croix, Geoffrey de, 89, 91
structured investment vehicles (SIVs).
        See finance capital; banking
        system
subprime mortgages. *See* finance capital,
    securitization
supply and demand, 65, 164, 175, 182
surplus labor. *See* labor, labor time, sur-
    plus and necessary labor
surplus value. *See* value, surplus value

T

Taylorism, 95, 99–101, 184
Taylor, Keeanga-Yamahtta, 229
tendency for the rate of profit to fall,
    174, 177–187
Thatcher, Margaret, 211
Theories of Surplus Value (Marx),
    154–155, 159, 161, 187
Trotsky, Leon, 101, 187–188
Trump, Donald J., 5, 91, 137, 236, 238

U

United Kingdom
  global financial systems and, 58
  health system and, 134
  imperialism and, 221–222
  Industrial Revolution and, 20–22
  neoliberalism and, 211
  pollution and, 141
  rise of capitalism and, 15–16, 18,
    24–25
United Nations, 59, 112, 126
United States
  class and inequality and, 3–5, 66, 89,
    90–91, 93, 95, 111–112, 184,
    212
  COVID-19 and, 1, 237–239
  economy of, 46, 71–72, 136, 170
  finance capital and, 198–199, 204–
    205, 207, 211, 213, 216, 218–220
  Great Recession and, 3, 148, 152
  housing bubble and, 201, 216–218,
    226–229, 231
  imperialism and, 59–60, 137, 222–224
  race and racism and, 85–86, 228–230,
    235–236
  rivalry with China and, 137, 173, 238
universal equivalent. *See* money, func-
    tion of

V

value. *See also* labor, labor theory of value
  destruction of, 171
  distinction from price and, 64–67
  equivalent and relative value and,
    51–52
  exchange-value and, 29–33, 37–45, 65,
    73–76, 155, 172, 233, 241
  money and, 50, 65–66
  surplus value and. *See also* profit
    absolute and relative surplus value
      and, 92–97, 174
    accumulation and, 72, 82, 111, 117
    exploitation and, 87, 184, 191. *See
      also* exploitation

finance capital and, 110, 224
imperative for, 162–163, 166
labor process and, 76, 79, 92–93,
  98–101, 174
organic composition of capital and,
  109, 177
process of exchange and, 72–73, 82,
  115–116
productivity and, 97, 108
rate of, 81, 178, 181
realization of, 104, 106, 155–156,
  164, 187, 198
use-value and, 29–31, 36–38, 71, 74,
  76, 79, 138, 172, 233
Value, Price, and Profit (Marx), 65
variable capital. *See* capital; variable
  capital
Vogel, Lise, 84

W

wages
  absolute and relative surplus value and,
    92–98
  class definitions and, 88–90
  level of, 66–67, 73–77, 84, 89, 112,
    148, 158, 198, 212, 240
  profitability and, 167, 174, 181–182
  rate of exploitation and, 80–82, 85–87,
    184, 212
  underconsumption theory and, 158,
    161–163
  wage labor and, 14–18, 22–23, 44
Wall Street, 4, 46, 88, 120, 205, 217–219,
  227–228, 234, 238
Walmart, 117–118
The Wealth of Nations (Smith), 17, 39–40
the working day. *See* value, surplus value
World Bank, 72, 220, 223–224

Z

Zweig, Michael, 88, 90

ABOUT HAYMARKET BOOKS

Haymarket Books is a radical, independent, nonprofit book publisher based in Chicago.

Our mission is to publish books that contribute to struggles for social and economic justice. We strive to make our books a vibrant and organic part of social movements and the education and development of a critical, engaged, international left.

We take inspiration and courage from our namesakes, the Haymarket martyrs, who gave their lives fighting for a better world. Their 1886 struggle for the eight-hour day—which gave us May Day, the international workers' holiday—reminds workers around the world that ordinary people can organize and struggle for their own liberation. These struggles continue today across the globe—struggles against oppression, exploitation, poverty, and war.

Since our founding in 2001, Haymarket Books has published more than five hundred titles. Radically independent, we seek to drive a wedge into the risk-averse world of corporate book publishing. Our authors include Noam Chomsky, Arundhati Roy, Rebecca Solnit, Angela Y. Davis, Howard Zinn, Amy Goodman, Wallace Shawn, Mike Davis, Winona LaDuke, Ilan Pappé, Richard Wolff, Dave Zirin, Keeanga-Yamahtta Taylor, Nick Turse, Dahr Jamail, David Barsamian, Elizabeth Laird, Amira Hass, Mark Steel, Avi Lewis, Naomi Klein, and Neil Davidson. We are also the trade publishers of the acclaimed Historical Materialism Book Series and of Dispatch Books.

ALSO AVAILABLE FROM HAYMARKET BOOKS

Blood and Money: War, Slavery, and the State
David McNally

The Debt System: A History of Sovereign Debts and their Repudiation
Éric Toussaint

Ecosocialism: A Radical Alternative to Capitalist Catastrophe
Michael Löwy

The Essential Rosa Luxemburg: Reform or Revolution and the Mass Strike
Rosa Luxemburg, edited by Helen Scott

From Marx to Gramsci: A Reader in Revolutionary Marxist Politics
Edited by Paul Le Blanc

Keywords: The New Language of Capitalism
John Patrick Leary

Marx's Capital Illustrated
David Smith, illustrated by Phil Evans

Socialism . . . Seriously: A Brief Guide to Human Liberation
Danny Katch

A Reader's Guide to Marx's Capital
Joseph Choonara

World in Crisis: A Global Analysis of Marx's Law of Profitability
Edited by Guglielmo Carchedi and Michael Roberts